INDETERMI

Terence Parsons presents a liv
sophical questions about iden
person's body? If a ship has a
ship identical with the origin
reassembled, is the newly asse
nal ship? Because these puzz
believe that they are questic
because the questions are in
that there is a problem with th
Parsons explores a different
answers because of the way t
the world is not); there is genu
world. He articulates such a v
host of criticisms that have b
sibility of indeterminacy in ide

Indeterminate Identity

Metaphysics and Semantics

TERENCE PARSONS

CLARENDON PRESS · OXFORD

OXFORD

UNIVERSITY PRESS

Great Clarendon Street, Oxford OX2 6DP

Oxford University Press is a department of the University of Oxford.
It furthers the University's objective of excellence in research, scholarship,
and education by publishing worldwide in

Oxford New York

Athens Auckland Bangkok Bogotá Buenos Aires Calcutta
Cape Town Chennai Dar es Salaam Delhi Florence Hong Kong Istanbul
Karachi Kuala Lumpur Madrid Melbourne Mexico City Mumbai
Nairobi Paris São Paulo Shanghai Singapore Taipei Tokyo Toronto Warsaw
and associated companies in Berlin Ibadan

Oxford is a registered trade mark of Oxford University Press
in the UK and certain other countries

Published in the United States
by Oxford University Press Inc., New York

British Library Cataloguing in Publication Data

Data available

Library of Congress Cataloging in Publication Data

Parsons, Terence.
Indeterminate identity : metaphysics and semantics / Terence Parsons.
p. cm.
Includes bibliographical references.
1. Identity (Philosophical concept) I. Title.
BD236 .P36 2000   111'.82—dc21   00-034027
ISBN 0-19-825044-4 (alk. paper)

1 3 5 7 9 10 8 6 4 2

Typeset by Best-set Typesetter Ltd., Hong Kong
Printed in Great Britain
on acid-free paper by
Biddles Ltd
Guildford & King's Lynn

To Peter Woodruff

PREFACE

I first addressed the topic of indeterminate identity in a short paper in the mid-1980s, resulting in Parsons (1987). A few years later I returned to the topic, and Peter Woodruff and I began discussing it in detail. We believed that it is coherent to hold that identity statements might be indeterminate, and that all of the a priori proofs to the contrary are clearly question-begging. But there might very well be other considerations that mitigate against this; for example, the determinacy of identities might be presupposed by other deeply held beliefs of ours. Besides, it is not an easy idea to grasp. We decided that we stood in need of some overall conception of what it would be like for some identities to be indeterminate. These conversations led to a study of Venn–Euler-like diagrams for "picturing" indeterminacy, diagrams that appear in some of our joint papers and in Chapters 7–9 of this book. These diagrams have often guided us in development of basic positions on matters of logic and semantics. We also wanted to set the basic theory on a sure footing, and this led in turn to an investigation of indeterminate set theory, which is summarized in Chapter 11.

In Spring 1998 I had an opportunity to lecture on Indeterminate Identity at the University of Salzburg. This required me to give a systematic overview of the topic of indeterminate identity, starting from scratch for people not already immersed in the literature. In doing this, I needed to indicate how my/our views are to apply to the identity puzzles that figure so prominently in the literature. I also needed to work out how the various thoughts that we have had on the topic mesh with one another, and with the ongoing literature on the subject. Those lectures led to this book. Although the book is singly authored, much of its theoretical content was originally developed in cooperation with Peter Woodruff. I am solely responsible for matters of exposition, and for various developments of the theory. Some of my own contributions (such as the notion of super-resolutions) can be identified, but in many cases I am not myself able to say whether I have new exposition of old ideas, or new ideas. I also want to emphasize that many of the general arguments given here in defence of the coherence of indeterminate identity are already present in some form in the literature. When I take a point to be common knowledge, I have not tried to trace its exact origins.

I wish to express my thanks to the Salzburg Philosophy department for its invitation to lecture there. Thanks are also due to those Fall 1998 participants in the UCI Logic Workshop who monitored and critiqued a presentation of a draft of this book, particularly: Jason Alexander, Jeff Barrett, Gary Bell, Penelope Maddy, Patricia Marino, and Kyle Stanford. My greatest debt, of course, is to Peter Woodruff, who is almost indeterminately a co-author.

Terence Parsons

U.C. Irvine
1999

CONTENTS

ANALYTICAL TABLE
OF CONTENTS

1. INTRODUCTION

Identity puzzles persist without consensus on any solution. This book explores the idea that they have no solutions because the identities are indeterminate—there is no fact of the matter about whether or not they hold. Four puzzles without determinate answers are discussed throughout the book: (i) is a person identical with that person's body? (ii) if a ship has its parts replaced and the old parts are assembled into a ship, which of the two resulting ships is identical to the original? (iii) if a person undergoes a crucial change, is the person after the change identical with the person before the change? (iv) given a cat with imprecise boundaries, which cat-like thing with precise boundaries is identical to the actual cat? The purpose of the book is to explore the view that there are no answers to these questions because of indeterminacy in the world (as opposed, for example, to imperfections in our language).

2. INDETERMINACY

Indeterminacy in the world is a genuine option within idealism, realism, or pragmatism. Indeterminacy pertains to states of affairs, such as whether a certain object has or lacks a certain property. If neither of these is the case, then the state of affairs is indeterminate, and a sentence reporting it lacks truth-value. A semantics is described for a logical notation in which sentences may lack truth-value. It contains a connective '!' for determinate truth: the sentence '!S' is true if 'S' is true, and is false if 'S' is either false or lacking in truth-value. The sign '$\triangledown$' represents indeterminacy: '$\triangledown S$' is true if 'S' lacks truth-value and is otherwise false. The logic of such a language which are true (false). It may also be read super-resolutionally: it is treated as true (false) if all worlds that result from some way of making our own world completely determinate would make the sentence true (false). These options account for data used by some writers in an attempt to refute indeterminate identity. A purported refutation of non-bivalence by Williamson is discussed; it is argued that his claims that all contradictory sentences must be false are plausible only if they are read in some special way, e.g. supervaluationally.

Several authors point out that if an object has indeterminate boundaries, this does not logically entail that it is indeterminately identical to something. Some mereological principles are given that would fill in this logical gap. Objects may or may not be subject to these principles. An example due to Cook is alleged to be hypothetically of this kind (given his assumptions); his disproof of indeterminate identity is examined and found to be inconclusive.

An argument by Noonan against an example (due to Broome) of indeterminate identity of clubs is shown to be implausible if the claims in it are read literally; those claims are plausible if read super-resolutionally, but then they do not conflict with indeterminate identity.

6. CONDITIONAL DISPUTATIONS

Truth-conditions for conditionals are discussed, and the Łukasiewicz conditional '$\Rightarrow$' is adopted; such a conditional is false when the antecedent is true and the consequent false, and true if the truth-value status of the consequent is at least as high as that of the antecedent (counting lack of truth-value as a status intermediate between truth and falsity). A conditional 'If A then B' is to be read either with this conditional ('$A \Rightarrow B$') or given the "if-true" reading ('$!A \Rightarrow B$'). The Łukasiewicz conditional satisfies *modus ponens, modus tollens*, hypothetical syllogism, and contraposition, but only a restricted form of conditional proof: taking 'A' as a premiss and deriving 'B' allows you to conditionalize and infer '$!A \Rightarrow B$', but not '$A \Rightarrow B$'. (No non-bivalent truth-status-functional conditional satisfies all of *modus ponens*, *modus tollens*, and conditional proof, so one can do no better.) If one wishes to state Leibniz's Law as a conditional, the bare Lukasiewicz conditional form is incorrect, but the "if-true" version is correct: '$!a = b \Rightarrow (\phi a \Rightarrow \phi b)$'. Broome gives a different version, which is logically equivalent to this one. Johnson criticizes these versions, but gives a conditionalized-conditional version that is also equivalent.

A second argument of Williamson is considered which defends bivalent versions of the Tarski biconditionals; it is held that his rationales for the biconditionals are subject to interpretation, and that interpretations that do not make them beg the question rationalize only non-bivalent versions.

7. UNDERSTANDING INDETERMINACY

The terminology used in explaining indeterminate identity is meant to be ordinary; 'identical' is not intended in a special sense. 'Indeterminate' may be definable within certain world views (such as idealism), but is otherwise taken as a primitive. The biggest impediment to understanding views that invoke indeterminate identity is our tendency to reason bivalently; this has nothing special to do with identity.

One can picture situations involving indeterminacy using Venn-like diagrams in which objects are represented by images with finite size. An object is pictured as being indeterminately P if its image lies partly inside of and partly outside of the region representing property P; objects are pictured as being indeterminately identical if their images properly overlap. Simple constraints on the picturing conventions entail that Leibniz's definition of identity in terms of coincidence of properties is built into the picturing. Picturings of the paradigm identity puzzles are given.

A more general notion of picturing can be defined that is not necessarily two-dimensional; a simple condition yields a kind of principle of plenitude for properties and the Leibnizian account of identity. A process is given to refine pictures into more determinate ones; under certain general conditions these refinements picture the resolutions discussed earlier in giving super-resolutional readings of sentences.

8. COUNTING OBJECTS

If we try to count objects in the face of indeterminacy, we sometimes get no determinate answer; this is due to indeterminacy of predication (producing indeterminacy regarding which objects are supposed to be counted), or indeterminacy of identity (producing indeterminacy regarding whether an object has already been counted), or both. Familiar formulas are given for making cardinality claims; e.g. "there are at least two ϕ's" is written as '$\exists x \exists y$ $(\neg x = y \;\&\; \phi x \;\&\; \phi y)$'. It is shown how to get the "right" answers; e.g. that in the ship case it is true that there are at least two ships, false that there are more than three, and indeterminate whether there are exactly two (or exactly three). Sometimes a question can be formulated in two ways: either austerely, or with a determinacy connective ('!') added; these formulations correspond to two natural "right" answers. Super-resolutional readings also explain certain of our intuitions.

9. DENOTING OBJECTS

Some authors have suggested that if it is indeterminate whether $a = b$, then it is not possible to determinately denote a; as a consequence, all identity sentences that lack truth-value suffer from some semantic defect. When it is indeterminate whether $a = b$, it is shown how to have singular terms that determinately denote a without denoting b at all, and terms that determinately denote a while also indeterminately denoting b, and terms that indeterminately denote each. So all options are possible.

10. ALTERNATIVES TO INDETERMINATE IDENTITY

Many writers believe that it is both possible and desirable to account for the lack of truth-value of identity sentences by appeal to indeterminacy in the semantics of our language or of the concepts employed by our language. It is shown here that several natural accounts of this sort do not yield a lack of truth-value in the puzzle cases without also wrongly yielding lack of truth-value in other cases as well. For example, in the case of a personal disruption, it ought to be true that exactly one person entered the room, and true that exactly one left, without its being either true or false that the person who entered is the person who left.

An account is examined that employs supervaluations to analyse indeterminacy in singular terms; as formulated, it does not seem to give the right pattern of truth-values in all cases. A second account is based loosely on a discussion by Lewis of how many cats exist in a given region; the account (not endorsed by Lewis) is objectionable; more importantly, it does not apply to the puzzle cases in general. Last is an account due to Stalnaker according to which we refine our concepts upon demand when faced with puzzle cases. This is the most promising approach; versions of it are refuted, and we are left uncertain whether it can be developed into a viable alternative.

11. SETS AND PROPERTIES WITH INDETERMINATE IDENTITY

Sets are things whose identities are defined in terms of their members: they are identical if they both determinately have and determinately lack the same members, they are distinct if one of them determinately has a member that the other determinately lacks, and otherwise it is indeterminate whether they are identical. A distinction is made between worldly sets and conceptual sets; the former but not the latter obey the DDiff principle for set membership: that if x is determinately a member of S and y is determinately not a member of S, then x is determinately distinct from y. A theory of objects together with worldly sets of those objects is formulated, and it is shown that there is indeterminacy of identity between such sets if there is any worldly indeterminacy at all, even if there is no indeterminacy of identity between objects. Salmon's argument against indeterminacy is shown to fail within this theory. If we construe worldly properties as extensional, then they can be identified with the sets under discussion, and the resulting theory is a formalization of the framework of objects and properties and identity sketched in Chapters 2 and 3. The theory can be extended to a transfinite hierarchy of sets, yielding an indeterminate version of Zermelo–Fraenkel set theory; the classical ZF theory is satisfied in a definable subdomain of this theory. Relations are definable as sets of ordered pairs, using a refinement of the usual definition of ordered pairs; this shows the consistency of an assumption made in Chapter 3 that if R is a relation between individuals, then bearing R to object o is a property.

A theory of conceptual sets results from removing the DDiff condition placed on worldly sets.

12. HIGHER-ORDER INDETERMINACY

We have indeterminacy if there is a question that has no answer; we have higher-order indeterminacy when it is indeterminate *whether* a certain question has an answer. There might not be any higher-order indeterminacy, but in case there is, two accounts of it are offered. The theory from earlier chapters can be accommodated within either account.

Appendix: Evans on indeterminacy

Some of Evans's remarks about modalities near the end of his 1978 paper have puzzled many commentators. Following a suggestion of Wiggins, it is shown that they make good sense if we assume that Evans saw indeterminacy as a kind, or mode, of truth, so that '$\triangledown S$' may be true when 'S' is true. On this reading, his argument is not relevant to the thesis of indeterminate identity discussed in the subsequent literature.

1

Introduction

1.1 IDENTITY PUZZLES

Throughout history philosophers have puzzled over questions of identity:

Is a person identical with that person's body? Of course, if the person lives on after the body no longer exists, they are distinct, and if the person ceases to exist at death but the body continues in existence, they are distinct. But what if they always coexist?

Suppose a ship sets sail, and while at sea it is completely rebuilt, plank by plank; is the resulting ship with new parts the ship that originally set sail? What if the discarded pieces of the original ship are assembled into a ship; is *that* the ship that originally set sail?

If a person has a brain transplant, or a memory transplant, or . . . is the resulting person the same person who antedated the operation, or has the old person ceased to exist, to be replaced by another?

These, and a host of puzzles like them, persist without adequate solutions. Each puzzle is actually a vague description of a spectrum of cases, some of which give rise to one answer, and some of which give rise to the opposite answer, with sufficient cases in between to bewilder just about anyone, regardless of their instincts; thus the puzzles persist.[1]

---

[1] This way of construing the puzzles carries out a theme of van Inwagen (1988), which describes a cabinet in which a person undergoes disruptive changes, so that you are uncertain whether the person who emerges is the person who entered. Van Inwagen suggests that anyone can fine-tune what happens inside the cabinet so as to yield a case about which the fine-tuner is uncertain.

Consider the ship case. Sometimes we can disassemble an object into parts and then reassemble those parts into the original object. I may have to do this in order to get my favourite desk into a new room; this is a way to move my desk into the new room, not a way of destroying it and replacing it with a new desk. (If you are not convinced by this, think of taking apart a blender to wash it and then putting it back together again.)[2] So sometimes reassembling parts yields the original object. But sometimes I repair an object by replacing a part; if I replace the radiator in my car with a new one I think I still own a car that I bought several years ago, not one that just sprang into existence. So sometimes replacing a part yields the original object. The "ship of Theseus"[3] example above illustrates a case in which our judgements about identity are supposed to be in clear conflict: the original ship has apparently been disassembled and reassembled, and the original ship has apparently been repaired by having new parts installed. But these cannot both be true, because two non-identical ships have resulted.

Perhaps you see one of the options as being clearly superior to the other? Then a minor adjustment in the case will bring them into conflict:

If you are sure the ship with new parts is the original ship, suppose that the new parts of the repaired ship are quite unlike the parts being replaced, making the ship with new parts unlike the original ship—as unlike as you need to weaken your judgement of identity. (You may also wish to suppose that the activity is part of a contest to see how creatively the contestants can disassemble a ship and reassemble it, thus favouring the reassembled ship as being the original ship.)

If you are sure the "reassembled" ship is the original ship, just reassemble most but not all of the discarded parts, mixing in a

---

[2] If you are inclined to be sceptical about even such a case as this, consider what *you* would say if asked where you purchased your blender. You would never say "I didn't purchase it, I created it after the parts were last washed." So you must admit that you talk *as if* an object can be reassembled. And you must admit that this is serious talk, worth explaining, so the idea that what you say is plausible because it is *literally true* is an option well worth exploring. That is enough to open the door to theorizing on the identity question.

[3] A ship example originates in Plutarch's *Life of Theseus*. This was updated by adding a second ship by Hobbes in *De Corpere*, 2, 11. I have added the twist that the repair/replacement takes place at sea; this is not essential to the example.

few new ones. Adjust the number of parts upward or downward until you are no longer sure about what to say. If necessary, leave some of the original parts in the ship with (mostly) new parts.

Some philosophers have been driven by examples of this sort to provide a *method* for answering any such question. The most popular methods are the simplest. For example, some propose that having the same parts is necessary for identity, and any change of parts whatever leads to non-identity; there is never any such thing as repair by replacement of a part. Others propose that continuity of size, shape, and function are required to maintain identity, so that there is never any such thing as reassembly. These are extreme positions; they are often admired for the ingenuity that goes into defending them, but they have few real adherents. Instead, most philosophers try to devise a subtler criterion for identity preservation that avoids such extreme judgements, a criterion that will allow us to say "Aha, that's it", whenever the criterion is applied. Such methods (when not overly vague) give natural answers in the problematic cases, but other clever philosophers inevitably devise new cases in which the "subtle" methods ride roughshod over our surest judgements. Proponents of such views then must either refine them, or explain why normal intelligent people are wrong to reject them. A great deal of ingenuity has gone into the defence of and attack on such views; none of that discussion will be reprised here. It is clear that none of the methods has won popular acceptance, and this motivates us to look elsewhere.

Because so many identity puzzles have remained unsolved for centuries, some observers have been led to speculate that these are questions that have no answers. But that raises other questions. Why don't they have answers? What would it take for them to have answers?

The most popular option in this century is that the questions have no answers because they are improperly formulated, typically because they incorporate a definite description that does not uniquely denote. Sometimes this is plausible. It is plausible in the "building" case. Suppose that Old Ivy Hall has an addition built onto it, tripling it in size without altering the structure of the original in any significant way, and the new large building is named Postmodern Hall. My office is in the old part and yours is in the new part. Someone asks "Is the building in which Parsons has his office the building in which you have your office?" It seems clear that this has no unique correct answer, and that this is because the definite description 'the building in which Parsons has his office' does not uniquely denote. Buildings can be parts of other buildings, and Old Ivy Hall is now a part of Postmodern Hall. My office is in Old Ivy Hall, and also in Postmodern Hall, and these are not the same building; one is part of the other. So there is no such thing as *the* building in which I have my office. And so the identity question is ill-formed.

This solution is plausible because buildings are parts of other buildings. It is less plausible to think that ships are parts of other ships (at least for normally designed ships), and quite implausible that persons are parts of other persons. Yet this is what it would take to solve the harder cases in parallel fashion. For example, you *could* say that the definite description 'the original ship' fails to uniquely denote, because there were actually two original ships: one that was later repaired with new parts, and one that was later reassembled from the original parts. This is not plausible.[4]

I do not believe that a systematic diagnosis of identity puzzles in terms of imperfections in our language, or in the concepts embodied in our language, will be satisfactory. This is certainly a natural option, and one that I need to discuss (Chapter 10). However, my main task is to explore an alternative that I find more plausible.

1.2 WORLDLY INDETERMINACY OF IDENTITY

I am inclined to think that an identity question can be completely coherent and well formed and yet lack an answer because of the way the world is (or because of the way the world is not). Not that there is an unknown answer, but rather that there is no answer at all. In the ship case above, the facts are these: there is a unique original ship, there is a unique ship with new parts, and there is a unique newly assembled ship. The ship with new parts is distinct

---

[4] I examine some closely related but more plausible views in Ch. 10.

from (non-identical with) the newly assembled ship. But there is no fact of the matter regarding whether the newly assembled ship is the original ship, or whether the ship with new parts is the original ship.

When there is no fact of the matter, a sentence reporting the purported fact lacks truth-value. So the following sentences have the indicated statuses:

the newly assembled ship = the ship with new parts	False
the newly assembled ship = the original ship	No truth-value
the ship with new parts = the original ship	No truth-value

These indeterminacies must cohere with certain others as well. It is indeterminate whether the newly assembled ship formerly left port when the original ship did, and likewise for the ship with new parts. It is indeterminate whether the original ship now has new parts. And so on.

Each of the sentences listed above non-defectively reports a state of affairs, a state of affairs of identity. The first state of affairs is made not to hold by the way the world is, but the second and third are not either made to hold or made not to hold by the way the world is. Thus there is genuine *indeterminacy of identity in the world*. This is not an illusion generated by indeterminacy as to how our language fits with the world; the indeterminacy is real.

There is now a growing literature on the question of worldly indeterminacy of identity, stimulated almost wholly by a one-page article by Gareth Evans (1978), giving a proof that there cannot be genuine indeterminacy of identity in the world. This proof has been attacked, defended, revised, expanded, and so on. The literature on this subject has now matured to the point where an extended look at the issues seems both timely and feasible. Discussion of the issues so far has proceeded on a number of fronts, and on a piecemeal basis. What does not yet exist is a single coherent presentation of a position that articulates and defends worldly indeterminacy of identity. That is the task of this book. There is little contained here that has not already been argued in the literature in one form or another. The contribution of this book is to choose from among the positive views a subset that can be maintained together, to express these in a common vocabulary, to assemble them in a presentation that can be mastered by someone new to the topic, and to add a few details that may advance the issues.

In presenting the thesis of worldly indeterminacy of identity I speak as an advocate on its behalf. This is not because I am convinced it is true; indeed, if I am right, that is a contingent matter on which nobody can be certain. But it makes for a more coherent exposition if I take a definite stance on the issue. I *am* convinced that the existence of worldly indeterminacy of identity is both coherent and possible.

My goal is primarily to articulate the view in detail and in generality. The articulation of the view I take to be a matter of hypothesis formulation, and this is immune from certain kinds of criticism. For example, I cannot be said to beg the question merely by formulating what one answer to the question is. The main task of the book is just that: to formulate a position. I will also argue that the position is immune to certain kinds of attacks that have been levelled at it in the literature. Here I can be said to beg the question—but only if I presume a point at issue. The bulk of this book will be occupied with these two tasks: formulation of the view and defences of its coherence and prima-facie plausibility in the face of purported refutations. Neither of these tasks, even if successful, will show the view to be true. For that, what is required is to see whether it explains better than competing views do why certain identity questions *seem* to be coherent and yet lack answers. Some competing views will be discussed in Chapter 10, but many will not. And so the ultimate fate of the view will be left uncertain.

Methodologically, I take a Peircean perspective. I begin with ordinary beliefs, which I will reject only if some reason is found to challenge them. These are my tentative data: *ordinary* beliefs—such as the belief that I have exactly one wife, that there is exactly one dog in my back yard, and that exactly one ship set sail before the problematic replacement/repair/reassembly process. I reject philosophical analyses that contradict these judgements, telling me, for example, that I actually have several dogs, or that there is not really any such thing as a dog—there are only basic particles that swarm into dog-like shapes. It is also part of my methodology that I do *not* take as data highly theoretical philosophical generalizations, such as "nothing is indeterminate", or "no two things can be in the same place at once", or the opposites of such views.

I see these as theoretical observations which are to be validated by how well they conform to the data, as opposed to the other way around. I may occasionally rely on some theoretical views myself, but only by accident, or when I see no other way to resolve an issue.

I do not necessarily expect the reader to share this methodology, or to apply it exactly as I do; I articulate it here to clarify what I will and will not be doing. Many proposed solutions to the puzzles involve taking a stand that requires us to reject some of the apparent data, for example, rejecting the view that exactly one person entered the room in which the disruption took place. Let me call any such position a "traditional solution". A traditional solution explains how and why we should *change* our beliefs, and shows how the puzzles are resolved if we do so. I will not discuss such solutions at all. There is an enormous literature devoted to this already, and there is no need for me to duplicate it. Instead I focus on proposed solutions that "preserve the data", solutions that explain how it is that

> The ordinary beliefs that we have about the identity puzzle cases are literally true.

I also limit myself by the working assumption that

> It is literally true that there is no answer to the identity questions in the puzzle cases.

I will develop one such explanation, and I will discuss others.

1.4 A STOCK OF PUZZLES

It will help to have at hand a small stock of cases to discuss, and an indication of what I take the data to be in each.

> *The person/body*: Assuming that a person exists when and only when their body exists,[5] is each person identical with his/her body?

---

[5] This assumption is crucial. For example, Stalnaker (1988: 354) says "we can distinguish intimately related things such as an artifact and what it is made of, a person and his or her body, by distinguishing their temporal properties." The person/body puzzle discussed here is a hypothetical one: *what if* there were no

Data: If I am alone in a room, then there is exactly one person in the room, and exactly one human body in the room.
Working assumption: There is no answer to the question whether the person in the room is the body in the room.

The ship: An assembly/repair process takes place as described above. Is the original ship identical with the ship with new parts, or with the newly assembled ship (or neither)?
Data: Exactly one ship left port, and exactly two ships docked.
Working assumption: There is no answer to the question whether the original ship is the ship with new parts, or whether the original ship is the newly assembled ship.

The personal disruption: A person enters a room where something disruptive happens to them that challenges our judgements about personal identity. Is the person who entered the room identical with the person who later leaves the room?
Data: Exactly one person entered the room, and exactly one person left the room.
Working assumption: There is no answer to the question whether the person who entered the room is the person who left the room.

The cat:[6] It is unclear exactly what the parts of a cat are. For example, it is unclear whether a molecule loosely attached to the end of a hair that is engaged in falling out is part of the cat. Consider all ways of answering such questions precisely. Call the object (if any) that answers to any such precise description of its parts a "p-cat". There are many p-cats, and they are distinct from one another, because they all have different parts. How is the cat related to the p-cats? Is it identical to any of them? To none of them? (Are the p-cats cats? If so, how many cats are on the table when we naïvely think there is only one?)
Data: There is exactly one cat, and there are many p-cats.
Working assumption: For any given p-cat, there is no answer to the question whether it is the cat.

---

clear examples of temporal properties in which they differ? Of course, if they do not temporally coincide, then presumably one will be a person-at-t and the other not a person-at-t, so they will be definitely distinct. The puzzle is: what if they always coexist?

[6] Patterned after an example in Lewis (1993).

You are asked in each case to adjust the details of the example so as to make the answer to the identity question most uncertain, based on *your* convictions. I will assume that I am addressing a reader who makes such adjustments to the cases under consideration.

For convenience later, I will refer to the above data together with the working assumptions as "extended data". This is not to insist that they are correct, but rather to emphasize that I will be trying to account for them, not to argue for them.

The first and last of these questions involve cases of identity-at-a-time, and the middle two are cases of identity-across-time. People sometimes distinguish these, calling the first "coincidence" and the second "persistence". I ignore the distinction because it is not relevant to any of the issues that I address.

1.5 PLAN OF THE BOOK

First I will address what is involved in there being indeterminacy in the world. Next, I will apply this to indeterminacy of identity. In both of these enterprises we need to clarify not only what a partially indeterminate world is like, but also how a language works that correctly describes such a world. Then I look at a number of arguments in the literature that attempt to show that positing indeterminacy of identity leads quickly to inconsistency. This is followed by a discussion of some variations of the inconsistency argument based on the logic and semantics of conditionals. Following this I discuss the complaint that we cannot conceive of identity's being indeterminate, and I give a useful "classical picturing" of situations involving indeterminacy, including indeterminacy of identity. This is followed by a discussion of how we can count objects whose identities are partially indeterminate, and of how we can uniquely refer to such objects. Then certain alternative views are treated, views that locate indeterminacy wholly in language or in our concepts; the question is whether such a view can provide a better account of the data than the view that posits real indeterminacy. After this there is a discussion of how it is possible to develop a coherent theory of sets that allows sets to have indeterminate members; properties with indeterminate identity are also discussed. Finally I briefly discuss what impact higher-order indeterminacy might have on this enterprise.

If I am successful, the reader will find a coherent statement of what it would be like if there were indeterminacy in the world, extending to indeterminacy of identity. (It would be what the world would be like if the world were exactly as we naïvely think it is.)

2

Indeterminacy

2.1 WHY TAKE INDETERMINACY SERIOUSLY?

The view under consideration sees the world as consisting of states of affairs. Some of these definitely hold, some definitely do not hold, and others are simply undetermined. Why should one think that the world might be like this? Because it is a possibility. For all we know, the world *is* like this.

Suppose that some form of idealism is correct, so that the world is a thing created by our minds. Then since our minds are finite, they are not likely to get around to finishing the job. So some aspects of the world will be left uncreated, or undetermined, and there will be indeterminacy. This option is sometimes foreclosed by supposing that there is an absolute mind that fills in for us whatever we ourselves leave undetermined. But why suppose that the absolute mind determines everything? If the absolute mind is anything like the traditional Judeo-Christian-Islamic deity, then this deity freely chooses both whether and what to create, so why assume that (s)he determines everything? It takes a rather special sort of deity to guarantee complete determinacy.

Ignore idealism. Michael Dummett[1] has made popular the idea that a test for a realist view is whether that view embodies "bivalence", the condition that every claim about the world is true or false. Suppose that a sentence expressing an undetermined state of affairs lacks truth-value. (This is an assumption that I will indeed make.) Then it appears that realism is incompatible with indeterminacy *by definition*! Perhaps this is so for Dummett's brand of realism, but not for mine. I assume that realism includes any view that how the world is is independent of my mind or how I conceive

[1] e.g., in Dummett (1978: 145–65).

of it. If this is so, there is no a priori reason to assume bivalence, and no reason to suppose that the world is completely determinate. Why should it be?

Another outlook is pragmatism, the idea that "the world" is whatever is revealed by scientific investigation and theorizing. Quine (along with other pragmatists) holds a view something like this. Quine sees the question of bivalence as a pragmatic method-ological choice we can make. A commitment to bivalence in our theorizing leads to methodological elegance and simplicity, while making it difficult to reconcile recalcitrant data; an abandonment of bivalence permits data to mesh more neatly with theory, while complicating the theory. (I am stating Quine's view here, not endorsing it.) Thus bivalence is a choice. Quine himself chooses bivalence over its "fuzzy and plurivalent alternatives" (Quine 1981: 94–5) but others may choose differently. Again, indeterminacy is an option.

Other views could be surveyed,[2] but the point is clear enough: there are plenty of reasonable conceptions of what the world is like that do not preclude at least some indeterminacy. And so we should investigate what the consequences would be if there were indeterminacy.

2.2 INDETERMINACY IN THE WORLD

I suppose that the world contains objects, properties of objects, and relations among objects. For any given object o and property p there are three options: either o definitely has p, or o definitely lacks p, or it is indeterminate whether o has or lacks p. For any given objects o_1 and o_2 and relation r there are also three options: the object o_1 definitely bears the relation r to o_2, or o_1 definitely does not bear the relation r to o_2, or it is indeterminate whether o_1 bears r to o_2.

For the moment[3] suppose we speak of o's having or lacking p as

---

[2] Cf. Burgess (1990), especially §§10–11, for a critique of certain contemporary views that reject all indeterminacy for reasons that he finds less than compelling.

[3] I say "for the moment" because in the detailed formulation of the theory I will not need to talk of states of affairs at all; I will only need to talk about objects, properties, and relations.

a state of affairs. Then these states of affairs either determinately hold (if *o* definitely has *p*), or determinately do not hold (if *o* definitely does not have *p*), or they are not determined either way. In the last case the state of affairs is indeterminate. I emphasize that it is the state of affairs that is indeterminate, not the objects or properties or relations composing it. Indeterminacy emerges at the level of states of affairs, and if we wish to call objects or properties or relations themselves indeterminate, we will mean by that merely that they enter into indeterminate states of affairs. There is nothing in the view discussed here which lays the blame for indeterminacy of states of affairs on either the objects or on the properties or relations. I thus set aside certain discussions in the literature addressing indeterminacy of identity which try to distinguish whether it is objects that are indeterminate, or the relation of identity itself.[4] I do not know how to apply the notion of indeterminacy below the level at which we make whole judgements, except derivatively; e.g. if one defines an indeterminate object as one for which there is some object with which it is indeterminately identical:

x is an *indeterminate object* $=_{df}$ ∃y[it is indeterminate whether x = y].

I am also neutral about whether or not properties and relations are "intensional" entities, that is, about whether there can be two *distinct* properties *p* and *q* that determinately hold of exactly the same objects and determinately fail to hold of exactly the same objects. It just happens that this issue does not bear on anything I have to say. So I will not discuss it, except briefly in Chapter 11. However, I am not neutral about realism for properties. The properties under discussion here must be genuine constituents of the world, not concepts in the mind or mere words. It is real properties in the

---

[4] Sainsbury (1989) defines a "vague property" as one that neither definitely applies nor definitely fails to apply to a sharp object, where a "sharp" object is one that does not have two precisifications such that some property definitely applies to one but definitely does not belong to the other. He does not define 'precisification'. Sainsbury (1994) argues more sceptically that there is no substantive thesis about whether there are vague properties. He suggests that one could define a vague *object* as one such that it is indeterminate whether some sharp property applies to it, but he doubts that one can clarify what a "sharp" property is. I am inclined to agree. Many writers suggest that there can be objects that possess genuinely vague boundaries, but the connection between this fact and indeterminate identity is debatable; see Ch. 5.

world that determine whether objects (real objects in the world) are or are not identical (really identical). So my theorizing is avowedly realistic. I have in mind no particular theory of properties, except that they must be genuine universals—they must be the sort of thing that are capable of being possessed by many objects. My discussion of identity is neutral among many different versions of such a view.[5]

Nominalists and conceptualists often believe that they can account for any phenomenon that realists can account for, by showing how to take talk about real things in the world and explain it in nominalistically or conceptualistically acceptable ways. I have no objection to such projects, but they need to be distinguished from what I am doing here. I am presenting a realist theory that might provide the input to nominalist or conceptualist reductions; I am not myself presenting a nominalist or conceptualist theory. (I do not know how to formulate the theory I discuss here in terms acceptable to nominalism or conceptualism.)

2.3 TRUTH-MAKING

States of affairs can make sentences true in different ways. In the most direct way, sentences may express states of affairs, e.g. the sentence may consist of an atomic predicate that stands for a property and a name that stands for an object. Such a sentence is true if the object named determinately possesses the property, false if the object determinately lacks the property, and it is otherwise lacking in truth-value. The sentence is made true, or false, or neither, directly by "the facts", i.e. by the status of how the object and property are related. Other sentences are made true, false, or neither, indirectly. For example, an existential "Something is *F*" whose

---

[5] For a survey of various theories of properties see Mellor and Oliver (1997). I take for granted that properties are universals (typically shared by many objects) in various places in this text. A referee for OUP suggests that the indeterminate identity view may be developed without this assumption. This may be true, but I have not explored that option.

predicate '*F*' stands for a property will be made true by a state of affairs that determinately holds; it will be made false by the determinate non-holding of all states of affairs involving any object and the property *F*; and it will be made truth-valueless by there *not being any* determinately holding state of affairs involving an object and the property *F*, together with there *being* some states of affairs of that form that do not either determinately hold or determinately not hold.

In addition to predicates that stand for properties, there are predicates that do not stand for properties. We will be able to prove below that if there is indeterminacy of certain sorts, then some predicates do not stand for properties, yet sentences containing them will be made true (or false or neither) by how the world is. For example, if 'F' stands for a property, then we might have a predicate meaning 'is neither determinately F nor determinately not F'. There is no reason to expect there to be a property answering to this latter predicate (though there might be)[6]; if there is not, such a predicate does not stand for a property, though it is clear how the truth of sentences containing it are validated (or not) indirectly by the facts. When we discuss existing predicates arising from philosophical examples, it may be uncertain whether they stand for properties; we will sometimes need to discuss issues that are formulated in terms of such predicates while being uncertain whether they stand for properties.

In order to clarify in general how aspects of the world make sentences about the world true (or false, or neither), we will need to say in detail how our language works and how it is related to the world. So we must discuss the semantics of the language that will be used in stating our metaphysical theses; this is the business of the next section. It turns out that we do not need to speak of states of affairs in order to do this, so they will henceforth vanish from our exposition. We do need to speak of objects, properties, and relations.

[6] Typically, whether a predicate *can* stand for a property depends on how the world goes. For example, if it is indeterminate whether $a = b$, then we can show that the predicate 'being a thing such that it is indeterminate whether it is *b*' will be a predicate that cannot stand for a property; see Chs. 4 and 7. But if *b* is not indeterminately identical with any object, there is no inconsistency in holding that 'being a thing such that it is indeterminate whether it is *b*' stands for a property.

2.4 LANGUAGE: SYNTAX AND SEMANTICS

The symbolism used herein consists mostly of the first-order predicate calculus. It contains names of objects, and predicates that are true (or false, or neither) of objects. There are connectives, and there are quantifiers to express generality. I postpone introducing a sign for identity until the next chapter, and I postpone introducing a conditional sign until Chapter 6; otherwise, what follows here is the language that will be used throughout the book.

Names: I assume we have a stock of names that name objects. Each name names a unique object. There are no denotationless names, and no names whose denotation is ambiguous. I make these assumptions for simplicity of discussion; the issues are sufficiently complex that we should not have to worry about whether, for example, a name lacks reference. (In Chapter 9, I discuss the claim that names *cannot* unambiguously denote objects which enter into indeterminate identities. My position is that they can, and I assume here that they do.)

Predicates: A one-place predicate may stand for a property, or it may not, and a two-place predicate may stand for a relation, or it may not. We need to allow for both options. In either case I assume that a predicate is true of some (or no) objects and is false of some (or no) objects. I decree that there is no object such that the predicate is true of it and also false of it. There may be objects the predicate is neither true nor false of. (Two-place predicates are true of/false of/neither true nor false of ordered pairs of objects.)

If a predicate stands for a property, then it is true of the objects that (determinately) possess the property, and it is false of those objects that (determinately) lack the property. So if an object neither determinately has nor determinately lacks the property, the predicate will be neither true of nor false of it. (Similarly for two-place predicates that stand for relations.)

Truth: The truth conditions for formulas and sentences are given here in a simple form. Most people knowledgeable about logic will know how to make this more rigorous (e.g. by defining satisfaction of formulas by infinite sequences of objects assigned to the variables), and most others will not be concerned.

Atomic sentences: An atomic sentence consists of a one-place predicate and a name, or a two-place predicate and two names. Such a sentence is true if the predicate is true of the object named by the name (or the pair of objects named by the names), and false if it is false of the object named by the name; otherwise the sentence has no truth-value.

Connectives and quantifiers: There are many different ways to define connectives and quantifiers for a language in which some sentences lack truth-value. We need to choose some particular conventions in order to have a definite framework, while remaining sensitive to the fact that other writers may interpret connectives differently. I make my own choice here, and discuss alternatives when they are relevant. For familiarity, I assume that all connectives and quantifiers behave in the usual ways when the formulas with which they combine possess truth-value. The quirks arise only for cases without truth-value. For these I choose the Łukasiewicz conventions, for their naturalness:

> *Negation*: A negation of a true sentence is false, and a negation of a false sentence is true. If a sentence lacks truth-value, so does its negation.
>
> *Conjunction*: A conjunction is true if both conjuncts are true, false if either is false, and otherwise lacking in truth-value.
>
> *Disjunction*: A disjunction is true if either disjunct is true, false if both are false, and otherwise lacking in truth-value.
>
> These connectives are summed up in Tables 2.1 and 2.2, in which the dashes stand for absence of truth-value.
>
> *Quantifiers*: The quantifiers $\exists$ and $\forall$ are understood as generalizations of conjunction and disjunction:
>
> > $\exists x \phi x$ is true if ϕx is true for at least one assignment to x, false if ϕx is false on every assignment to x, and otherwise $\exists x \phi x$ is lacking in truth-value.
> >
> > $\forall x \phi x$ is true if ϕx is true for every assignment to x, false if ϕx is false on at least one assignment to x, and otherwise $\forall x \phi x$ is lacking in truth-value.

The determinate truth connective: It will be useful to have a "non-classical" connective for truth. I use '!' for this. The convention is:

> '!S' is true if 'S' is true, and otherwise false.

TABLE 2.1. TABLE 2.2.

A	B	A&B	A ∨ B		A	¬A
T	T	T	T		T	F
—	T	—	T		—	—
F	T	F	T		F	T
T	—	—	T			
—	—	—	—			
F	—	F	—			
T	F	F	T			
—	F	F	—			
F	F	F	F			

I call this the "truth" connective, though it is probably better called the "determinately" connective. That is, you should *read* '!S' as 'Determinately, S'. The notion of truth gets in only in the metalanguage, when we state the *truth*-conditions for the elements of our language: 'Determinately, S' is true if 'S' is true, and false if 'S' is false or lacks truth-value.

Using this notation we can express other ideas. For example, the falsehood of 'S' is expressed by its negation being (determinately) true: '!¬S'. We can also express indeterminacy. There is an established sign for this in the literature, originating in Evans (1978): we express a claim that S is indeterminate by writing '∇S', defined as:

$$\nabla S =_{df} \neg !S \ \& \ \neg !\neg S$$

This means that it is not determined *whether* S. Thus ∇S is incompatible with S's being true and with S's being false. A sentence of the form '∇S' is true if and only if 'S' itself lacks truth-value. These conventions are summed up in Table 2.3.

This is most of the language we will use throughout. The language is not "bivalent" in the usual sense because it allows the possibility that sentences may lack truth-value. But it is also not "multivalent" as this is usually understood, since this usually means that there are more than two truth-values. For the language used

TABLE 2.3.

S	(determinate) truth !S	(determinate) falsity !¬S	indeterminacy ∇S
T	T	F	F
—	F	F	T
F	F	T	F

here, there are only two truth-values, true and false, though there are three truth-value *statuses*: true, false, and neither.[7]

2.5 DETERMINACY IN NATURAL LANGUAGE ASSERTIONS

A sentence expressing an indeterminate state of affairs lacks truth-value. When we assert sentences, we generally put them forth *as true*, so an assertion of 'S' will commit the assertor to the claim that the state of affairs that S determinately holds.[8] This means that for assertions it is generally redundant to use the adverb 'determinately' to modify the whole sentence used to make the assertion. With regard to subclauses of assertions, however, it may or may not be redundant to add 'determinately'. Since it is not always immediately obvious whether it is redundant or not, I will occasionally burden my sentences with redundant uses of 'definitely' and 'determinately' so that the reader will not have to pause to figure out whether determinacy is entailed (or required) or not.

How do we deal with *indeterminacy* in real life discussion?

---

[7] For most purposes it does not matter whether one assumes that a sentence which is neither true nor false has no truth-value, as I do, or assumes that it has a special "neuter" value. I take the former option merely because it does not require explaining what an additional "truth"-value is which is neither truth nor falsehood.

[8] It is possible to commit oneself merely to the non-falsehood of the proposition asserted, but this usually takes a special convention. See Woodruff (1970) for a study of "hedged assertion" in formal languages, and Parsons (1984) for natural languages. These options are especially relevant to work on the semantic paradoxes. Since the paradoxes are not at issue here, I omit discussing them.

Presumably, if we think a claim is indeterminate we avoid making either that claim or its negation (which is also indeterminate). But what if we are called upon to take sides? We have one of two resources. One option is to retreat to a meta-level and say something like "You can't say one way or the other", or "That can't be determined", or "There's no answer to that question", or some variant of these. If we are philosophers, we will feel called upon to say more, but in ordinary conversations such a comment will usually suffice. A second option is to "deny" the claim, usually with a special emphasis on negation; this is followed up, if need be, by denying the opposite as well. If asked whether the ship that docked in a given port is the same as the one that left the original port, you might say "It's *not* the same, but it's not *different* either; there's just no telling", or even "It's not the *same*, but it's not *not* the same either." Denying that it is the same ship is not the same as asserting the negation of the claim that it is the same ship, because that would make you take sides, which is exactly what you think should not be done. So a denial is either an assertion of a special kind of negation, or it is itself a special kind of speech act—an act which denies the content "that it is the same ship", as opposed to an act which asserts the different content "that it is not the same ship". In this book I take the conservative option, which is to see this kind of denial as assertion of the special kind of negation called "exclusion negation".[9] Unlike normal negation, the assertion of the exclusion negation of a claim merely denies that claim, it does not endorse its opposite (its ordinary negation). Whereas the ordinary negation of a claim S is another assertion, 'not S', which lacks truth-value if S does, exclusion negation is used in such a way that 'ex-not S' is an assertion that is true when S lacks truth-value (Table 2.4).

This, then, is the kind of negation that we are trying to express when we reject a claim with special intonation in order to distance ourselves from taking sides regarding it. Exclusion negation is

---

[9] It is hard to say which of these is the best account, or even if there is a difference between them. But some such account is needed, because there must be (and is) an alternative to asserting the negation of a claim that you think is indeterminate. I have argued in Parsons (1984) that in some recalcitrant cases (cases involving semantic paradox) we are forced sometimes to see denial as a speech act separate from assertion, rather than see it as the ordinary assertion of a special kind of negation. Since this book is not about the paradoxes, I here take the simpler line of preserving a single kind of assertion and employing a special kind of negation when needed. It is not a trivial task to repackage a theory developed using exclusion negation into one that appeals to a special kind of denial.

TABLE 2.4.

S	negation not S	exclusion negation ex-not S
T	F	F
—	—	T
F	T	T

easily defined in terms we have available from above; the exclusion negation of 'S' is just '¬!S'. If we want to say in the object language that a claim lacks truth-value, we just exnegate both it and its negation, saying '¬!S & ¬!¬S'. Indeed, this is our proposal above for introducing a connective for indeterminacy. This kind of notation corresponds to things we actually say when forced to confront claims in real life that we think are indeterminate.[10]

---

[10] Here and throughout this book I am making a simplification that is strictly wrong, but convenient. This is to ignore certain instances of what Frege calls indirect contexts. I argue in Parsons (1996, 1997) that whenever we have a *that*-clause or a *whether*-clause we have a case of indirect discourse, a context in which we have shifted to talk of the meaning of the contents of the clause. This is obvious in 'She means that snow is white', or 'She believes that snow is white'; I think it is equally true for 'It is true that snow is white' and 'It is not the case that snow is white'. (In Fregean terms, the sentences 'It is true that snow is white' or 'That snow is white is true' attribute truth to a thought, which is referred to by the that-clause.) As a consequence, there is no such *connective* as 'it is not the case that'; the phrase 'it is not the case that' is a complex phrase that *contains* a connective, 'not', but that is not itself a connective; it is *more than* a connective since it also creates an indirect context. Nonetheless we are inclined to call it a connective because it resembles the behaviour of one in spite of its complexity: the 'that' makes the phrase that follows refer to its meaning, and the 'it is the case' correctly characterizes that meaning if and only if the sentence following the 'that' is true when normally interpreted. As a result, these two phenomena cancel each other out, and the complex phrase 'it is not the case that' has the same overall effect as 'not' all by itself, with the exception that the long phrase goes uniformly in front and the 'not' must usually go someplace inside. Something like that is at work in the suggested readings above for the determinate-truth connective. It is not strictly correct to read '!S' as 'it is true that S', or 'determinately, S', because '!' is not itself to be pronounced at all; its effect in speech shows up only as a special intonation or stress on the sentence that follows it. Exclusion negation '¬!' is also just pronounced 'not', but with a special stress that settles on the 'not' itself or some part of the sentence that follows. Since stress is rarely unambiguous in what it contributes to meaning, I will persist below in the inaccurate but clearer policy of reading '!S' as 'it is (determinately) true that S' and '¬!S' as 'it is not (determinately) true that S', with the understanding that the notation is intended to be my way of symbolizing some uses of '*not* S', as the occasion demands.

2.6 LOGIC

When we wish to be precise in using a language that permits truth-valueless sentences, the logical truths that result and the inferences that are valid differ subtly from the ones we are used to when we idealize and assume bivalence. There is nothing difficult or mysterious about this, but because of lack of familiarity it may not be obvious without some thought, and even some analysis, what is permitted and what is not. This is especially so for people who have been trained in logic, for they have developed quick instincts for what is the case, and these instincts must sometimes be overcome. In any event, it is worth taking some time to go over the consequences for logic of admitting the possibility of lack of truth-value.

Things are simple in one way: the language described above (and used throughout this book) contains no non-extensional contexts. I omit these because they have no bearing on any of the issues to be discussed. So one may "quantify into" any context. That is, if '... a ...' is a sentence containing a name 'a', the following is always valid:

$$\frac{\ldots a \ldots}{\exists x (\ldots x \ldots)}$$

And when we introduce identity (in the next chapter), this inference will always be valid:

$$a = b$$
$$\frac{\ldots a \ldots}{\ldots b \ldots}$$

Validity: I assume that when we discuss validity we are discussing truth-preservation. That is:

An argument is *formally valid* if and only if any instance of it that has all true premises also has a true conclusion.

One could mean different things than this by validity, and some people do. For example, one might require of a valid argument that it preserve truth and also preserve non-falsehood, so that no instance of a valid argument can lead from premises that lack truth-value to a conclusion that is false.[11] I do not require this additional complication because I judge that this is never needed to assess arguments that are actually given in the literature. (Of course, if you are arguing from true premisses, the differences will not matter.) This leaves open the possibility that in some of the philosophical discussion addressed below there might be misunderstanding due to a conflict of assumptions about what is meant by validity. I think this does not actually happen, but the reader should be on guard.

The semantics described in §2.4 determines the valid inferences. These valid inferences may also be studied by using formal proofs that are based on the semantics. I give a set of rules of proof here. Except for abstraction principles, these include all of the rules of proof that will be appealed to in this book.

In order to state all the rules here, I need to add a conditional connective. I use the symbol '$\Rightarrow$' for this connective. Its definition is that '$\phi \Rightarrow \psi$' is true if 'ϕ' is false or 'ψ' is true or both 'ϕ' and 'ψ' lack truth-value; it is false if 'ϕ' is true and 'ψ' is false; it is otherwise lacking in truth-value. This connective will be discussed and its choice justified in Chapter 5; I include it here in order to state a set of rules that will not need to be supplemented later. I also include the rules for identity, though they will not be discussed until the next chapter.

The following are (partly redundant)[12] rules for a natural deduction system in which premisses are introduced at will, and subproofs can appear at any later point. A line *dominates* a later line if the dominating line is not within a previously completed subproof. Almost any currently popular version of natural deduction (modified as indicated below) will do. In the system given here, when a rule indicates that something may be inferred from certain given things, those things may be anywhere in the proof so long as they dominate the line being derived.

Except for the quantifier/determinacy commutation rules and the non-falsity rules for quantifier inferences, these rules look quite

---

[11] Van Inwagen (1988) does this, as does Cowles (1994) following him. This must be kept in mind when assessing any of the claims of those papers. My views are much closer to the views expressed by van Inwagen and Cowles than one might think, since apparently conflicting claims turn out not to conflict once the alternate meanings of 'valid' are unpacked.

[12] For ease of use, more rules are stated here than are logically required; e.g. RAA can be inferred from CP and Rule T.

TABLE 2.5.   Rules for a natural reduction system

Rule T: Infer anything on a line if it is tautologically implied by a set of sentences on lines that dominate that line.

Rule RAA: If there is a subproof whose sole hypothesis is 'ϕ' and whose last line is of the form '$\psi \& \neg\psi$', then the subproof may be followed by '$\neg!\phi$'.

Rule CP: If there is a subproof whose sole hypothesis is 'ϕ' and whose last line is 'ψ', then the subproof may be followed by '$!\phi \Rightarrow \psi$'.

Self-Identity: '$\forall x(x = x)$' may be written on any line.

Leibniz's Law: From '$s = t$' and 'ϕs' infer 'ϕt',
where 'ϕt' results from 'ϕs' by replacing some or all occurrences of 's' in 'ϕs' by 't'.

Quantifier Rules: We adopt the usual rules of Universal Specification, Universal Generalization, Existential Specification, Existential Generalization.

Quantifier Rules for Non-falsity: We also adopt "non-falsity" versions of the rules of Universal Specification, Universal Generalization, Existential Specification, Existential Generalization by prefixing their formulas with '$\neg!\neg$'. For example, the non-falsity version of Universal Specification is that from '$\neg!\neg\forall xFx$' one may infer '$\neg!\neg Fa$'.

Quantifier Interchange: '$\exists x\phi$' may be interchanged with '$\neg\forall x\neg\phi$' in any context; likewise for '$\forall x\phi$' and '$\neg\exists x\neg\phi$'.

Quantifier/Determinacy Commutativity: '$!\forall x\phi$' is interchangeable with '$\forall x!\phi$' everywhere. Likewise '$!\exists x\phi$' and '$\exists x!\phi$'.

---

normal. Their principal novelty lies in the modified reductio and conditional proof rules, and in the fact that tautological implication has different forms than in bivalent logic. Tautological implication is defined as follows:

> A set of sentences *tautologically implies* a given sentence if and only if every assignment of truth-value statuses to the non-molecular parts of the sentences which makes all the sentences in the given set true also makes the given sentence true.

This definition relies on the truth-table accounts of the connectives, including the non-standard '!' and '$\triangledown$' connectives and the '$\Rightarrow$' conditional. Since these truth-tables are new, so are the resultant tautological inferences. I summarize here some points of comparison with ordinary bivalent logic.

First, consider sentences of the ordinary predicate calculus as described above that do not contain the connectives '!' or '∇' or '⇒'. Then:

1. Classical tautologies (those made without the use of the special connectives) are not provable. Classical tautologies are not tautologies here because of the possibility of lack of truth-value. For example, A ∨ ¬A is not a tautology because if A lacks truth-value, so does ¬A, and so does the disjunction. The "Law of Excluded Middle" does not obtain.

2. Most inferences from premisses, however, work in the usual fashion. That is, if you have some premisses, and a conclusion that classically follows from those premisses, then that inference is usually valid here. This is because 'follows' means that if the premisses are true the conclusion must be true too. Assuming that the premisses are true very often amounts to assuming that there are no gaps in them in positions that could make a classically valid conclusion lack truth-value. The commonest exceptions to this are cases of "irrelevant" inferences; e.g. in bivalent logic you can infer 'A ∨ ¬A' from 'B ∨ ¬B', and you cannot do that here. But you can infer 'A' from 'A ∨ B' and '¬B', and you can infer '¬A ∨ ¬B' from '¬(A & B)', and so on.

3. *Reductio ad absurdum*: You can show that something is *not true* by deriving a contradiction from it. But that does not show that its negation is true. And so the proof technique of indirect proof (Rule RAA: show that '¬S' is true by deriving a contradiction from 'S') cannot take its usual form. Illustration:

> If you assume A&¬A as a hypothesis, you can easily infer a contradiction from it (itself). Classical indirect proof would then let you infer ¬(A&¬A). But if A lacks truth-value, so does ¬(A&¬A), so you are not allowed to infer that.

When the truth connective (the "determinately" connective) is included, the following hold:

1. This connective does not interfere with any of the inferences we just discussed. If you *can* prove something in a way

I just described, the presence of the other connectives does not interfere with this.

2. The truth connective commutes with quantifiers. So you needn't worry about properly ordering it with respect to the quantifiers. For example, !∃xFx will always have exactly the same truth-value status as ∃x!Fx.

3. The truth connective distributes across & and ∨:

!(A&B) is equivalent in truth-value status to !A&!B, and !(A∨B) is equivalent in truth-value status to !A∨!B.

This connective does not, however, commute with negation; ¬!A is not generally equivalent to !¬A.

4. There are tautologies and logical truths involving '!'. For example, A ∨ ¬!A is a tautology, and ∀x(Fx ∨ ¬!Fx) is logically true.

5. There is a form of indirect proof. If you derive a contradiction from S, then although that doesn't show ¬S, it does show ¬!S. So although this is *not* valid:

NO: | S
    |————————
    | A & ¬A
  ¬S

the following *is* valid:

YES: | S
     |————————
     | A & ¬A
   ¬!S

Contrapositive reasoning: The above principles are natural and easy to recall. A subtler point is this: if you have a valid inference pattern, contrapositive forms of that pattern need not be valid. For example, if this is a valid form:

A
————
∴B

then you cannot assume that this form is valid:

¬B
————
∴¬A
.

As a counter-instance, it is plain that this inference pattern is valid:

$$\frac{A}{\therefore !\,A}$$

because if the premiss is true, so is the sentence that says it is true. But the contrapositive principle is not remotely compelling:

$$\frac{\neg !\,A}{\therefore \neg A}.$$

If A lacks truth-value, then the premiss is true and the conclusion is not true, because it lacks truth-value. This failure of contrapositive reasoning does not rely on any esoteric doctrine; it is an inevitable and natural result of admitting the possibility of a sentence's lacking truth-value.

There is, of course, a reliable form of "near-contrapositive" reasoning, using the truth connective. If this is valid:

$$\frac{A}{\therefore B}$$

then so is this:

$$\frac{\neg B}{\therefore \neg !\,A}.$$

In my opinion the major cause of ongoing controversy regarding indeterminacy in general and indeterminacy of identity in particular is our tendency to take for granted contrapositive reasoning when using propositions that may lack truth-value. This type of reasoning is so natural to us when dealing with truth-valued claims that we instinctively pursue it when dealing with meaningful claims that may lack truth-value, where it is straightforwardly fallacious. I will touch on this point a number of times throughout the book.

The point just made about contrapositive reasoning depends on the use of a negation connective that produces a sentence without truth-value when appended to a sentence that lacks truth-value. This is the sort of negation that is usually intended when people discuss issues of indeterminacy.[13] If one uses "exclusion" negation,

---

[13] This is based on my reading of the literature; others might disagree. Fortunately, people usually specify how they intend their negations to be taken.

things are different. Recall that the exclusion negation of a sentence, produces a sentence that is true when 'S' lacks truth-value:

ex-not S $=_{df}$ ¬!S

The use of exclusion negation removes all truth-value gaps, and so contrapositive reasoning *is* valid using it. But exclusion negation has idiosyncrasies of its own; for example, the law of double exnegation does not hold. (From 'ex-not ex-not S' one may *not* infer 'S', though the reverse is valid.) I find it more revealing to think of exclusion negation as a way of denying the *truth* of a claim, and writing this *explicitly* using '¬!' instead of a single connective 'exnot'. When discussing the views of others, I need to be careful to match their own use of negation, and the reader needs to be alert that no questions are begged because of unclarity over what kind of negation is used.

2.7 WHAT IS NOT AT ISSUE

Certain topics are not discussed here, though they may be called to mind by some of the discussion so far.

Semantic and/or set-theoretic paradoxes: Much work in the last few decades on systems of logic that allow for truth-value gaps have been motivated by the study of semantic paradoxes or, to a lesser extent, by the paradoxes of set theory. Those topics are not under consideration here.

Vagueness: People sometimes use 'vagueness' to express what I call indeterminacy. I avoid the word 'vague' because it suggests a very different study of one or more very different notions.

> 1. Vagueness is usually thought of as a property of language or of concepts. Some people think that this kind of vagueness is to blame for identity puzzles, but I do not, and we need to keep the views straight. The topic here is indeterminacy in the world, not vagueness of words or concepts. It may be difficult to distinguish these in practice, but it is essential to use terminology that at least allows the distinction a chance to be made.[14]

---

[14] The use of 'vague' makes a transition between language and the world overly natural. Consider Pelletier (1989). He quotes me in Parsons (1987) talking about indeterminacy of truth-value, using 'indeterminacy' to describe this. He rewords this as "vagueness, or indeterminateness" (Pelletier 1989: 492), and then he concludes

2. When people use 'vague' to characterize things in the world, they often speak of vague *objects* or of whether *the identity relation* itself is vague. As explained early in this chapter, I see indeterminacy as applying at the level of states of affairs, and I do not attempt the additional step of blaming it on either the objects or the properties or relations making up those states of affairs. One can define a "vague object" as an object x such that for some object y it is indeterminate whether $x = y$. This, however, does not blame vagueness on x itself, as opposed to y, or to the identity relation.

3. Studies of vagueness often include cases in which the vagueness is due to a borderline case, where it is a matter of degree whether a predicate applies to an object, whereas I develop a theory in which indeterminacy is not a matter of degree; in language it leads to a lack of truth-value, not to degrees of truth-values. Perhaps this is an inadequate way to view things, but it would be misleading to use a term that suggests the theory is something it is not.

4. It is common to assume that along with vagueness comes higher-order vagueness; not only is it vague whether this is orange, it may be vague *whether* it is vague whether this is orange. Indeterminacy is not like this, at least in the version of the theory I discuss in most of the book. Higher-order indeterminacy is discussed briefly in Chapter 12.

Fuzzy logic: Fuzzy logic is a study that has been much discussed over the last couple of decades because it has been taken as a slogan for a certain kind of computer programming; it refers to software systems that are designed to allow for "risky" reasoning, inferences to conclusions that are not deductively validated by the given data. It sometimes concerns reasoning to conclusions that have definite truth or falsity, but their truth or falsity is yet unknown, and the scale of "truth-values" in fuzzy logic is often taken as representing degrees of knowledge. My enterprise is not epistemological at all. When I say that a sentence lacks truth-value this is because the world gives it none, not because we are presently ignorant of what it is.

"vagueness ought to be viewed as a semantic notion, and investigated by means of different evaluation techniques." (ibid.). I agree totally with his conclusion, but the subject has changed. One kind of vagueness is indeed a (semantic) notion essentially involving language. Its study leaves untouched the indeterminacy I am investigating.

As originally developed, "fuzzy logic" has a technical definition; it is a semantical system in which there are additional truth values between 0 and 1, usually an infinite number of them, representing degrees of truth. Again, I have only two truth-values: true and false, and three possible truth-value statuses: true, false, and neither; I do not think of "neither" as a *degree of truth*, though I am not sure what difference this would make.

Non-extensional contexts and modality: These issues are not directly relevant to anything discussed in this book. I discuss only language with extensional contexts, and no modal notions are invoked in the analysis.

3

Identity

3.1 WHAT IS IDENTITY?

When are objects *a* and *b* identical? I accept the Leibnizian doctrine that defines identity between objects in terms of coincidence of their properties. If there is indeterminacy in the world, then it may be indeterminate *whether a* and *b* coincide in the properties that they share. Consequently, it will be indeterminate whether they are identical. Specifically:

> *x* is determinately identical with *y* if and only if: every property that *x* determinately possesses *y* also determinately possesses (and vice versa) and every property that *x* determinately does not possess *y* also determinately does not possess (and vice versa).

> *x* is determinately not identical with *y* if and only if: there is some property that *x* determinately possesses that *y* determinately does not possess, or some property that *x* determinately does not possess that *y* determinately possesses.

> It is indeterminate whether *x* is identical with *y* if and only if *x* and *y* are neither determinately identical nor determinately not identical. This will happen where there is no property that *x* determinately possesses that *y* determinately does not possess, and vice versa, but there is at least one property that *x* determinately possesses such that it is indeterminate whether *y* possesses it, or vice versa, or at least one property that *x* determinately does not possess such that it is indeterminate whether *y* possesses it, or vice versa.

More succinctly:

x is determinately identical with *y* if and only if *x* and *y* determinately possess and determinately lack exactly the same properties.

x is determinately not identical with *y* if and only if there is some property regarding whose possession *x* and *y* determinately disagree.

Otherwise it is indeterminate whether *x* is identical with *y*.

This account is meant to be a "real definition", not a "nominal definition". That is, the account is not meant to explain what I take 'identical' to *mean*. I mean by 'identical' exactly what others mean by it; this is the only way I know to guarantee that we are discussing the same issue. I assert the equivalences above as truths about identity. That is, the theory under examination is a theory that embodies these equivalences as substantive claims about identity.[1]

I use 'distinct' for 'not identical'. (That *is* a nominal definition.) Indeterminacy of identity between *a* and *b* thus coincides exactly with indeterminacy of distinctness.

The account of identity given above in terms of properties says nothing about relations. Suppose that *x* and *y* coincide completely in terms of their properties, but differ determinately in terms of their relations to objects?[2] Then they should be distinct, not identical. So a better account than the one above would read:

x is determinately identical with *y* if and only if *x* and *y* determinately possess and determinately lack exactly the same properties, and determinately stand in, and determinately do not stand in, the same relations to the same objects.

x is determinately not identical with *y* if and only if there is some property regarding whose possession *x* and y determi-

---

[1] Here and throughout the text I ignore the complication of time, assuming e.g. that the properties in question are things like "being yellow at t" as opposed to "being yellow", where the latter is a property that one and the same thing possesses at one time and not at another. If I were to appeal to the latter notion of property, identity would have to be defined in terms of "having all the same properties at all the same times", instead of just "having all the same properties". I use the former notion because the account is less complicated; I think that nothing of substance turns on the choice.

[2] An old illustration is of a universe consisting of nothing but two spheres of the same size, composition, etc., existing some distance apart; the spheres are supposed to be two objects that differ only with respect to their relations. (One is distant from a certain object—the other sphere—and the other is not distant from that object.)

nately disagree or some relation to some object regarding which they disagree.

Otherwise it is indeterminate whether x is identical with y.

Officially I adopt this more refined account as the official view. But it is clumsy to state, and there is a simple way to merge the options. Suppose that for any relation R and any object o there is a property P which is determinately possessed (or determinately dispossessed) by exactly those objects that determinately bear R (or that determinately do not bear R) to o. Then the accounts coincide. I will indeed make this assumption. It is a controversial assumption, but so far as I can see it is irrelevant to any of the issues about indeterminate identity to be discussed. If it becomes relevant, we should retreat to the account of identity that explicitly takes relations into account.

Is identity itself a relation? It can be, but it need not be; the assumptions made so far leave this open. This is primarily because so little has been assumed. For example, I have not even assumed that if P and Q are properties, then their conjunction is a property. (I have not assumed that there is *some* property U that determinately holds of exactly the objects that both P and Q determinately hold of, and determinately fails to hold of exactly the objects that either P or Q determinately fail to hold of.) Later I discuss applications in which I assume a principle of plenitude for properties that will yield such conjunctive properties, as well as others, but nothing controversial will turn on that. These questions about how properties are related to relations, and to one another, are important, but they are technical and they are distracting, and they are not crucial to the ontological issues discussed here.

It should be clear that I reject as basic any account of identity in terms of coincidence of the predicates in some language that combine truly with the names of the objects in question. Such an account can be wrong in two ways. First, if the language is too impoverished, we may not have the words to express a difference in properties between x and y when one exists. Second, there is no automatic guarantee that predicates stand for properties, and if they do not then it might be possible for such a predicate to combine truly with a name of x and falsely with a name of y even when it is not determinate whether x is y. This can (and will) happen sometimes when the content of the predicates is partly

linguistic or semantic. Cases of this sort will be discussed exten-
sively below.

I take it as obvious that identity between objects in the world is
basically a matter of what the world is like, and only secondarily a
matter of how language functions. I know of no conclusive way to
argue this point, so I merely state it.[3] This leaves me at odds with
certain philosophers who take the contrary view. For example,
Harold Noonan urges that identity be defined in terms of the
behaviour of predicates and names, and he suggests that if identity
is defined in terms of properties, and if satisfying a predicate does
not necessarily count as a property, then one is speaking merely of
'a kind of *relative identity*: a relation which ensures indiscernibility
of its terms in some, but not all, respects' (Noonan 1984: 118).
I think that Noonan is mistaken in this claim about relative
identity; this will be discussed below. For now, I state the conflict
so as to contrast my own position.

3.2 INDETERMINATE IDENTITY

The ontological picture introduced in the last chapter is neutral
about whether any indeterminacy obtains at all. It is consistent to
append to the account the assumption that every property is actually determinately possessed or determinately not possessed by
every object. It is also consistent to assume otherwise, and I will
continue with that assumption in effect, since otherwise the theory
has no interesting application.

If there is indeterminacy in the world, then it is still left
open whether it extends to identity. Perhaps there is a great deal
of indeterminacy, but for any objects *a* and *b* either their own
indeterminacies completely coincide or else they determinately
disagree about possession of some property. Then there would be
indeterminacy without indeterminacy of identity of objects.[4] We
cannot settle a priori whether this happens. I will presume that

---

[3] See Keefe (1995: 185 ff) for considerations in favour of this position.

[4] I leave open for the present whether there might be indeterminacy of identity
of sets of objects even when there is no indeterminacy of identity for the objects
themselves. A positive answer to this question is consistent and interesting; it is
discussed in Ch. 11.

identity itself is sometimes indeterminate, for this is the interesting case, but it is a contingent matter.

It is sometimes convenient to speak of an identity between two objects as being indeterminate; this is always elliptical for the proposition that it is indeterminate *whether* the objects in question are identical.

3.3 LAWS OF IDENTITY

The semantics for the identity sign are:[5]

> The predicate '=' is true of exactly those pairs of objects $<x,y>$ such that x is determinately identical to y.

> The predicate '=' is false of exactly those pairs of objects $<x,y>$ such that x is determinately not identical to y.

Given this explanation together with the semantical and meta-physical theses laid out above the following two principles must automatically hold for the identity sign:

> *Reflexivity*: Any sentence of the form '$a = a$' is logically true.[6] Likewise, the sentence '$\forall x(x = x)$' is logically true.

> *Leibniz's Law*: The following holds, where '. . . t . . .' represents any sentence containing the term 't' in one or more places:

> $s = t$

> $\underline{. . . s . . .}$
> $. . . t . . .$

> That is, given any identity between terms, and any sentence whatever containing one of those terms, you may infer the same sentence with the one term replaced by the other in as many of its occurrences as you like.

---

[5] The first of these two clauses is emphasized in Stalnaker (1988: 350). When indeterminacy is possible, we must consider the "anti-extension" of a predicate as well as its extension; identity is no exception.

[6] Again, this is because only names with unique denotations are permitted in the language. If there were denotationless names in the language, sentences of the form '$a = a$' would not be logically true. In Ch. 9, I argue that it is possible for a name to have a unique denotation even when it names an object which is indeterminately identical with some object that the name does not denote.

We can show that Leibniz's Law holds by an inductive proof. We have three base cases:

1. Suppose first that the sentence '. . . *s* . . .' is atomic; for simplicity, suppose it consists of a one-place predicate '*F*' followed by '*s*'. Assuming that '*s* = *t*' is true, the object named by '*s*' is identical to that named by '*t*'. Assuming that '*Fs*' is true, it must be that '*F*' is true of the object named by '*s*'. So '*F*' is true of the object named by '*t*'. So '*Ft*' is true.

By similar reasoning, the inference holds when '. . . *s* . . .' is '¬*Fs*' (just replace 'true' by 'false' and add a clause for negation).

By similar reasoning, the inference holds when '. . . *s* . . .' is '∇*Fs*'. Here, since '∇*Fs*' is true, '*Fs*' lacks truth-value, so '*F*' is neither true nor false of the object named by '*s*'. So it is neither true nor false of the object named by '*t*'. So '*Ft*' lacks truth-value, and '∇*Ft*' is true.

2. The law can be shown for more complex formulas by induction on the complexity of the formula.

This proof itself uses Leibniz's Law in the metalanguage, and this might lead one to suspect that some question is being begged here. Perhaps in some sense it is, but this is no different in principle than any other law of logic. For example, when one shows that a certain classical first-order system of logic obeys the principle of universal instantiation, one uses universal instantiation in the metalanguage. If one insists on more than this, then no system can ever be shown to validate any law of logic. In the face of extreme logical scepticism, the most that one can show is that certain principles cohere, that is, that using the principle in the metalanguage does indeed allow you validate it for the object language.

Since I intend the metaphysical theory under discussion to possibly be true of the actual world, then I must be using the same logic in my metalanguage as in the object language.

Recall that validity means preservation of truth. If the identity premiss is true, then the objects named by '*s*' and by '*t*' are indistinguishable with respect to any of their properties and relations. Further, given that the language contains no non-extensional contexts, Leibniz's Law holds. Indeed, if Leibniz's Law were not to hold for such an extensional language, this would cast serious doubt on whether our sign of identity were actually expressing identity, as opposed to some weaker relation.

(Leibniz's Law is expressed here as a principle of inference, as opposed to a schema for conditional statements. This is because we have not as yet discussed conditionals. Conditionals bring with them their own idiosyncrasies and controversies, and it is better not to get those issues entangled with issues about Leibniz's Law. Conditional formulations of Leibniz's Law are discussed in Chapter 6.)

Leibniz's Law together with reflexivity lets us derive some of the other well-known principles of identity, such as:

Symmetry:

$$\frac{s = t}{\therefore t = s}$$

Transitivity:

$$\frac{\begin{array}{l} s = t \\ t = u \end{array}}{\therefore s = u}$$

It is crucial, however, that *contrapositive* versions of Leibniz's Law do *not* hold. We do not have:

$$\frac{\begin{array}{l} \ldots s \ldots \\ \neg(\ldots t \ldots) \end{array}}{\therefore \neg s = t} \qquad \text{NO!}$$

Recall the point made in the last chapter: if a pattern of inference is valid, that does not guarantee that contrapositive versions of it are valid. Leibniz's Law is a crucial example of this. As we will see in the next chapter, if contrapositive versions of Leibniz's Law were valid, it would be possible to disprove the truth of any assertion of indeterminate identity. Thus the theory under discussion *must* deny the validity of the contrapositive version of Leibniz's Law.

But how can there be a counter-example to this principle? If the premises are both true, then it appears that *s* and *t* must disagree with respect to the property expressed by the context '. . . *x* . . .'. But then the objects denoted by '*s*' and '*t*' disagree with respect to that property, and thus they are *by definition* determinately not identical, which is all that the conclusion states! The answer to this is that the context '. . . *x* . . .' *may not express a property*, and it is only in this sort of case that the principle fails. We will see examples of this in the next chapter.

The following principle remains valid in any case:

$$\frac{\begin{array}{l} \ldots s \ldots \\ \neg(\ldots t \ldots) \end{array}}{\therefore \neg! s = t}$$

So the loophole cases are ones in which s and t are neither determinately identical nor determinately not identical; they will be cases of indeterminate identity. With this in mind, it is easy to give a specific counter-example to a contrapositive version of Leibniz's Law. Let the first premiss say that a is determinately identical with a, and the second premiss say that a is not determinately identical with b:

$$!a = a$$
$$\neg! a = b$$

Obviously we do not want to conclude from the fact that a is not determinately identical with b that it is (determinately) not identical with b:

$$\frac{\begin{array}{l} !a = a \\ \neg! a = b \end{array}}{\therefore \neg a = b} \quad \text{NO!}$$

At least I do not want to conclude this, though it is clear that others do. The theory of indeterminate identity must hold the contrapositive of Leibniz's Law to be invalid, at least for some instances, such as the one just displayed. In later chapters I will dispute various arguments to the effect that the contrapositive of Leibniz's Law *must* be valid.

By denying the validity of this principle I may be charged with begging the question in favour of indeterminate identity. I countercharge that to assume the validity of the principle is to beg the question on the other side. So we must let each side take sides, and consider what independent considerations there might be to resolve the issue.

(One might worry whether using the converse of Leibniz's Law *in the metalanguage* would force the converse of Leibniz's Law to hold for the object language. Yes, that is true. So it is only by adopting the desired logic in the metalanguage that I can say that the semantics I have described works as I say. But this should be no embarrassment. Again, I assume that my metalanguage works just as my object language does. The remaining worry is whether I can do all this consistently. That is not difficult. Consistency can be established by an assignment of artificial entities to the language, described in a classical set-theoretic setting. That can easily be done by appeal to the 'pictures' described in §7.6.)

3.4 RELATIVE IDENTITY?

We may now return to Noonan's charge that defining identity in terms of properties and relations instead of in terms of linguistic interchangeability will yield only a kind of relative identity. 'Relative identity' is a phrase made popular by Peter Geach (in Geach 1967), who focused on the fact that we often wish to say things like

> 'the first letter in "aardvark" is the same type as the second one, but not the same token.'

Geach took the locution 'x is the same F as y' and called it 'relative identity', 'relative' because of the relativity of choice of 'F', and 'identity' because of the use of the word 'same'. It is clear that relative identity is not the same as the non-relative identity that I have been discussing. The most crucial difference between them is that Geach's relative identity does not validate Leibniz's Law; if it did, 'x is the same F as y' would entail 'x is the same G as y', and this is supposed not to follow. So a good test for relative identity is whether it does or does not sanction Leibniz's Law. The identity I am discussing does sanction this law, and thus it cannot be a species of relative identity. If Noonan means by 'relative identity' what Geach means, his criticism does not apply to the theory given here.

Noonan may not have meant 'relative identity' in Geach's sense. He may merely have meant that identity defined in terms of properties and relations is just a kind of limited indiscernibility that does not guarantee general indiscernibility. This is the crux of the matter; if it is true that $a = b$, then there should not be any statement made using one of these names (outside of non-extensional and quotational contexts) that changes truth-value status when that name is replaced by the other. Again, it is Leibniz's Law that is given as a test for whether we are talking about real identity. On this test our theory yields real identity.[7]

Here is a fuller quote from Noonan. He suggests that if identity is defined in terms of properties, and if satisfying a predicate does not necessarily count as a property, then one is speaking merely of

a kind of *relative identity*: a relation which ensures indiscernibility of its terms in some, but not all, respects—in particular, not in respects only expressible by predicates containing '$\triangledown$' or synonyms of such predicates. Noonan (1984: 118)

The implication here seems to be that an identity will not sanction indiscernibility of its terms within contexts governed by the indeterminacy connective '$\triangledown$'. But this is not so. At least, it is not so in the theory under discussion here. The following is a valid pattern no matter how the blanks are filled:

$$a = b$$
$$\frac{\triangledown(\ldots a \ldots)}{\therefore \triangledown(\ldots b \ldots)}.$$

Our identity *does* guarantee complete indiscernibility, even in contexts containing '$\triangledown$'. What Noonan has in mind may be a converse principle: that if there is a *discernibility in language*, then this guarantees *distinctness*. That is, that this is valid:[8]

$$!(\ldots a \ldots)$$
$$\frac{!\neg(\ldots b \ldots)}{\therefore \neg a = b}.$$

In Noonan (1990) he cites this principle, which he calls "the Principle of the Diversity of the Definitely Dissimilar", and in Noonan

---

[7] I do not mean to suggest that Leibniz's Law is itself beyond question. For example, Zemach (1991) rejects it. He relativizes identity to ideologies, and holds that objects may be identical with respect to one ideology but not with respect to others. He adopts a kind of relative identity as a "substitute" for Leibniz's Law. His theory of "vague objects" is thus quite different from the one I am developing.

[8] I have simplified Noonan's formulation by representing his 'ϕ & $\Delta\phi$' as '!ϕ', where '$\Delta\phi$' means 'it is determinately true or determinately false that'. These are equivalent in truth-value status. Also, Noonan formulates the principle as a conditional, whereas I use a principle of inference. This is sometimes a crucial difference, for the conditional formulation is often a stronger principle. But when the premisses (antecedents) are bivalent in virtue of form, as is true of any formula that begins with '!', the various conditional formulations all coincide with the principle of inference.

(1991) he calls this a "weaker" principle than Leibniz's Law. But it is not weaker in the logical sense (the logical sense being that Leibniz's Law entails it but not vice versa), for it is not entailed by Leibniz's Law. The principle in question is just another equivalent to the contrapositive of Leibniz's Law. (This is because putting a determinate-truth connective '!' on the front of a whole premiss is always redundant.)[9]

Perhaps the contrapositive of Leibniz's Law is valid; perhaps not. But it is not obvious. It is the point at issue.

3.5 APPLICATIONS

According to the account of identity just described, if it is indeterminate whether $a = b$, then there is no property with respect to which a and b disagree, but there is at least one property (typically, many) that one of them determinately possesses (or determinately does not possess) such that it is indeterminate whether the other has it. If we think that we have a case of indeterminate identity, then we should be able to point to some such property. I review here the four identity puzzles cited above with this in mind.

Me and my body: The theory allows one to say that it is indeterminate whether I am identical with my body. This says little in detail about which properties I and my body share. For example, suppose that my body takes up space, and suppose that taking up space is a property. Then I myself

---

[9] To make this clear in the case in question, suppose first that the contrapositive version of Leibniz's Law holds; then so does Noonan's principle:

1.	$!(\ldots a \ldots)$	Noonan's premiss
2.	$!\neg(\ldots b \ldots)$	Noonan's premiss
3.	$(\ldots a \ldots)$	From 1
4.	$\neg(\ldots b \ldots)$	From 2
5.	$\therefore \neg a = b$	By the contrapositive of Leibniz's Law

Second, suppose that Noonan's principle holds. Then so does the contrapositive version of Leibniz's Law:

1.	$(\ldots a \ldots)$	Premiss of contrapositive of Leibniz's Law
2.	$\neg(\ldots b \ldots)$	Premiss of contrapositive of Leibniz's Law
3.	$!(\ldots a \ldots)$	From 1
4.	$!\neg(\ldots b \ldots)$	From 2
5.	$\therefore \neg a = b$	By Noonan's principle

must either have the property of taking up space, or else it must be indeterminate whether I have this property. Both options are open. Conversely, if it is true that I think, and if thinking is a property, then either my body thinks, or it is indeterminate whether it thinks. Somewhere there must be some indeterminacy of property in order for me and my body to not be determinately identical. But the case abstractly described does not give details. If I and my body and nothing else are in a certain room,[10] then there is at least one thing in the room and at most two, though it is indeterminate whether there is exactly one thing, and indeterminate whether there are two. (Such cardinality judgements are discussed in Chapter 8.)

Perhaps I and my body differ only in *modal* properties. Perhaps we share all non-modal properties, such as taking up space, and thinking. But perhaps I *could* live on *without* my body (although we both cease to exist at death, or God, contingently, sees fit to resurrect my body for my comfort). What does the theory say then? Well, if such modal properties are properties, then if I have this property and my body does not, we are distinct, and the puzzle has a traditional solution. If modal predicates do not stand for properties, then the theory does not yet take sides. The theory does not tell us what properties there are; it only says what the consequences are for identity of possessing properties. I am inclined to view modal properties as properties, but that is me, not the theory. The issues discussed here are not likely to turn on considerations of modality.[11]

The ship: Suppose that being located at a certain point in space at a given time is having a property. Let o be the place from which the original ship set sail at time t_0, and let d_1 and d_2 be the places that the ship with new parts and the newly assem-

---

[10] Of course, my body can't be in a room unless its parts are there too, so the example is fanciful; I think, however, the point is clear.

[11] The options for how to do modal semantics are so numerous that just about any view about indeterminate identity may be reconciled with just about any view about whether modal predicates do or do not stand for properties. Cf. Keefe (1995) and Stalnaker (1988: 355 ff) for some discussion. In my opinion, the additional complexities (and complexities abound!) are all contributed by artefacts of modal semantics, and shed no light on the basic question of whether identity might be indeterminate (in this world). This is why I do not discuss them.

bled ship respectively dock at time t_n. Then the ship with new parts determinately has the property of being at d_1 at t_n, and the newly assembled ship determinately lacks that property (since it is determinately elsewhere then); as a result, the ship with new parts and the newly assembled ship are determinately distinct. It is indeterminate whether the original ship is at d_1 at t_n, since otherwise it would be determinately distinct from one of the resulting ships, and the puzzle would have a traditional solution.

This example shows that indeterminate identity is not transitive: the newly assembled ship is indeterminately identical with the original ship, which is indeterminately identical with the ship with new parts, but the newly assembled ship is not indeterminately identical with the ship with new parts. Before the repair job began there was exactly one ship; afterwards there are exactly two. All told, there are at least two and at most three, with either exact answer being indeterminate.

The disrupted person(s): It is indeterminate whether the person who originally entered the room is the person who later left the room. Assuming that leaving the room is a property or entails the possession of certain properties, it is indeterminate whether the person who entered the room left the room. Exactly one person entered the room, and exactly one person left the room. It is indeterminate whether there is exactly one person overall or exactly two persons overall, but false that there are fewer than one and false that there are more than two.

The cat and the p-cats: There is exactly one cat on the table, though probably millions of p-cats. For each p-cat, it is indeterminate whether it is identical with the cat. Since there is only one cat, for each p-cat it is indeterminate whether it is a cat (if it were determinately *not* a cat it would be determinately distinct from the cat; if it *were* a cat, then by parity so would be the others, and there would be millions of cats on the table).

In describing these cases I have not only said how I think the theory is supposed to work, I have also reviewed what I take to be some of the data against which any theory should be tested. That is, if you grant that each identity puzzle has no answer, then the rest of the things that I say about the puzzling situations are what I think any thoughtful person uncorrupted by a philosophical theory would say. I say this here partly to urge agreement, but also to let the reader know something about how subsequent discussion will go: the theory under consideration has the virtue of agreeing with these points, and competing theories are compelled to deny some of them.

4

The Evans Argument, Properties, and DDiff

> One should be suspicious of any argument that purports to
> get substantive metaphysical conclusions out of the logic of
> identity.
>
> Stalnaker (1988: 357)

4.1 THE EVANS ARGUMENT

In 1978, Gareth Evans published a one-page article, "Can there be
Vague Objects?" In spite of its title (vague *objects*), the aim of the
paper was to prove that no statements of indeterminate identity
can be true. Specifically, no statement of the form '∇$a = b$' can be
true. This paper has become a focal point for a growing body of literature, including the present book. It is thus important to consider
what Evans's argument is, and what it shows.

I set aside two potentially distracting issues:

First, it is not clear that Evans intended to address the question
that I and other commentators call indeterminacy of identity. There
is some reason to suspect that Evans saw indeterminacy as a sub-
class of truth, as opposed to a lack of truth-value. That is, he may
have intended '∇S' to mean " 'S' is true, but indeterminately so", as
opposed to meaning that 'S' lacks truth-value altogether. If so, his
argumentation is irrelevant to most of the subsequent literature
that it inspired. But it is the discussion that the paper inspired that
I am interested in, so I will ignore the fact that Evans might have
meant something different. I speak of "the Evans argument" as an
argument aimed at refuting the possibility of indeterminacy of
identity as I (and most others) understand indeterminacy of identity. (I say more about the alternative interpretation of Evans in the
Appendix.)

Second, as a number of commentators have pointed out, it is obvious that a statement of the form '$a = b$' *can* lack truth-value if the singular terms making it up do not have clear and unambiguous reference. Evans could not possibly give a conclusive argument to refute this possibility. I agree with the majority[1] in interpreting his argument as trying to show that a statement of the form '$\triangledown(a = b)$' cannot be true *if* the singular terms making it up have clear and unambiguous reference. So interpreted, the argument is a direct attack on the central thesis of this book.

The argument: The argument is a *reductio ad absurdum* of the view that a statement of the form '$\triangledown a = b$' is true. It goes as follows:[2]

(1) $\triangledown(a = b)$	The hypothesis to be refuted
(2) $\lambda x[\triangledown(a = x)]b$	Abstraction from (1) ["Abstract introduction"]
(3) $\neg\triangledown(a = a)$	Truism[3]
(4) $\neg\lambda x[\triangledown(a = x)]a$	Reverse abstraction from (3) ["Abstract elimination"]
(5) $\neg(a = b)$	(2), (4) by Leibniz's Law

Before critiquing the argument, it needs to be completed. A *reductio* argument should end in a contradiction, and this one does not. Evans discusses this point and makes some complicated remarks about it, which I ignore here.[4] For in the theory under

---

[1] Including Burgess (1989), Garrett (1988), and Lewis (1988).

[2] Evans (1978: 208)—which is the *only* page of the article. I use Evans's notation except for replacing his negation sign '~' with mine '¬', and using the slightly more common notation '$\lambda x[...]$' for property abstraction than his '$\hat{x}[...]$'. He does not explain either piece of notation, so one can assume that it means nothing unorthodox. I have also replaced '$x = a$' by '$a = x$' in lines (2) and (4); this bring the argument into conformity with the rationale that Evans gives for the steps. Without this change the argument is missing two steps that appeal to the symmetry of identity within indeterminacy contexts. This is a valid principle, but it complicates the proof, which does not need to rely on it.

[3] Evans does not call (3) a truism; he merely cites it without justification. In order for (3) to be justified we need to assume that the term 'a' is not referentially flawed. We may need a similar assumption about 'b' to justify step (2).

[4] It is Evans's complex remarks about how to complete the proof that provide the best evidence that he meant something different by indeterminacy than most commentators (see the Appendix to this book). His discussion has inspired a number of speculations about what he might have had in mind; cf. Gibbons (1982), Pelletier (1984, 1989); nobody has come up with an interpretation of these remarks which makes them plausible without changing the subject matter away from the kind of indeterminacy we are discussing.

discussion in this book, the argument is easy to complete. Since validity is just truth preservation, if (5) is true so is (6):

(6) $!\neg(a = b)$.

As we have construed indeterminacy, line (1) means:

(1′) $\neg!(a = b)$ & $\neg!\neg(a = b)$,

and (6) clearly contradicts the second conjunct of (1′). So if the proof is correct as given, it is easily fleshed out into a full *reductio*.[5]

The complexity of the argument is due partly to the presence of the property abstracts. Their importance can be best understood if we initially see what the argument would be like without them. So remove the lines in which they occur, and consider the following three-line variant:

(1) $\triangledown(a = b)$　　The hypothesis to be refuted
(3) $\neg\triangledown(a = a)$　　Truism
(5) $\neg(a = b)$　　(1), (3) by Leibniz's Law

This shortened version of the argument gives the strategy in a succinct form:

> Step (1) says something about *b*: that *b* is indeterminately identical to *a*. Step (3) denies this about *a*. So *a* and *b* cannot be identical.

The response to this shortened form is clear. The argument does not use Leibniz's Law at all, but rather its contrapositive. This is the principle discussed and rejected in the last chapter. The argument thus begs the question.

However, we also noted in the last chapter that the contrapositive of Leibniz's Law is valid if the formula in question stands for a property. And this is the point of the additional abstraction steps in the full argument; they introduce the required properties:

[5] This fleshing out of the argument is not possible if Evans's negation is meant to be exclusion negation, in which case line (5) would mean what we would express as '$\neg!(a = b)$'. So there is an interpretation of the argument on which it fails to arrive at a full *reductio*, thus making it irrelevant to the theory under discussion. Garrett (1988) adopts this interpretation.

(1) $\triangledown(a = b)$ The hypothesis to be refuted

(2) $\lambda x[\triangledown(a = x)]b$ Abstraction from (1) ["Abstract introduction"]

(3) $\neg\triangledown(a = a)$ Truism

(4) $\neg\lambda x[\triangledown(a = x)]a$ Reverse abstraction from (3) ["Abstract elimination"]

(5) $\neg(a = b)$ (2), (4) by Leibniz's Law

Evans says as much in justifying line (2); he says:[6]

> (1) reports a fact about b which we may express by ascribing to it the property '$\lambda x[\triangledown(a = x)]$'.

So the strategy is to see (1) as attributing a property to b, and make this explicit in (2), and then to see (3) as denying that very same property of a, and make that explicit in (4). Step (5) is the contrapositive of Leibniz's Law, but applied in a special case in which it is valid. So criticism of the full proof must focus on the transitions from (1) to (2) and (3) to (4). And here it is apparent what must be said by any defender of indeterminate identity: there is no property of "being indeterminately identical to a", and so the property abstract '$\lambda x[\triangledown(a = x)]$' does not stand for a property. The inference from (1) to (2) is fallacious, because there is no reason to think that the sentence in (1) can be recast in terms of attribution of a property to an object. And the proof itself gives a reason to think that (1) cannot be so recast, for there are no other flaws in the proof, and the proof attempts the impossible: to prove a priori the inconsistency of indeterminate identity.

Actually, there are two distinct ways to criticize the proof, depending on how one interprets the use of property abstracts. *Way 1*: In the first way of interpreting abstracts, one supposes that the use of a property abstract is legitimate when, and only when, that abstract actually stands for a property which holds of the objects that satisfy the formula inside the abstract (and determinately fails to hold of the objects that dissatisfy the formula, and indeterminately holds of the objects such that it is indeterminate whether they satisfy the formula). This is the interpretation employed in the previous paragraph. On this interpretation, the fact that step (1) is true does not automatically tell you that there is a *property* which reflects the semantic behaviour of the

---

[6] Again I have replaced '$x = a$' by '$a = x$'; see note 2 of this chapter.

formula in the abstract. On this interpretation, the inference from (1) to (2) is fallacious. *Way 2*: In the second way of interpreting the abstracts, one does not assume that an abstract needs to stand for a property; abstracts are just ways of reexpressing other formulas that do not use this mode of expression, and the semantics of formulas containing abstracts is completely parasitic on that of the formulas one gets by eliminating the abstracts. If the abstracts of Evans's proof are interpreted in this way, the inference from (1) to (2) is above reproach (as is the inference from (3) to (4)). But on this interpretation, step (5) is again fallacious. Recall that the contrapositive of Leibniz's Law does not hold for formulas in general, though it holds for the predication of genuine properties. On this second way of interpreting abstracts, the abstracts in the proof are not guaranteed to stand for properties, and so step (5) is fallacious. (The argument reduces to the shortened version discussed above.)[7]

---

[7] There is yet a third way of interpreting the abstracts; one might require that abstracts can only be used if they stand for properties, but not require that the property that an abstract stands for holds of exactly those objects which determinately satisfy the contained formula, *and* determinately fails to hold of exactly those objects which dissatisfy the formula, *and* indeterminately holds of exactly those objects which indeterminately satisfy the formula. Specifically, it is possible to give a *non-standard* account of abstraction in which an abstract is always guaranteed to stand for a property, but in such a way that the abstraction principles are not necessarily satisfied. (This is similar to Frege's "chosen-object" treatment of definite descriptions; a definite description always denotes an object, but not necessarily one that the description part of the definite description describes.) We describe such a non-standard interpretation of abstracts in Parsons and Woodruff (1995). This non-standard interpretation of the abstracts does not improve Evans's proof, for on this interpretation, although step (2) of the Evans argument indeed turns out to be valid, step (4) becomes invalid. I ignore an extended discussion of this non-standard interpretation because it does not improve the proof, and because the interpretation itself is somewhat artificial.

(The non-standard interpretation is this: we suppose that an abstract stands for whatever property determinately holds of exactly the objects that determinately satisfy the contained formula, and indeterminately holds of exactly the objects that indeterminately satisfy the formula *or* that do not determinately satisfy the formula but that are indeterminately identical to objects which determinately satisfy the formula; it determinately fails to hold of the rest. On the assumptions used in §4.3 below there will always exist such a property, and if the formula inside the abstract does express a property (as described in §4.3), it will express a property which agrees perfectly with the property assigned to the abstract. Otherwise, the formula will be determinately dissatisfied by certain objects which the property assigned to the abstract indeterminately holds of. This happens for the formula '$\nabla(a = x)$'; it is determinately dissatisfied by a (making step (3) true) but it is indeterminate whether a possesses the property that the abstract stands for (making step (4) lack truth-value).)

4.2 WHY THERE IS NO PROPERTY
OF INDETERMINATE-IDENTITY-
WITH-AN-OBJECT

The argument above proves that belief in indeterminacy of identity forces one to deny that there is a property of being indeterminately-identical-with-*o*, where *o* is an object which is indeterminately identical to something. But why should this be the case?

It is apparent that a property abstract purportedly expressing such a property must "quantify into" an indeterminacy connective; the abstraction operator on the outside must bind a variable within the scope of the indeterminacy connective:

$$\lambda x[\triangledown(\underline{x} = o)].$$

This leads one to suspect that we might be dealing here with some kind of non-extensionality, or some kind of modal fallacy.[8] I think this is not the case at all. As noted in the last chapter, the connectives '!' and '∇' do not create non-extensional contexts; one may freely existentially generalize on terms within their scopes, and one may freely intersubstitute coreferential names. The phenomenon at work here is unrelated to oddities of non-extensionality or of semantic paradoxes; it is more closely associated with the paradoxes of naïve set theory. This can be seen without talking about identity at all if we replace identity by its definition in terms of properties. Instead of writing '*a* = *b*', write:

$$\forall P(Pa \Leftrightarrow Pb),$$

where the quantifier ranges over properties, and where the biconditional is defined to be true if both sides have the same truth-value status (true, false, or neither) and false if they disagree in truth-value (one side is true and the other is false). Then the indeterminate identity of *a* with *b* is expressed as:

$$[*]\triangledown\forall P(Pa \Leftrightarrow Pb).$$

The question whether there is a property of "being indeterminately identical with *a*" is then the question whether the following abstract stands for a property:

---

[8] e.g. Burgess (1990: 269) suggests that if the Evans argument is not valid, then one must hold that the indeterminacy connective introduces a referentially opaque context.

$\lambda x[\triangledown \forall P(Pa \Leftrightarrow Px)]$.

Suppose it does. Then we can refute [*]. For then *a* lacks that property:

$\neg \lambda x[\triangledown \forall P(Pa \Leftrightarrow Px)]a$

because this is false:

$\triangledown \forall P(Pa \Leftrightarrow Pa)$.

And *b* has that property:

$\lambda x[\triangledown \forall P(Pa \Leftrightarrow Px)]b$

because [*] is true.

So *b* has the property and *a* lacks it:

$\lambda x[\triangledown \forall P(Pa \Leftrightarrow Px)]b \ \& \ \neg \lambda x[\triangledown \forall P(Pa \Leftrightarrow Px)]a$.

Existentially generalizing on the abstract denoting the property then yields the following as true:

$\exists P(Pb \ \& \ \neg Pa)$.

But the truth of this sentence contradicts the truth of [*]. So if the abstract stands for a property that is in the range of its own property variable, we can show that [*] is not true.

The force behind the reasoning thus comes from the fact that identity is defined in terms of what properties there are, and a problematic property is defined using an abstract that quantifies over *those* properties. The condition in the abstract is cleverly designed to conflict with its yielding one of the properties quantified over (if any objects are indeterminately identical with *a*). The reasoning thus resembles that of the Russell paradox in set theory. (Identity between sets is defined in terms of what sets they have as members, and a problematic set is defined using a set abstract that quantifies over *those* sets. The condition in the set abstract is cleverly designed to conflict with its yielding one of the sets quantified over.)

I see no way around the facts discussed above. We thus have a choice to make: either deny that indeterminate identity is possible or deny that abstracts covertly employing quantification over properties (such as the one above) always pick out a property from among the ones quantified over in the definition of identity. *Either option is consistent.* So the opponents of indeterminate identity can happily give the Evans argument as an illustration of their point of view, and defenders of indeterminate identity can happily reject its abstraction steps as illustrative of their point of view. Neither of these stances can refute the other side. My stance, of course, is the latter.

4.3 DDIFF: THE CONDITION OF DEFINITE DIFFERENCE

It is convenient to speak of abstracts as standing for or not standing for properties, and of the formulas that generate such abstracts as expressing (or not expressing) such properties. In what circumstances does a formula of one free variable express a property? The framework sketched earlier is silent about this question for atomic predicates, but it is sometimes informative about complex predicates. Coupled with our definition of identity, the framework gives us a necessary condition for a formula to express a property. Let ϕx be a formula with one free variable x. Then a necessary condition for ϕx to express a property is that satisfaction and/or dissatisfaction of it by objects make a definite difference in their identity. Following Peter Woodruff,[9] I call this condition "DDiff" for "definite difference". The condition says that there are no objects x and y such that x definitely satisfies ϕ and y definitely dissatisfies ϕ and yet it is indeterminate whether x is y. In notation:

$$\text{DDiff:} \quad \neg\exists x\exists y[!\phi x \,\&\, !\neg\phi y \,\&\, \triangledown x = y].$$

Equivalently:[10]

---

[9] Woodruff and Parsons (1997). Woodruff is responsible for the name 'definite difference'. Noonan (1990) and (1991) calls the principle that DDiff holds of every formula the "Principle of the Diversity of the Definitely Dissimilar".

[10] The clauses in the conditional form of DDiff contain determinacy and indeterminacy connectives that force both the antecedent and the consequent to be truth-valued. So all conditionals that agree with the classical material conditional for parts that have truth-value are equivalent in this context, and the choice of one of these conditionals over another is not crucial here. For consistency, I have used my favourite conditional connective, which is used throughout the text. (See §6.1 for discussion of the alternatives.)

DDiff: $\forall x \forall y[!\phi x \ \& \ !\neg\phi y \Rightarrow \neg\triangledown x = y]$.

If ϕx does *not* satisfy DDiff, then it cannot express a property. For if it did express a property, that property would be definitely possessed by an object x and definitely lacked by an object y, and thus, by our definition of identity, x would definitely not be identical with y, contrary to the clause in DDiff of the form '$\triangledown x = y$'. So this is not an independent thesis; it is just a logical consequence of the worldly Leibnizian definition of identity that we are using.[11]

In certain circumstances, we can prove that certain formulas do not express properties, because we can prove that they do not satisfy DDiff. The formula '$\triangledown(a = x)$' discussed above is an example of this (if there is at least one object that is indeterminately identical to a). The converse is sometimes possible as well. Suppose that a formula is constructed entirely from primitive predicates that

---

[11] This can be seen as follows. Using property quantifiers, our definition of identity is:

$a = b =_{df} \forall P(Pa \Leftrightarrow Pb)$.

With this definition, DDiff takes this form:

DDiff: $\neg\exists x\exists y[\triangledown\forall P(Px \Leftrightarrow Py) \ \& \ !\phi x \ \& \ !\neg\phi y]$.

Now suppose that ϕ does express a property, Q. Then the instance of DDiff for ϕ is equivalent to this form:

DDiff: $\neg\exists x\exists y[\triangledown\forall P(Px \Leftrightarrow Py) \ \& \ !Qx \ \& \ !\neg Qy]$,

where it is understood that 'Q' stands for a property, and thus is the sort of thing that the quantifier '$\forall P$' may be instantiated for. We need to show that this form of DDiff must be true. For that, it is sufficient to show that a formula of this form *cannot* be true:

$\triangledown\forall P(Px \Leftrightarrow Py) \ \& \ !Qx \ \& \ !\neg Qy$.

So suppose it is true. Then an inference based on the last two conjuncts yields:

$\triangledown\forall P(Px \Leftrightarrow Py) \ \& \ \exists P(!Px \ \& \ !\neg Py)$.

But the last conjunct entails

$\neg\forall P(!Px \Leftrightarrow !Py)$.

Since the smallest ingredients of this formula are preceded by '!', the whole formula is bivalent in virtue of its form, and thus it entails

$!\neg\forall P(!Px \Leftrightarrow !Py)$.

But this is inconsistent with '$\triangledown\forall P(Px \Leftrightarrow Py)$' when '$\triangledown$' is expanded by its definition; that is, it is inconsistent with:

$\neg!\forall P(Px \Leftrightarrow Py) \ \& \ \neg!\neg\forall P(Px \Leftrightarrow Py)$.

stand for properties and relations, and that the logical symbols in the formula include only the identity sign, the connectives &, ∨, ¬, and the quantifiers ∃ and ∀. Then if ϕx is such a formula with one free variable, it satisfies DDiff. Only if we include a connective such as '!' or '∇' or '⇒' do we get formulas that do not satisfy DDiff[12] (or if we start out with primitive predicates that do not stand for properties).

I will assume hereafter that any formula of one free variable that satisfies DDiff expresses a property, and that abstracts constructed from such formulas stand for those properties. This commits one to a certain principle of plenitude for properties. If a formula satisfies Ddiff, then we know it *can* express a property. But does it? That depends on what we assume about properties. We can assume that there are hardly any properties at all, e.g. that logical combinations of predicates expressing properties typically do not themselves express properties. On this assumption if '*Fx*' expresses *Fness* and '*Gx*' expressed *Gness* then there may be no property of being *F and G* for '*Fx & Gx*' to express. Or we can assume instead that there are lots of properties, and that logically complex formulas (made without '!' or '∇' or '⇒') whose parts express properties typically also express properties. I find it convenient to use "property" talk, and so I will indeed make the maximal assumption that any formula expresses a property if it is constructed entirely from atomic predicates that stand for properties, and from identity, and the quantifiers, and the connectives '&', '∨', and '¬'. For the philosophical issues discussed below, it won't matter whether we adopt this principle or something weaker. This is because the important point always turns out to be the converse: any formula that does not satisfy DDiff cannot express a property.

4.4 ABSTRACTS AND PROPERTIES

In the discussion above it became clear that some abstracts, such as the one employed in the Evans argument, cannot stand for one of the properties in terms of which we define identity. We did not show that the abstracts cannot stand for some *other* kind of prop-

---

[12] See Keefe (1995) for a discussion of why we should not expect prefixing a predicate with '∇' to preserve propertyhood.

erty. In the account of indeterminacy that began in Chapter 2 we talked about properties and relations "in the world"; this is an onto-logical notion of property. People sometimes talk about properties in another way, using 'concept' and 'property' interchangeably, sometimes even construing properties as the *meanings* of predi-cates. Suppose there are two sorts of things that are commonly called "properties": real things in the world, on the one hand, and parts of our conceptual apparatus for representing the world, on the other. I am not certain this distinction can be clearly made, but I think these two different ways of viewing things are quite common. If the distinction can be made, then it is clear that the theory I am discussing sees real identity in the world as arising with the worldly properties, not the conceptual ones. When people feel that abstracts *must* stand for properties, they may be thinking of the other sort of properties, those that are part of our conceptual apparatus. We can happily admit that Evans's abstract '$\lambda x[\triangledown(a = x)]$' expresses a *conceptual* property. But there is no reason that I know of for assuming that conceptual properties validate the con-trapositive of Leibniz's Law, which involves the worldly sort of properties.

It is essential for my purposes that we distinguish abstracts that can stand for worldly properties from those that cannot. It is much less important what we decide to do with the ones that cannot stand for mundane properties. One may or may not want to say that such an abstract stands for a conceptual property. (Conceptual proper-ties are investigated a bit more in Chapter 11.) When I say without qualification that a predicate does not stand for a property, it will be the worldly sort of property that I have in mind.

5

Non-Conditional Disputations

In this chapter I discuss a number of attempts to prove that there can be no such thing as indeterminate identity. The arguments discussed here are limited to ones that do not turn on the logic or semantics of conditionals. These are straightforward arguments, mostly to the effect that positing indeterminate identity is inconsistent with some known truth. Other sorts of arguments are confronted later, including arguments based on the logic of conditionals, arguments asserting that indeterminate identity makes it impossible to refer to objects, arguments to the effect that indeterminate identity cannot be understood, and arguments to the effect that there are better accounts of the data.

It does not make sense to survey the whole literature on this topic. I include a representative sampling of the sorts of arguments that people commonly find persuasive. I begin with the three considerations that, aside from Evans's proof, have been mentioned to me most often by others.

5.1 QUINE: NO ENTITY WITHOUT IDENTITY

W. V. Quine has made famous the slogan "No entity without identity", and some people construe this as ruling out the possibility that there might be objects between which a claim of identity has no answer. Does Quine's slogan conflict with the view under consideration here?

I don't find Quine's slogan, as intended by him, incompatible with the possibility of indeterminate identity. The slogan is fuelled by a discussion of merely possible entities in "On What There Is", in which he expostulates:

Or, finally, is the concept of identity simply inapplicable to unactualized possibles? But what sense can be found in talking of entities which cannot meaningfully be said to be identical with themselves and distinct from one another? Quine (1961: 4)

What Quine rejects here is a kind of entity to which the *concept* of identity is inapplicable. An endorsement of indeterminate identity does not deny that the concept of identity is applicable to objects, it merely claims that in certain circumstances when you apply the concept you get no answer. Not because the objects are the wrong *sort* of things to which to apply identity, but just because that is the way things go (or fail to go). Furthermore, all objects *are* identical with themselves, and all *are* distinct from one another if 'an*other*' is read strongly to mean "definitely not the same". Further, it is meaningful to ask of *any* objects *a* and *b* whether *a* is *b*, and to expect a correct response from the alternatives *yes*, *no*, or *neither yes nor no*. Quine's slogan does not rule out indeterminate identity because it does not address the issue.

Suppose we reinterpret the slogan so as to require a determinate *yes* or *no* answer to an identity question whenever posed? Since Quine did not propose the slogan under that interpretation, it is no surprise that he gives no arguments for it under that interpretation. The slogan is now simply a statement of what is at issue, and its fame alone has no efficacy.

5.2 METHODOLOGICAL BIVALENCE

As mentioned in Chapter 1, Quine sees the question of bivalence as a methodological choice. There is no fact of the matter about whether our utterances are bivalent or not; there is only a decision to be made about how to theorize. In any given science, it is possible to maintain a methodology committed to bivalence; it is possible because it is always possible to interpret recalcitrant data in such a way as to preserve our methodological choice. It is also possible to abandon bivalence if that makes things go more smoothly.

It should be clear that if it is a methodological choice that we face, then this fact by itself does not refute indeterminacy. For a refutation, we need to see why the choice should be made against indeterminacy. I think that one factor that leads people to suppose that one should choose bivalence is fears about what an alternative will bring. The first fear is that centuries of accomplishments that are formulated under the assumption of bivalence will need to be jettisoned. But this is not so. If you have a particular bit of subject matter that is nicely accounted for by a theory based on bivalence, then it needn't be abandoned at all. Giving up bivalence as a general principle does not mean abandoning it in every case. All that you need to do for your bivalent subtheory is to explicitly assume bivalence of application for its primitive predicates. Then no classical consequences are lost. You lose classical consequences only when you do not assume bivalence for the claims with which you are working. An example of both points is given in Chapter 11 where classical Zermelo–Fraenkel set theory is found as a bivalent subtheory of a general non-bivalent theory of sets.

A second fear is that abandoning bivalence will leave you in a position of not knowing what follows from what. When Quine (1981: 94–5) rejects the "fuzzy and plurivalent alternatives" to bivalence, he may not have had in mind the clear and well-behaved logic sketched in Chapter 2. It is true that if you simply abandon bivalence without settling on any particular alternative at all, then you open a Pandora's box of alternatives, including options that hardly anybody understands, and that is not a wise methodology for anybody. But that is not what is suggested in this book. The non-bivalent framework used here is really quite conservative and well behaved. It is especially important in this connection to recall that *reductio ad absurdum* is retained in this framework as a *refutation* technique. You *can* show that a claim is not true by deriving a contradiction from it. You merely cannot use this to establish that its negation is true, unless you have reasons to believe that the claim is a bivalent one.

A mark of science is supposed to be that hypotheses are confirmed by their instances. I see no reason why this would be different in a non-bivalent framework.[1] Another mark is that a hypothesis is a serious scientific option only if it is falsifiable (can

[1] It may be important in this connection to explore how probability theory might be affected by non-bivalence. This can be done by replacing negation by exclusion negation in the basic axioms (i.e. replace '¬S' by '¬!S'), and expanding the available tautological equivalences by the principles of logic from Ch. 2. I have not explored the philosophical consequences of doing this.

be shown to be false) within one's current methodology. In a non-bivalent framework this must be liberalized to: a hypothesis is a serious scientific option only if it is refutable (can be shown not to be true) within one's current methodology.

It is possible to imagine that the world contains indeterminacies, but why would anyone choose to do science on that basis? The answer may lie in theoretical simplicity. It is conceivable that you will find yourself confronted with data that can be accommodated neatly with a non-bivalent theory, and not so neatly with a bivalent one. This seems to have been the actual view of a substantial number of people, both scientists and philosophers, working in quantum mechanics. One reads over and over in this literature that there is no truth to the matter of whether a certain particle has simultaneously both position and momentum. I don't claim that this view is correct; the foundations of quantum mechanics are unsettled at this point in time. The point is rather that many thoughtful scientists and philosophers have in actual fact been willing to abandon bivalence for the sake of having the simplest theory. Whether they were right to do so is beside the point. It is their thoughtful willingness to do so that illustrates that abandoning bivalence is a genuine and reasonable option in doing science.

Even if bivalence were chosen within the respective sciences by individuals and communities of scientists, this cannot be decisive about claims that occur *between* and across the individual sciences. In fact, some of the most troublesome cases in the history of identity puzzles come from this locale.[2] Suppose a person undergoes a kind of disruption, e.g. a partial brain transplant, that is easily explainable in physical terms. There is no puzzle here about the identity of physical systems with which physics deals, nor of the psychological human development and interaction with which psychology deals; the question of whether the same person emerges is not a question in either physics or psychology. Bivalence within these sciences leaves this puzzle unaddressed.

Perhaps the personal disruption is a question in sociology? Sociology, based on normal occurrences, does not deal with such disruptions. And if such disruptions became commonplace, the science would probably pose a new category in terms of which to study it— speaking perhaps of *disruptees*. The indeterminacy would be thus

---

[2] See Parsons (2000). Compare also Zemach (1991), who thinks of identity puzzles as arising between *ideologies*, with bivalence holding within each ideology.

avoided, for such is the commitment of each science on its own (or so we are supposing). But to avoid it is not to solve the identity puzzle. Perhaps science works better by formulating bivalent theories using newly invented concepts that are carefully crafted to fit into bivalent scientific laws. This does not refute indeterminacy, it ignores it. We already knew that we could refocus our search for scientific laws by employing new categories. The philosophical task is to address the puzzles raised by the original ones. The tendency of scientists to search for new concepts leaves unsettled the issues posed in terms of other concepts. It is certainly not obvious how old problems disappear—if they do so—when new categories are introduced.

Other puzzles similarly arise in the interfaces; the person-and-their-body at the interface of biology and some science of persons, the cat and the p-cats at the interface of biology and physics, and so on. Of course, one might hope that the sciences will eventually grow together, so as to accomplish the much discussed reduction of everything to physics, or something of this sort. But that is not accomplished at present, and we don't know what form it will take if it does occur, or whether and how identity puzzles will be affected, if at all. In the meantime, a methodological commitment to the search for bivalence *in* each science is not sufficient to close the door on an exploration of other options for claims *between* the sciences.

5.3 SALMON'S ARGUMENT BASED ON ORDERED PAIRS

Nathan Salmon attempts to refute the possibility of indeterminate identity, arguing as follows:[3]

[S]uppose that there is a pair of entities x and y . . . such that it is vague (neither true nor false, indeterminate, there is no objective fact of the matter) whether they are one and the very same thing. Then this pair $<x,y>$ is quite definitely *not* the same pair as $<x,x>$, since it is determinately true that x is one and the very same thing as itself. It follows that x and y must

---

[3] Some writers see Salmon's argument as identical in structure to Evans's (e.g. Burgess (1990: n. 7)). If it is, I already discussed it in the last chapter. Others see it as a distinct argument, which is why I discuss it independently here.

be distinct. But then it is not vague whether they are identical or distinct.
Salmon (1981: 243)

The argument appears to have this structure:[4]

(1) $\triangledown(x = y)$ Hypothesis to be disproved
(2) $\neg\triangledown(x = x)$ Truism
(3) $\neg(\langle x,y\rangle = \langle x,x\rangle)$ From (1) and (2)
(4) $\neg(x = y)$ From (3), by the theory of ordered
                                     pairs
(5) $\neg\triangledown(x = y)$ From (4)

I agree with every step except for the inference from (1) and (2)
to (3). This is fallacious; if it is indeterminate whether $x = y$ then it
is indeterminate whether the pair $\langle x,y\rangle$ is identical with the pair
$\langle x,x\rangle$. No principle of bivalent logic or of bivalent set theory (or
ordered-pair theory) should be taken to validate the inference to
(3), since the inference crucially involves non-bivalency. Salmon
cites no reason for (3), so we can only speculate about how to
validate it.

A natural way to think of filling in the proof would be to use
indirect proof, assuming the principles of ordered-pair theory: if the
pairs in (3) *were* identical, that would contradict (1) and (2). The
additional steps between (2) and (3) would then be:

(2a) Suppose $\langle x,y\rangle = \langle x,x\rangle$ Hypothesis for indirect
                                          proof
(2b) Then $x = y$ From (2a) by the theory of
                                          ordered pairs: pairs are
                                          identical iff their first and
                                          second members are.
(2c) $\neg\triangledown(x = y)$ From (2b) by preservation
                                          of truth.
(2d) $\triangledown(x = y)$ & $\neg\triangledown(x = y)$ From (1) and (2c)
(3) $\neg(\langle x,y\rangle = \langle x,x\rangle)$ From (2a)–(2d) by indirect
                                          proof.

Every step of this subproof is fine, but its conclusion is not. Indirect proof is invalid in a logic that permits sentences that lack

---

[4] Following Salmon's words precisely would require us to place a determinately
sign '!' in front of lines (3) and (4). This complicates the notation without having
any particular effect on the validity of the steps.

truth-value, and so disproving (2a) is not sufficient to validate its negation, it is only sufficient to conclude that (2a) is *not true*. Instead of (3) you *can* conclude:

(3′) ¬!(<*x*,*y*> = <*x*,*x*>)   From (2a)–(2d) by indirect proof.

But this is not sufficient to complete the original proof.

There are a number of other ways to try to fill out the above reasoning, but I know of no alternatives that turn it into a conclusive proof. This type of argument does however raise the question of whether, and to what extent, ordinary principles of set theory may be applied in the presence of indeterminate identity. If we had to abandon set theory in the face of indeterminate identity, this would be very serious, and one might then argue against indeterminate identity on grounds of utility. In Chapter 11, I argue that set theory meshes nicely with indeterminate identity.

5.4 SUPERVALUATIONS AND SUPER-RESOLUTIONS

A popular way to deal with sentences that lack truth-value is to invoke supervaluational readings. I do not appeal to supervaluations in formulating the theory of this book. But I can't avoid talking about them. This is for two reasons. First, I will discuss alternative accounts, and some of them are based on supervaluational readings of sentences. So we need to know what supervaluational readings are. Second, the theory I develop here without supervaluations will sometimes contradict data-like sentences that we are inclined to accept. Such contradiction fuels refutations of the theory that are discussed in the remainder of this chapter. I will suggest that we are inclined to accept some sentences in a way that apparently contradicts the theory of indeterminate identity because we naturally read them non-literally. We either tend to read them supervaluationally or superresolutionally, and when they are read in this way they do not contradict the theory.

5.4.1 Ways of reading sentences

In doing semantics one often encounters sentences that elude a simple classification in terms of truth-value. For example, it is apparent that when asked to judge the sentence 'The king of France is not bald', some people see the sentence as obviously false, since there is no king of France to be bald, others see it as true, since it contradicts a false sentence, others (e.g. Frege) see it as lacking truth-value, since there is no king of France to be bald or not, and still others (e.g. Russell) see it as ambiguous between true and false. Since these are reactions of native speakers who are in possession of all the facts, and since the sentence is so simple, many people, myself included, see the sentence as one whose surface syntax does not single out a unique meaning. One gets different meanings depending on how one interprets, or "reads", the sentence. Semantic theory is then challenged to explain how these many different readings may arise from such a simple sentence. In inspecting the phenomenon of indeterminacy, we will have to confront examples in which speakers naturally interpret sentences differently, and these different "readings" will need to be accounted for.

I take for granted that the reader is familiar with scope ambiguities, such as in a sentence like 'An observer saw every ship', which can either mean that some one observer was such that (s)he saw every ship, or that every ship was seen by some observer, though not necessarily by the same observer. In this text we will have occasion to focus on additional sources of multiple readings of sentences.

5.4.2 Supervaluations

Supervaluations provide a *way of reading* sentences, a way that sometimes gives truth-values to sentences that would otherwise lack them. The supervaluation technique is typically used for one of two purposes:[5]

> (1) One application is to ambiguous sentences. Call an ambiguous sentence "supertrue" if it is true on all ways of resolving the ambiguity and "superfalse" if it is false on all ways of resolving the ambiguity. If the sentence comes out true on some resolutions and false on others, then it is "supertruth-valueless". This successfully mirrors ways that we often assess

---

[5] Supervaluations were originally proposed in van Fraassen (1966). Fine applies the technique to (semantic) vagueness. Fine (1975: 284) emphasizes the application to ambiguity: "An ambiguous sentence is true if each of its disambiguations is true."

real-life utterances that are subject to different interpretations; we call such an utterance true without bothering to resolve the ambiguity if it is true no matter how the ambiguity is resolved.

(2) A second application of supervaluations is to sentences which lack truth-value for reasons other than ambiguity. To evaluate a sentence supervaluationally, you focus on the basic units of the sentence that are responsible for its lack of truth-value, and you consider how to flesh out these units consistent with whatever determinacy is already there. For example, the lack of truth-value may be because a predicate does not apply either truly or falsely to certain objects, so you consider how to extend its extension (the objects it is true of) and its anti-extension (the objects it is false of) so as to cover these additional objects. Or else the lack of truth-value is due to the fact that some singular term lacks a referent, and you consider various ways of arbitrarily assigning it a referent. Call any way of extending the original semantics so as to get a truth-value for every sentence an "extended valuation". Then a sentence is supertrue if it is true on all extended valuations, superfalse if it is false on all extended valuations, and otherwise supertruthvalueless. The advantage of reading sentences supervaluationally in this way is that sentences that are not logically true because of the possibility of truth-value gaps may be logically supertrue because of the way the gaps get filled in. For example, classical tautologies are often not logically true when gaps are allowed, but they are logically supertrue, and this restores a measure of neatness to one's logical system.[6]

In theory formulation, I avoid supervaluational readings for the same reason others invoke them: they make the assessment of a sentence less directly a matter of how its parts relate to the world than do literal readings. For example, '$Fa \vee \neg Fa$' is supertrue

---

[6] There are limits to the neatness of supervaluational logic. For example, as with my own approach, contraposition of validity does not generally hold in supervaluational logic. Note that the general theory of supervaluations is more complicated than my survey of it indicates; complications abound when one has notation *in the object language* for *both* 'true' and for 'supertrue'. I avoid this; my '!' converts a true sentence into a true one and all others into a false one. It does *not* necessarily convert a *super*true sentence into a true one.

because of its logical form, quite apart from whether 'Fa' is true, false, or neither. The connection between the truth-value status of a sentence and how its parts relate to the world is typically simpler to calculate than the connection between its supervaluational status and how its parts relate to the world. Since I am primarily concerned with depicting the world, the more direct semantics is preferable. I also think that certain key claims involving indeterminacy are more easily formulated presuming a literal reading than a supervaluational one, when supervaluational readings let logical form wipe out differences of content. Simply put, I am interested in *assessing the causes* of truth-value gaps, not in elegant ways of *avoiding* such gaps by interpreting them away.

Although I avoid using supervaluations in formulating my own theoretical views, I will certainly appeal to them on occasion to explain why we tend to judge certain sentences true when my theory says they lack truth-value. For example, if 'S' lacks truth-value, then on my view so does 'S or not-S', yet we are inclined to think that 'S or not-S' is in some sense correct. This is exactly the sort of data that supervaluations were introduced to account for; we *do* tend to read complex sentences supervaluationally sometimes, and I have no reservations about agreeing with this. What must be kept in mind is that a supervaluational reading is always parasitic on another, which I call the "literal" reading. The theory produces the literal reading, and that is the one I typically focus on. You can always *read* the results supervaluationally. But you should not reject a claim that a sentence, read literally, lacks truth-value, just because the same sentence, read supervaluationally, has a truth-value.

5.4.3 Super-resolutions

In discussing the worldly theory of indeterminacy, we will need to consider an additional method of reading sentences. Supervaluations are a nominalistic creation; one typically deals with pieces of language and how they relate to the world, without any discussion of properties and without assuming that the world itself is indeterminate. So when we try to combine the traditional method of supervaluations with the theory under discussion here there are a couple of oddities that need to be addressed. First, suppose that a predicate 'P' stands for a property. Making 'P' more precise by an

extended valuation may result in its no longer standing for a property. Since whether 'P' stands for a property or not may affect how
it interacts with identity, we need to worry about how this change
may affect the readings of sentences that contain it and that also
contain identities of objects that have the original property. (An
example will be given below.) Second, it is generally assumed in the
case of supervaluations that all of the "input" indeterminacy is
semantic, to be resolved by clarifying the referents of names and
the extensions of predicates. But in our framework, we may have
an identity statement without truth-value even though the referents of the names are clear (as discussed in Chapter 9). How should
a supervaluation treat such a statement? If identity can have its
extension "clarified" at will, then it loses its special relation to the
having and lacking of properties, but if its extension cannot be
altered, supervaluations will not produce supertruth when they are
expected to.

Here is an example that combines these two concerns. Suppose
that 'P' stands for a property, and consider the sentence:

$$Pa \ \& \ \neg Pb \ \& \ a = b.$$

This sentence might lack truth-value when read literally. (Suppose
that 'P' stands for the property p, which holds of a and neither holds
nor fails to hold of b, and that it is indeterminate whether a is b.
Then 'Pa' is true, and 'Pb' lacks truth-value, and so does '$a = b$'.) It
is also the sort of sentence that could not be true because of its
form, and thus it is the sort of sentence that supervaluations are
supposed to address; we are supposed to be able to address the
apparent logical falsehood of the sentence by showing that
although it lacks truth-*value*, it is *superfalse*, that is, it is false on
every extended valuation that gives it a truth-value. But the method
of supervaluations alone does not give this result without supple-
mentation. If no constraints are placed on the extended valuations,
then there are extended valuations that make the sentence true,
and ones that make it false, resulting in a sentence which is
supertruthvalueless, just as the original is.

(To make the sentence false, just extend the extension of 'P' to
include b, and the second conjunct will then be false. To make it
non-false, just extend the anti-extension of 'P' to include b, which
makes the second conjunct true. That leaves the third conjunct, the
identity, to consider. If 'P' still stands for a property, then the iden-

tity must be false, since the first two conjuncts force *a* to have that property and *b* to lack it. But there is nothing in the method of supervaluations to require that '*P*' still stands for a property; in extending it we may have converted it to one of those predicates that do not stand for properties, in which case the identity clause is not yet determined. So how do we treat the identity? As mentioned above, we might either leave it alone, or we might adjust its extension at will. If we leave it alone, the third conjunct stays indeterminate, and we have produced an extended valuation that makes the whole sentence lack truth-value. If we adjust its extension at will, we can let it be true of *a* and *b*, and thus the whole sentence comes out true. In either case, the extended valuation makes the sentence non-false, and thus it is not superfalse as desired.)

What is desired is a technique similar to the bare supervaluation approach that respects the details of the theory under discussion. Here is one such. Suppose that the world is not completely determinate. Now consider various ways in which it might become determinate by determining undetermined states of affairs. That is, by taking a property that neither determinately applies nor fails to apply to any given object and making it determinately apply or determinately not apply to that object. Call the result of such a way of making world *w* completely determinate a *resolution* of *w*. If *r* is such a resolution, we can ask about the truth-values of sentences that result from altering the semantics of predicates that stand for properties so as to correspond to the new ways that those properties behave under *r*, and from readjusting the extension of the identity predicate as required by the Leibnizian definition of identity in terms of properties and relations. Then in any resolution, identity will be completely determinate for any pair of objects. If a sentence contains only primitive predicates that stand for properties, and identity, we can ask whether it is true in a resolution *r* of *w*. This is to ask about truth resulting from resolution of the world without alteration of the language that depicts the world. And we can ask further which sentences are true in *every* such resolution. Call this "super-resolved truth". Super-resolved truth is like the supertruth due to supervaluations, except that it is truth that results from considering making the world more determinate, instead of truth that results from making our language more determinate. In a large number of cases, super-resolved truth will coincide with unresricted supervaluational truth, even though they are arrived at quite differently. But not always. The example discussed above is super-resolvedly false. This is because super-resolutions respect the ontology. We alter the extension and anti-extension of '*P*' indirectly by extending what the property that it stands for is true or false of. If we make the world more determinate by letting the property *p* above be false of *b*, then there is a *property* that holds of *a* and not of *b*, and the identity is forced to be false.[7]

The reason for keeping super-resolutions in mind is the same as for unrestricted supervaluations: sometimes we make judgements that certain sentences are true, or false, when the theory says that they lack truth-value. In some cases (according to many philosophical logicians, and I agree), this is because we are reading the sentences supervaluationally. And in some other cases in which unrestricted supervaluations yield no (super)truth-value, I think we are reading the sentences in a super-resolved way. Certainly I need some explanation of why people uncorrupted by philosophical theory are tugged in the direction of saying that for any two things, either they're the same thing or they're not:

$$\forall x \forall y (x = y \vee \neg x = y).$$

I myself feel this pull, and when I ask myself why, I find that I am inclined to say something like:

Well, however things *are*, they have to be like that.

If the 'are' is read as 'determinately are', then I am asking about resolved truth, not truth simpliciter. The sentence '$\forall x \forall y (x = y \vee \neg x = y)$', read literally, lacks truth-value according to the theory, but it is true on all resolutions; it is super-resolvedly true. (Its supervaluational truth status depends on how the theory of supervaluations is extended to handle worldly indeterminacy of identity.)

The remaining three topics in this chapter bring in molecular sentences in one way or another, so let me summarize my position on these. If both disjuncts of a disjunction lack truth-value, so does the disjunction—if it is read straightforwardly as I have explained it

---

[7] The super-resolutional account can be interpreted as an *application* of the supervaluational account; simply limit the extended valuations of names and predicates to valuations that they could have *in some resolution*. I will continue to use the term 'super-resolution' because it suggests the details of how the valuations are to be determined; I call the approach that uses all arbitrarily chosen extended valuations the "unrestricted supervaluation" approach.

above. However it is sometimes natural to read a disjunction super-valuationally. It is always natural to read it this way when the statement has the form of an explicit instance of the Law of Excluded Middle: "*A* or not *A*". Read straightforwardly, '*A* or not *A*' lacks truth-value when '*A*' lacks truth-value. Read super-valuationally, '*A* or not *A*' is true, since any way of assigning a truth-value to '*A*' makes the whole disjunction true. The same holds for super-resolutional readings. When I make statements myself I always intend that they be taken straightforwardly, not supervalu-ationally or super-resolutionally, but when considering statements made in other contexts we must be alert to other ways of inter-preting them.

5.5 AN ARGUMENT BY WILLIAMSON AGAINST NON-BIVALENCE

Timothy Williamson's book *Vagueness* (Williamson (1994)) is devoted primarily to linguistic or conceptual issues about vague-ness, but he touches briefly on the possibility of indeterminacy of identity. Tracing through his reasoning,[8] the line of argument depends crucially on his rejection of multivalent logic, and his defence of bivalence. Although I employ only two truth-values, true and false, I admit three truth-value statuses: true, false, and neither, and variants of Williamson's arguments apply to this stance as well.

Williamson's position is a broad one, not directed merely at inde-terminacy of identity; he believes that there is no worldly indeter-minacy of any kind. He phrases this as an attack on the idea that statements might have some degree of truth other than 0 (complete falsity) or 1 (complete truth). Anyone who believes in some other degree of truth must give a coherent account of how our language embodies this. He considers a view substantially like the one dis-cussed here, in which something like a "truth-functional" language is used. Specifically, he argues against the claim that: "the degree of

---

[8] Williamson discusses indeterminate identity in his §9.2 *Determinacy in the World*; he rejects it there (1994: 255) because it requires a formulation in terms of many-valued logic, which has been rejected in §§4.11–4.14. I focus here on the main point of §4.14.

truth of various compounds is a function of the degrees of truth of their components" (1994: 135).

If we read 'degree of truth' as 'type of truth-value status' then his discussion is pertinent to the view under consideration here. He argues as follows:

> Now imagine someone drifting off to sleep. The sentences 'He is awake' and 'He is asleep' are vague. According to the degree theorist, as the former falls in degree of truth, the latter rises. At some point they have the same degree of truth, an intermediate one. By what has just been argued, the conjunction 'He is awake and he is asleep' also has that intermediate degree of truth. But how can that be? Waking and sleep by definition exclude each other. 'He is awake and he is asleep' has no chance at all of being true. Our man is not in an unclear area between the cases in which the conjunction is true and those in which it is false, for there are no cases of the former kind. . . . Since the conjunction in question is clearly incorrect, it should not have an intermediate degree of truth. It is clearly incorrect, although neither conjunct is; one must be careful to distinguish what can be said of the conjunction from what can be said of each conjunct. Thus degree-functionality fails for conjunction.
>
> The same point can be made with 'He is not awake' in place of 'He is asleep'. . . . How can an explicit contradiction be true to any degree other than 0? (ibid. 136)

I do not hold that any contradiction can be true to any degree other than 0 (falsity). I do, however, hold that a contradiction can *lack* truth-value if its parts do. Williamson's discussion of 'He is awake and he is not awake' needs to be addressed because it appears to rule out lack of truth-value as well as intermediate degrees of truth-value.

What happens if 'He is awake' lacks truth-value? I hold that the conjunction 'He is awake and he is not awake' also lacks truth-value. Williamson is right in questioning whether this is how a person would normally intend such an utterance. But this is hard to assess, since it isn't an utterance that one would normally make. But suppose someone actually asserts 'He is awake and he is not awake'; what *would* they be likely to mean? The most natural interpretation would be that they are saying this to emphasize that he is *sort of* awake and *sort of not* awake. Under this interpretation, both Williamson and I are wrong, for so used, the sentence would be true. But on that interpretation it is not a contradiction at all; this is because the 'sort of' modifies the meanings so that the second

conjunct does not deny what the first asserts. So under this interpretation the utterance is not relevant to Williamson's query "How
can an explicit contradiction be true?"

This is not what Williamson intended to discuss. So let us fasten
on a reading in which the second conjunct *is* the negation of the
first, in a situation in which the first conjunct is as midway between
truth and falsity as you can get it. I am then comfortable in saying
that both conjuncts lack truth-value, and the whole does as well.
Williamson thinks that the whole must be fully false. He says this
apparently because he thinks this must be true of any contradiction: "How can an explicit contradiction be true to any degree other
than 0?" The answer to his question is straightforward: "by having
parts that lack truth-value".

This answers Williamson's question, but not his concern, for
there really is something odd about seeing explicit contradictions
as indeterminate. This is probably because an explicit contradiction
cannot be true. This, however, does not make it false, unless it has
a truth-value. But suppose we want somehow to be able to construe any sentence that cannot be true in such a way that it is
thereby false. This is what supervaluational readings are for; a sentence read supervaluationally is automatically false (or a sentence
read normally is automatically superfalse) if its form prevents it
from being true, and any explicit contradiction is like this. It *is*
appropriate to read a sentence supervaluationally if you are
judging it based more on form than on content, which is what
Williamson urges that we do with explicit contradictions.

Succinctly put: Williamson objects to the lack of bivalence of any
view that admits "truth-value status functionality" because, so read,
some explicit contradictions are not false (they lack truth-value).
But any sentence *can* be read supervaluationally. So anyone who
has a potentially non-bivalent language has a language that *can*
read contradictions as false when you focus on form over content.
So the existence of instincts to call explicit contradictions false
cannot refute such a view.

Elsewhere (Chapter 5), Williamson argues that a consistent use
of supervaluational readings yields unnaturalness in some contexts.
I agree with many of the points he makes, though the discussion is
too wide-ranging to sum up here. But I draw a different lesson.
There is a wide variety of contexts in which definite truth and falsity
cannot be assumed, and no uniform approach to non-bivalent

language will be most natural in all of them. The best we can do is to be clear about how our own language is to be taken, and to be careful not to misconstrue others. Occasional contexts in which truth-status-functional readings of connectives are unnatural cannot tell against a theory formulated with such readings, so long as one does not assert that such readings of connectives are the ones intended by all speakers of natural language in all contexts. And I make no such claim.

Williamson has other relevant arguments; I discuss one which relies on the logic of conditionals in the next chapter, and I discuss higher-order indeterminacy in Chapter 12.

5.6 FUZZY OBJECTS AND INDETERMINATE IDENTITY

One widely discussed issue is not strictly a refutation, though it often plays much the same rhetorical role. It turns on the relation between the existence of "fuzzy objects" and the existence of indeterminacy of identity. Several writers suggest that people believe in indeterminacy of identity because they mistakenly think that it follows from the existence of fuzzy objects. But it does not; so a major rationale for believing in indeterminacy of identity is thus undercut. If the only evidence one could ever have for indeterminacy of identity is easily reconstruable as evidence for fuzzy objects, the thesis of indeterminacy of identity could not ever be validated.

An example: a mountain has indeterminate boundaries. Pick a rise in the landscape with boundaries such that it is indeterminate whether they are the boundaries of the mountain. Does it follow that it is indeterminate whether the rise is the mountain? Not automatically; certainly not without some additional argumentation.

A "fuzzy object" is an object with indistinct boundaries. The indistinctness of boundary is usually construed as an indistinctness in whether a certain portion of space is inside or outside the object or not, and this is then recast as the question of whether the stuff in the disputed region is or is not part of the object. If indistinctness is interpreted as indeterminacy, a fuzzy object then becomes an object such that it is indeterminate what its parts are. For our purposes, then, a fuzzy object may be taken to be as follows:

> *x* is a *fuzzy object* =$_{df}$ there is some *y* such that it is indeterminate whether *y* is part of *x*.

As many writers either point out or argue at length,[9] the existence of a fuzzy object in this sense does not logically entail that there are objects such that it is indeterminate whether they are identical. Most people leave it at that. But there is a bit more to be said. For there are situations in which one *can* infer the indeterminate identity from the existence of fuzzy objects.

5.6.1 *Inferring indeterminate identity from fuzzy objects*

Although the existence of fuzzy objects does not entail that there is any indeterminate identity, it may do so with the help of some additional assumptions. Here are some assumptions that would make the transition feasible. The assumptions are ingredients of a theory of mereology (the study of parts and wholes). We use 'part' here in the sense in which each object is part of itself.

> *Mereological identity*: For any objects *x* and *y*, *x* is identical with *y* if and only if *x* and *y* have the same parts.
> *Transitivity*: If *x* is part of *y*, and *y* part of *z*, then *x* is part of *z*.
> *Mereological sums*: For any objects *x* and *y* there is an object *z* which is their mereological sum, in the sense that
>   (i) *x* is part of *z*, and
> (ii) *y* is part of *z*, and
> (iii) everything that *x* and *y* are both parts of, *z* is part of also.
> *Uniformity of indeterminate parts*: If it is indeterminate whether *y* is part of *x*, there is no part of the sum of *x* and *y* which is determinately not part of *x*.

These assumptions are to be understood strongly. For example, the claim of *mereological identity* is that '*x* is identical to *y*' is to be *true*, *false*, or *neither*, exactly when the claim '*x* and *y* have the same parts' is *true*, *false*, or *neither*. In *mereological sums* it is understood that for any objects *x* and *y* it is determinately true that there is an

---

[9] e.g. Burgess (1990).

object z which is the sum of x and y, where the explanation of "sum" is definitive as just explained. I clarify these assumptions in this way not because I believe that they are true when so clarified, but rather because I am giving an example of assumptions that *would* connect indeterminacy of parts with indeterminacy of identity. These assumptions are not true of objects in general, because there are many sorts of objects that either have no parts in a straightforward sense, or they have parts in a sense that does not allow us to infer their identity from the fact that they share parts. But in some limited domains, the assumptions may be quite plausible. In such a domain one *could* infer indeterminate identity from the existence of fuzzy objects. Consider an object a and some object b where it is indeterminate whether b is a part of a. We could argue as follows:

> By *mereological sums* there is an object c which is the sum of a and b. We will show that it is indeterminate whether c is identical to a. By *mereological identity* it will be sufficient to show two things:
>
> (1) There is something that is determinately a part of c and not determinately a part of a. This rules out the possibility that a and c are determinately identical.
>
> (2) There is nothing that is determinately part of a that is determinately not part of c, and vice versa. This rules out the possibility that a and c are determinately distinct.
>
> Arguments:
>
> (1) By hypothesis it is indeterminate whether b is part of a, and by construction of c as the sum of a and b, it is determinate that b is part of c. So a is not determinately the same as c.
>
> (2) By construction of c as the sum of a and b and by transitivity it follows that every determinate part of a is a determinate part of c. And by the *uniformity of indeterminate parts*, there is no determinate subpart of the sum of a and b (that is, no determinate subpart of c) that is determinately not part of a.

So there are assumptions with which one can argue from the existence of fuzzy objects to the existence of indeterminacy of identity, and they may be quite plausible when applied to certain sorts of objects. But in other cases the assumptions may not be plausible at all. For example, I am a person. It is up for grabs whether I am a mereological object or not. I do indeed have a spatial location, but it is unclear whether my identity is dependent on this, so the principle of mereological identity may be false when applied to me. If so, I may be a fuzzy object, but there may be nothing with which I am indeterminately identical.

Are mountains mereological entities of which these assumptions hold? I suspect not, though I am not certain. If they were, they would yield hosts of examples of indeterminate identity.

5.7 COOK'S BUILDING

The following example involves considerations of parts and wholes. Cook (1986) takes the position that the Evans argument is flawed, but that there is nonetheless no such thing as indeterminate identity. To make this plausible he argues generally against indeterminate identity, and he also explains how at least one apparent case of indeterminate identity is instead merely a case of a fuzzy object.

Cook considers a building, somewhat different from the one I discussed in Chapter 1. He assumes a structure with a kind of dumbbell shape, consisting of two modules, A and B, connected by a narrow walkway, C. Smith is lecturing somewhere within module A, and Jones within module B. The question will be whether the building in which Smith is lecturing is the same as the building in which Jones is lecturing.

My own instinct is that there are three determinate buildings: A, B, and ABC, with each of A and B being parts of ABC. If this is so, there are two distinct buildings (B and ABC) in which Jones is lecturing, and thus 'the building in which Jones is lecturing' is a definite description that has no unique reference, and the example raises no genuine puzzle about identity. But Cook assumes otherwise, and his view leads to an interesting case.

Let 'J' abbreviate 'the building in which Jones is lecturing', and 'S' abbreviate 'the building in which Smith is lecturing'. Cook assumes that 'J' has a unique reference, and so does 'S', but it is indeterminate exactly what the *parts* of J are, and likewise for S:

"The denotation is not indeterminate; the boundaries of what is denoted are indeterminate" (1986: 182).

He rejects the idea that clarifying what counts as a building is even relevant to the question of denotation or identity:

When we sharpen the notion of a building, we are not making the denotation of 'the building in which Smith is lecturing' determinate; we are making it determinate whether this building includes [B]. (If the colour of my car is on the borderline between red and orange, then it is indeterminate whether the colour of my car is red. 'The colour of my car', however, has a determinate denotation. If we sharpen the notion of being red, we don't make the denotation of 'the colour of my car' determinate, we make it determinate whether the colour of my car is red.) (ibid: 183)

Cook's position is that 'S' and 'J' each uniquely denotes an object with indeterminate parts, but there is no indeterminate identity of objects.

5.7.1 An argument from fuzzy buildings to indeterminate identity

Let me digress for a moment to consider whether this might be a case in which indeterminacy of parts actually does entail an indeterminate identity. Assume that the only parts of the building that are relevant in this example are A, B, and C, and sums made of them. We may also in this case make a crucial assumption that cannot be made about all cases: that the buildings in question *would* be identical if they determinately had exactly the same parts, and that they *would* be determinately distinct if one of them determinately had a part that the other determinately lacked. S has A as a determinate part, since S is determinately the building in which Smith is lecturing, and it is determinate that Smith is lecturing in A; similarly J has B as a determinate part. Now we can argue as follows:

> Suppose that J is determinately identical to S. Then J and S have the same parts. Since A is determinately a part of J, it is also determinately a part of S, and since B is determinately a part of S, it is determinately a part of J. So each of J and S have both A and B as determinate parts. If we assume that in this case there are no scattered buildings, C must be determinately

part of each as well.[10] It follows that neither J nor S has any indeterminate parts at all, contrary to the initial assumption. So J cannot be determinately identical to S.

Suppose that J and S are determinately distinct. Then we have determinately distinct objects J and S, with each of them having a determinate part (B for J and A for S). They must determinately disagree with respect to some part, for this is necessary for them to be determinately distinct. By parity, C must be part of both or part of neither or an indeterminate part of each, so they will not disagree with respect to C. So it must be that A is determinately not a part of J and B is determinately not a part of S. Since they are fuzzy objects, they must have indeterminate parts. As a result, it must be that C is an indeterminate part of each. This is coherent, but entirely unmotivated by our understanding of the setup. Why should it be determinately false that B is part of S, yet indeterminate whether C is? Indeed, suppose that we move the parts A and B closer and closer together until C has shrunk to nothing at all and A and B share only a doorway. Then there is no remaining part to be an indeterminate part of both J and S, and the example collapses. Yet it is just as plausible in that case to say that J and S are fuzzy objects as it is in the original case.

The mereological assumptions in this argument are certainly not beyond challenge, but they seem to me plausible. I conclude that this is a case in which the indeterminacy of parts does plausibly lead to indeterminacy of identity. Or, it would if the parts were indeterminate, which is what Cook assumes.[11] Sometimes there can be indeterminate parthood without indeterminacy of identity, and sometimes there cannot be; one has to look at the details of the case to tell.

---

[10] We could also assume at this point that C is an indeterminate part of one of the buildings, and argue by symmetry that it must be an indeterminate part of the other as well. The conclusion would then follow that J and S agree in all their parts.

[11] To be clear: I disagree with Cook that this is a case in which there is determinate reference to buildings but in which it is indeterminate what their parts are. I think that in this particular case one should deny that the descriptions have unique denotations, and one should not conclude that there is indeterminacy of identity in the world because of such a case.

5.7.2 Cook's refutation of indeterminacy of identity

I have argued that if Cook is right about J and S having indeterminate parts, they are indeterminately identical. But Cook has an argument that this is not possible, and we need to look at that. Cook rejects the Evans argument; he says that being indeterminate identical with *a is* a property, but that one cannot conclude from the fact that *b* determinately possesses it and *a* does not that *a* and *b* are distinct. (I agree with this only on the assumption that he has in mind what I above called conceptual properties.) But he thinks a better argument against the indeterminacy of identity can be given, one involving the law of excluded middle (LEM). Briefly, he holds that indeterminacy of identity conflicts with LEM, but LEM can be defended.

Here is the statement of the conflict between indeterminacy of identity and LEM:

[I]f indeterminacy is in the world then LEM does not hold—objects can be in three mutually exclusive states: they can be identical, they can be non-identical, and they can be indeterminately identical. To defend LEM, then, is to attack the view that objects can be indeterminately identical. (Cook 1986: 183)

The defence of LEM is explained as follows:

The trick to seeing that borderline cases do not force us to give up LEM is (a) seeing that a disjunction can be true even though neither disjunct is true, and (b) seeing that this does not prevent the disjunction's being exhaustive. (ibid. 184)

Expanding on (a) he says:

[O]ne will not be able to explain the truth conditions for the statement that the car is red in a straightforward truth-functional way. Here I think one should appeal to something like true-under-an-acceptable-sharpening. Thus, one might say that 'red or orange' is true of an object if under all acceptable sharpenings of 'red' and 'orange' either 'red' or 'orange' is true of it. (ibid.)

He goes on to explain how 'J = S' can be seen as a similar case, because the identity contains a concealed appeal to 'part of the same building', which is vague in a way similar to the way in which 'red' is vague.

The immediate problem with this explanation is that it is no longer clear why indeterminate identity is supposed to conflict with

LEM. The conflict was asserted above, but that explanation makes it clear that the conflict arises when the disjunction '$a = b$ or not $a = b$' is treated truth-functionally. However, the defence of LEM rests on the claim that a disjunction may be true even if neither disjunct is true; this is to treat the disjunction non-truth-functionally, and this undercuts the assertion that indeterminate identity inevitably conflicts with LEM. Thus the argument against indeterminate identity vanishes.

The explanation, I think, is that Cook does not think that *real* indeterminacy of identity admits of the same treatment as vagueness, and so when LEM is applied to a case of indeterminate identity, the truth-functional reading is the only one available. And he is consistent in his treatment of the building case, for Cook sees '$J = S$' as lacking in truth-value, but not because of indeterminacy of identity; he thinks that this is only an apparent case of indeterminacy of identity. It is an identity statement with a concealed vagueness in it, but a vagueness in 'part of', not a vagueness in '='. Thus he may consistently hold that a disjunction may be true when neither disjunct is true, if the lack of truth-value depends on vagueness, while also holding that if there were real indeterminacy of identity, a disjunction made up of parts that lack truth-value for this reason would still lack truth-value.

This puts us on common ground, at least for the language I have adopted here: if a is indeterminately identical with b then '$a = b$ or not $a = b$' really does lack truth-value, and "sharpenings" of concepts or vague terms is irrelevant to this. I then accept this as a counter-example to LEM, a law which Cook defends. But on this understanding it appears to me that Cook has not defended LEM for the case in point. He explains how apparent counter-examples to LEM *due to vague terms* are not real counter-examples, but this explanation does not apply to the case of indeterminate identity. So violations of LEM due to indeterminacy of identity have not been addressed, and indeterminacy of identity remains unrefuted.

5.8 BROOME'S CLUB

In a paper objecting to Evans's argument, John Broome (1984) proposes a plausible example of a case of indeterminate identity.

SCENARIO: A club comes into existence and continues for five years, at which point it ceases functioning. A few years later a group of people, including many members of the club previously mentioned, get together and act as a club for an additional twenty-five years. The reader is invited to fill in the details in such a way that it is indeterminate whether the earlier club was revived when the new meetings began.

Broome suggests that this is a case in which there is an earlier club, and a later club, with no fact of the matter as to whether they are the same. (If they were the same, then it would be determinately true that the earlier club was revived, and if they were not the same it would be determinately false that the earlier club was revived.) I am inclined to agree.

Noonan (1984) argues that this cannot be a case of indeterminacy of identity. He asks that we consider the predicates:

lasted for at most five years
lasted for at least twenty-five years
lasted for at most five years or lasted for at least twenty-five
   years

He claims that it is indeterminate whether the first predicate is true of the earlier club, and indeterminate whether the second predicate is true of the earlier club, but determinate that the third predicate is true of the earlier club. He concludes that he cannot understand how there can be such an object. The argument is subtle, so I quote it in full:

[I]f 'the earlier club is the later club' is indeterminate in truth value for [the] reason [that the objects are indeterminately identical], then the predicate 'lasted for at most five years' will be neither determinately true nor determinately false of the object denoted by the term 'the earlier club' (for if the identity *were* false that predicate would be true of the earlier club, and if the identity *were* true it would be false of the earlier club). Similarly, the predicate 'lasted for at least twenty-five years' will be neither determinately true nor determinately false of the earlier club (for if the identity were true that predicate would be true of it, and if the identity were false it would be false of it). On the other hand, the predicate 'lasted for at most five years or lasted for at least twenty-five years' must be determinately true of the earlier club (for the object determinately denoted by 'the earlier club' has certainly lasted for at least five years on Broome's account, and there is no other longer-lived entity, apart from the later club—which has lasted for at least twenty-five years—with which it might be identical, so its lifespan must either be a maximum of five, or a minimum of twenty-five, years). The earlier club, then, on Broome's account, must be an object which determinately satisfies the predicate 'lasted for at most five years or lasted for at least twenty-five years' but neither determinately satisfies the predicate 'lasted for at most five years' nor determinately satisfies the predicate 'lasted for at least twenty-five years'. But I do not understand how there can be such an object. (Noonan 1984: 119)

Noonan's bewilderment (as he goes on to explain) is not with the general case of a disjunctive predicate being true of a thing when neither disjunct is, for he believes that this occurs naturally with borderline cases such as being either-orange-or-red; the puzzlement is over examples like that above, where the description ('at most five or at least twenty-five') prohibits such a borderline. I have difficulty with such cases as well. But I am not convinced that we have such a case at hand. I agree that each of these predications are indeterminate:

> The earlier club lasted for at most five years
> The earlier club lasted for at least twenty-five years.

But I think the disjunctive predication is indeterminate as well:

> It is indeterminate whether the earlier club lasted for at most five years or at least twenty-five years.

Why does Noonan think the disjunctive predication is true? His argument has this structure:

> The predicate 'lasted for at most five years or lasted for at least twenty-five years' must be determinately true of the earlier club.
> For: (i) the object determinately denoted by 'the earlier club' has certainly lasted for at least five years,
> and: (ii) there is no other longer-lived entity, apart from the later club—which has lasted for at least twenty-five years—with which the earlier club might be identical,
> so: (iii) its lifespan must either be a maximum of five, or a minimum of twenty-five, years.

I agree with (i), but (ii) is difficult to interpret. Part of the trouble is the 'might' in:

> (ii') there is no entity x such that x is distinct from the later club and x lasts more than five years and such that the earlier club might be x.

If the 'might' is read modally, then the conclusion (iii) does not follow. If it is merely rhetorical, as in:

(ii′) there is no entity x such that x is distinct from the later club and x lasts more than five years and such that the earlier club is x.

the clause is much too strong; it is equivalent to the claim that the earlier club is identical with the later club. This yields the conclusion, but it begs the question.

Probably what is meant is:[12]

(ii′) there is no entity x such that x is distinct from the later club and x lasts more than five years and such that it is not determinately true that the earlier club is not x.

that is:

(ii″) $\neg \exists x[\neg(x = l)$ & (x lasts more than five years) & $\neg!\neg(e = x)]$.

But this is not true in the example envisaged. Not because it is false, but because it is indeterminate. For there is an instance of (ii″)—the earlier club itself—which makes (ii′) indeterminate in truth-value. The instance is:

Indeterminate: $\neg(e = l)$ & (e lasts more than five years) & $\neg!\neg(e = e)$.

This is indeterminate because each of its first two conjuncts are indeterminate (and its last conjunct is true). Since this is indeterminate, its existential generalization:

$\exists x[\neg(x = l)$ & (x lasts more than five years) & $\neg!\neg(e = x)]$

is either indeterminate or true. But this is the negation of (ii″), which is thus indeterminate or false. So the argument is not successful.

Of course, one might interpret 'apart from the later club' to mean '*determinately* distinct from the later club. Then (ii′) has the form:

$\neg \exists x[(!\neg x = l)$ & (x lasts more than five years) & $\neg(!\neg e = x)]$.

This does entail:

---

[12] I am indebted here to an anonymous referee for OUP.

$\neg(!\neg e = l) \vee \neg(e$ lasts more than five years$) \vee (!\neg e = e)$.

The last disjunct drops off, yielding:

$\neg(!\neg e = l) \vee \neg(e$ lasts more than five years$)$.

But the additional '!' in the first conjunct prevents us from inferring:

$(e = l) \vee \neg(e$ lasts more than five years$)$

which is what we need to infer:

$(e$ lasts a minimum of twenty-five years$) \vee \neg(e$ lasts more than five years$)$.

Instead, one gets:

$\neg!\neg(e$ lasts a minimum of twenty-five years$) \vee \neg(e$ lasts more than five years$)$.

which is not the desired result.

I see no other way to interpret the point that makes it strong enough to yield the conclusion without presupposing what is at issue. (I return to a speculative interpretation later in this section.)

It is worth noting that if this kind of reasoning were to be persuasive, it would be a problem for indeterminacy in general, not just for the indeterminacy of identity. For a conundrum like that which Noonan presents occurs without identity being involved at all. Notice that identity was not mentioned in the original scenario; the question directly posed was whether or not the original club was revived. Suppose we ignore 'the later club' and simply ask whether the original club lasted at most five years, or at least twenty-five years, or either at most five or at least twenty-five years? It is easy to simulate a puzzle like Noonan's for the original club:

[I]f it is indeterminate whether the original club was revived, then the predicate 'lasted for at most five years' will be neither determinately true nor determinately false of the object denoted by the term 'the original club' (for if that predicate were determinately true of the original club, it would be determinately false that the original club was revived, and if it were determinately false of the original club, it would be determinately true that there was a revival). Similarly, the predicate 'lasted for at least twenty-five years' will be neither determinately true nor determinately false of the original club (for if that predicate were determinately true of the original club, it would be determinately true that the original club was revived, and if it were determinately false of the original club, it would be determinately false that there was a revival). On the other hand, the predicate 'lasted for at most five years or lasted for at least twenty-five years' must be determinately true of the original club (for the object determinately denoted by 'the original club' has certainly lasted for at least five years on Broome's account, and there is no club with a life-span between five and twenty-five years, so its lifespan must either be a maximum of five, or a minimum of twenty-five, years). The original club, then, on Broome's account, must be an object which determinately satisfies the predicate 'lasted for at most five years or lasted for at least twenty-five years' but neither determinately satisfies the predicate 'lasted for at most five years' nor determinately satisfies the predicate 'lasted for at least twenty-five years'. But how can there be such an object?

If this reasoning is good, it shows there is no such thing as indeterminacy. But the central parenthesis here clearly involves an illegitimate appeal to excluded middle. This is the part of the argument that Noonan fills in with the remarks about identity examined above.

5.8.1 Super-resolutional readings

I could rest here, but I am bothered, for in spite of the inconclusiveness of Noonan's reasoning, I find I am tempted (somewhat) to agree that the disjunction he cites is true:

> The earlier club lasted for at most five years or at least twenty-five years.

Why is this? When I try to examine my own instincts I find it is partly my inclination to respond to disjunctive questions with the Sherlock Holmes principle:

> "When all the alternatives have been ruled out, whatever remains must be true, no matter how unlikely."

And in the case of the disjunction, the alternative is ruled out; it is ruled out that the earlier club lasted more than five but less than twenty-five years. But the Holmes principle yields the disjunction above only if "no answer" is not one of the alternatives. If it is one of the options, the principle is misapplied.

Another closely related theme that moves me towards accepting the disjunction is to read it:

No matter how things *turn out*, either the earlier club lasted for at most five years or at least twenty-five years.

Something like this is a possible construal of the passage from Noonan quoted above:

[the earlier club] has certainly lasted for at least five years . . . , and there is no other longer-lived entity, apart from the later club—which has lasted for at least twenty-five years—with which it might be identical, so its lifespan must either be a maximum of five, or a minimum of twenty-five, years.

It is indeed true that in any *determinate extension* of this world, the lifespan of the earlier club *must* be either a maximum of five, or a minimum of twenty-five, years. But to read the sentence in this way is to read it super-resolutionally; the sentence is true in every *resolution* of the world. But if this is how we read it when we endorse the disjunction, then we *can* understand how a disjunction can be true when its parts are indeterminate. The parts are indeterminate because there is no one way they turn out in every resolution, but in every resolution, one of them turns out true, and that is why the disjunction is super-resolutionally true.

So there are ways in which the disjunction may be true when its parts lack truth-value, but their existence does not tell against the indeterminate identity at all.

5.9 WHY CONSIDERING CONJUNCTIONS OR DISJUNCTIONS IS INEVITABLY INCONCLUSIVE

There is a theme to the last few arguments we have considered. In each case, what is at issue is whether a certain claim can lack truth-value because of what the world is like. The strategy is to focus not on this claim, but on a complex sentence having that claim as a part, for example, on a disjunction containing the claim as a disjunct, or a conjunction containing it as a conjunct. The advantage of this is supposed to be that we have clear instincts that the disjunction is true (or that the conjunction is false), thus refuting the claim that its disjuncts lack truth-value. This strategy has two weaknesses. The first is that the data to the effect that the disjunction is true are not compelling. The second is that when the disjunction is read so as to make its truth compelling, this appears to force a reading in which the disjunction is true *in spite of* the possible lack of truth-value of its parts, and so one may not reason from the truth of the whole to the truth-values of its parts. I don't know any way around this. If there is a reading on which the disjunction is true, that seems to go nowhere in attacking indeterminacy.

6

Conditional Disputations

Some people have thought that indeterminacy of identity can be refuted by considerations gleaned from the logic of conditionals—the logic of statements of the form 'If A then B'. I think that this cannot be right; indeterminate identity can be stated and assessed without the use of conditionals, and considering conditionals merely brings in irrelevant complications. But others have thought differently, and it is incumbent on me to provide a coherent response to their objections. Besides, although it is possible to avoid the use of conditionals, it is awkward.

I begin by saying what I mean by 'if . . . then . . .', and then I discuss constraints on other options for treating conditionals. We then look at various ways in which Leibniz's Law can be formulated as a conditional. This is followed by some ways in which the logic of conditionals and biconditionals has been used in attempts to refute indeterminate identity. (The sections after §6.1 are not presupposed by later chapters.)

6.1 THE CONDITIONAL AND THE BICONDITIONAL

For reasons given earlier I ignore supervaluational readings and I concentrate entirely on conditionals for which the truth-value status of the whole is determined by the truth-value statuses of the parts. I take for granted that any feasible rendition of the conditional will agree with the classical material conditional when the parts of the conditional have truth-values. I also assume that a conditional with a false antecedent and a truth-valueless consequent is just as true as one with a false antecedent and a false consequent; so it is true. Likewise for a conditional with a true consequent and

an antecedent without truth-value. So any truth-table will be got
by filling in the cases left open in Table 6.1.

If we use the classical definition of the material conditional in
terms of disjunction and negation:

$$\phi \supset \psi =_{df} \neg\phi \vee \psi,$$

then our previous analysis of disjunction yields a conditional whose
truth-table is got by making all the open cases above be truth-value
gaps (Table 6.2).

This conditional is well defined, but it does not seem to reflect
what people have in mind when they choose to say 'if . . . then . . .'
instead of 'not . . . or . . .'. At the very least, there is a much stronger
inclination to treat 'If S then S' as automatically true than to treat
'S ∨ ¬S' as automatically true. Doing this requires that the line in
the truth-table for 'if . . . then . . .' with two gaps be T. I will assume
this in what follows. So the question is how to fill in the other two
empty cells in the table. I choose the most popular version, the so-
called "Łukasiewicz" interpretation, which makes the remaining
empty cells be gaps (Table 6.3).

I call this "sustaining if-then": the truth-value status of a conditional is determined by how far the consequent drops below
the antecedent in truth-value status, counting T as highest and F
as lowest. If there is no drop at all, the conditional is true, if there

TABLE 6.1.

ϕ	ψ	If ϕ then ψ
T	T	T
T	—	? ←
T	F	F
—	T	T
—	—	? ←
—	F	? ←
F	T	T
F	—	T
F	F	T

TABLE 6.2.

ϕ	ψ	$\phi \supset \psi$
T	T	T
T	—	—
T	F	F
—	T	T
—	—	—
—	F	—
F	T	T
F	—	T
F	F	T

is a drop all the way from T to F it is false, and otherwise the conditional lacks truth-value. The resulting conditional validates most of the laws one naturally expects from a conditional, such as *modus ponens*, *modus tollens*, hypothetical syllogism, and contraposition.

The conditional just defined also yields a natural biconditional. That is, if '$\phi \Leftrightarrow \psi$' is defined as '$(\phi \Rightarrow \psi)\&(\psi \Rightarrow \phi)$', then one obtains a biconditional that is true when ϕ and ψ have the same truth-value status, false when they differ in truth-value, and otherwise indeterminate (Table 6.4).

The "if-true" use of conditionals: Woodruff (1969) points out that there is a use of 'if . . . then . . .', which he calls the "if-true" use, in which what one means by saying 'if ϕ then ψ' is 'if ϕ is true then ψ'. This is a hypothesis about people's behaviour in interpreting conditionals, and a substantial justification of it would take more discussion than I can devote to it here, but I think it is right, and it is important to take into account when assessing arguments that people actually give in a non-classical setting. I regard this as a special *use* of 'if . . . then . . .'. This use is easily expressed with the notation at hand: if someone says 'if ϕ then ψ' intending the "if-true" meaning, their claim should be symbolized as '$!\phi \Rightarrow \psi$'.

The "if-true" use of conditionals is important to capture because we need to confront the fact that the literal reading of the

	TABLE 6.3.				TABLE 6.4.	
ϕ	ψ	$\phi \Rightarrow \psi$		ϕ	ψ	$\phi \Leftrightarrow \psi$
T	T	T		T	T	T
T	—	—		T	—	—
T	F	F		T	F	F
—	T	T		—	T	—
—	—	T		—	—	T
—	F	—		—	F	—
F	T	T		F	T	F
F	—	T		F	—	—
F	F	T		F	F	T

Lukasiewicz conditional, '$\phi \Rightarrow \psi$', does not validate conditional proof. This is easy to see from the conventions already adopted. Suppose that ϕ lacks truth-value, and consider the following three-line argument using conditional proof:

1. | ϕ Hypothesis for CP
2. | $!\phi$ From 1
3. $\phi \Rightarrow !\phi$ By CP from 1–2   NO!

If this proof were good, '$\phi \Rightarrow !\phi$' would be a truth of our logic, but it is not; it lacks truth-value when ϕ does. So the '$\Rightarrow$' connective does not validate classical conditional proof. This is important, since people often take conditional proof techniques for granted in their reasoning. Woodruff's suggestion is that when people instinctively use conditional proof in a non-classical setting they are assuming that ϕ is true, and then deriving ψ from ϕ, and then concluding *correctly(!)* that they have shown 'if ϕ is true, then ψ'.[1] In a classical setting, this is no different from concluding 'if ϕ then ψ', and no harm is done. But in a non-classical setting one needs to be attuned to the difference. The difference is that conditional proof is not valid for the literal reading of '$\Rightarrow$', but it is valid for the "if-true" reading of '$\Rightarrow$'. We do not have:

NO: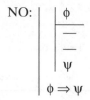

but we do have:

YES: | | ϕ
| | ─
| | ─
| | ψ
| $!\phi \Rightarrow \psi$

---

[1] If this is done above, line 3 will read '$!\phi \Rightarrow !\phi$', which *is* a truth of logic.

6.2 CONSTRAINTS ON ALTERNATIVES

Why settle for a conditional that does not obey conditional proof without giving it the "if-true" reading? Why not use a conditional that satisfies *all* the laws we expect from a well-behaved conditional? The answer is that no such conditional exists. We can do no better than the options already discussed. Suppose that you want a conditional that, like the material conditional, is true whenever its antecedent is false, and whenever its consequent is true, and that makes '$\phi \Rightarrow \phi$' always true. There is *no* such conditional definable in terms of truth-value status that sanctions these three rules:[2]

    (i) *modus ponens*
    (ii) *modus tollens*
    (iii) conditional proof

The proof is simple. If we had classical conditional proof, we could prove 'if ϕ then !ϕ', as we showed above, so any sentence of this form would be true. When ϕ lacks truth-value, 'if ϕ then !ϕ' would then be a true sentence with its antecedent lacking truth-value and its consequent false. Since the truth-value status of the parts determine that of the whole, *any* sentence with a truth-valueless antecedent and a false consequent would be true. Let 'If A then B' be such a true sentence. Then *modus tollens* would lead from the truths 'If A then B' and 'not B' to the truth-valueless sentence 'not A'.

So you cannot have everything you want. Nobody may fault the conditional chosen in the last section merely because it does not do everything one might want; that is not a reasonable goal. Likewise, one cannot propose an alternative treatment of conditionals without also failing to achieve all desirabilities. Given these facts, I am inclined to see the Lukasiewicz conditional as the best of all, since it validates both *modus ponens* and *modus tollens*, and we can explain good versions of conditional proof as resulting from if-true readings of it, that is, as proofs that correctly conclude a sentence of the form 'if !ϕ then ψ'.

---

[2] Likewise, no such conditional satisfies all of (i) *modus ponens*, (ii) contraposition, (iii) conditional proof. Here is the argument. Conditional proof would allow us to prove 'if A then !A', so that would be true. If A lacks truth-value, this would yield truth for any conditional 'if G then H' where G lacks truth-value and H is false. By contraposition, 'if $\neg H$ then $\neg G$' would then be true, when $\neg H$ is true and $\neg G$ lacks truth-value. But then *modus ponens* would lead us from truths ('If $\neg H$ then $\neg G$' and '$\neg H$') to a conclusion ('$\neg G$') that lacks truth-value.

6.3 LEIBNIZ'S LAW AS A CONDITIONAL

It has been suggested that indeterminate identity may be refuted as follows. First, formulate Leibniz's Law in conditional form:

[LL?]   If $s = t$ then (ϕs iff ϕt).

Then use a simple variant of the Evans argument to refute indeterminate identity:

1. $\nabla a = b$	Hypothesis for refutation
2. $\neg\nabla(b = b)$	Logical truth
3. $\neg(\nabla a = b$ iff $\nabla b = b)$	From 1,2 by truth-functional logic
4. If $a = b$ then ($\nabla a = b$ iff $\nabla b = b$)	[LL?]
5. $\neg a = b$.	From 3, 4 by *modus tollens*, contradicting (1)

Whether this is a good argument or not depends on how the connectives are symbolized. Using the Łukasiewicz conditional and biconditional the steps are indeed valid:

1. $\nabla a = b$	Hypothesis for refutation
2. $\neg\nabla(b = b)$	Logical truth
3. $\neg(\nabla a = b \Leftrightarrow \nabla b = b)$	From 1,2 by truth-functional logic
4. $a = b \Rightarrow (\phi a \Leftrightarrow \phi b)$	[LL?] using $\Rightarrow$
5. $\neg a = b$.	From 3, 4 by *modus tollens*

So there appears to be a problem for indeterminate identity.

The source of the problem is the formulation of Leibniz's Law. I have accepted a version of this law as a principle of inference, and this automatically validates the following "if-true" version of Leibniz's Law:

Leibniz's Law: $!a = b \Rightarrow (\phi a \Leftrightarrow \phi b)$.   [Good Version]

But I have rejected the contrapositive version of the law. Since the '$\Rightarrow$' conditional satisfies contraposition, it is easy to show that the following simpler version of Leibniz's Law must not be accepted:

NO: $a = b \Rightarrow (\phi a \Leftrightarrow \phi b)$.   [Bad Version]

This is the version of Leibniz's Law used in the above proof, and it must be rejected. If the good version of Leibniz's Law is used instead, the last line of the proof does not follow by *modus tollens*, nor does it follow by any acceptable inference pattern:

1. $\triangledown a = b$ Hypothesis for refutation
2. $\neg\triangledown(b = b)$ Logical truth
3. $\neg(\triangledown a = b \Leftrightarrow \triangledown b = b)$ From 1,2 by truth-functional logic
4. $!a = b \Rightarrow (\phi a \Leftrightarrow \phi b)$ Leibniz's Law as a conditional: good version
5. $\neg a = b$ From 3, 4 by *modus tollens*   NO!

Instead, one can infer:

5′. $\neg!a = b$.

But (5′) is compatible with the claim that $\triangledown a = b$, and it achieves no refutation of it.

Any defender of indeterminate identity is thus forced to accept certain conditional formulations of Leibniz's Law, and reject others. A good version is:

Leibniz's Law: $!a = b \Rightarrow (\phi a \Leftrightarrow \phi b)$.

I see no difficulty in rejecting the other version above, only the inevitable awkwardness that comes with using conditionals in a framework that takes indeterminacy seriously.

In conversation, I have occasionally been confronted with the following sort of argument:

> Granted, we disagree about indeterminate identity, and we don't seem to be able to find grounds to resolve our disagreement directly. So we should turn instead to an independent discussion of conditionals, about which we have intuitions having nothing to do with identity. We clearly expect conditionals to be minimally well behaved, and our only assumption about identity is that we expect Leibniz's Law to have a conditional formulation. But then the proof at the beginning of this section is valid, and it disproves the existence of indeterminate identity.

The answer must be that there is indeed a conditional formulation of Leibniz's Law, using the "if-true" reading of the conditional. With that version of the Law, the above proof is fallacious, as discussed. If you insist on formulating Leibniz's Law using that same conditional without the "if-true" reading, then I explicitly disagree, but this is not a new issue; it is the same old question about the validity of the contrapositive of Leibniz's Law couched in terms of how to formulate Leibniz's Law as a conditional. And if you wish to use some other conditional with which to formulate the Law, then we must see what its logic is, and whether it can accommodate the invalidity of the contrapositive of Leibniz's Law and also satisfy *modus tollens* (which is needed in the proof above). No new issues arise; we merely repackage old ones.

For example, suppose that you are inclined to agree with me on issues concerning indeterminate identity, but you feel that there *must* be a conditional form of Leibniz's Law which requires no special "if-true" reading. That is easily accomplished. Define a new connective with this truth-table (Table 6.5).

Then formulate Leibniz's Law as follows:

Leibniz's Law $a = b \Rightarrow (\phi a \Leftrightarrow \phi b)$.

This is completely adequate from my point of view, since it is equivalent to the "if-true" reading of the version of Leibniz's Law given above, and it itself requires no special reading. This new connective validates both *modus ponens* and conditional proof. (It does not, however, validate *modus tollens*, or contraposition, so it does not save the flawed proof above. Again, you can't have everything you want in a conditional.)

I assume (when this does not beg a question) that the principal options for interpreting conditionals are Łukasiewicz's "sustaining"

TABLE 6.5.

ϕ	ψ	$\phi \Rightarrow \psi$
T	T	T
T	—	—
T	F	F
—	T	T
—	—	T
—	F	T
F	T	T
F	—	T
F	F	T

if-then conditional, or that same conditional given its "if-true" reading. If other writers use conditionals differently, I will need to be sensitive to that fact. But nobody can appeal to the "naturally desirable conditional": the one that is truth-status-functional and that validates all natural logical principles, for no such conditional exists if there are truth-value gaps. As a corollary, I will insist that the awkwardness of any one of the existing non-classical conditionals not be used as an objection to some unrelated claim. Most important, when we use a conditional, we must keep straight what meaning is intended by it when a claim is made using it, so that the meaning does not shift during discussion.

6.4 TWO EXAMPLES OF ALTERNATIVE CONDITIONALS

I have suggested that discussion of formulations of conditionals does not change anything of substance about indeterminate identity; it only repackages the issues. Here are two illustrations of this.

Broome (1984) discusses Evans's argument, and asks what sort of conditional would be needed to express a correct version of Leibniz's Law for use in the proof. He assumes that the Law should take this form:

If $a = b$ then (Ea iff Eb)

and he argues:

The ground of Leibniz's Law is that if a is identical to b then a and b are one object, and an object has a property if and only if it has it. This licenses us to say only that

If '$a = b$' is true then '($Ea \equiv Eb$)' is true.

In other words, it rules out that '$a = b$' should be true and '$Ea \equiv Eb$' false, and also that '$a = b$' should be true and '$Ea \equiv Eb$' undetermined. (1984: 9)

He then claims that in order to express Leibniz's Law in conditional form, the conditional '$\supset$' in the Law must have one of the two truth-tables (Table 6.6 which makes the conditional be automatically bivalent or Table 6.7). Broome observes that neither of these tables validates *modus tollens*, and that

	TABLE 6.6.			TABLE 6.7.	
ϕ	ψ	if ϕ then ψ	ϕ	ψ	if ϕ then ψ
T	T	T	T	T	T
T	—	F	T	—	—
T	F	F	T	F	F
—	T	T	—	T	T
—	—	T	—	—	T
—	F	T	—	F	T
F	T	T	F	T	T
F	—	T	F	—	T
F	F	T	F	F	T

Evans's argument formulated with such a version of Leibniz's Law fails.[3]

Broome's second table is the table for the symbol '⇨' introduced temporarily above, the connective that embodies the "if-true" reading of the '⟹' conditional. Thus his proposal is almost the same as the form I have suggested for a correct version of Leibniz's Law. *Almost* the same; it depends on how we read the biconditional in the consequent of Broome's version. It is natural to assume that this is the conjunction of two conditionals,[4] so Broome's version of the law would likely be:

---

[3] Garrett (1988) adds that if this is correct then an argument from Wiggins (1986) against indeterminate identity also fails. But Wiggins means something else by indeterminate identity (personal communication); he is disputing a view according to which a statement might be indeterminate while *having* a truth-value. So the view Wiggins disputes does not require formulation in a non-bivalent language, and his own argument is entirely classical.

[4] One might speculate that Broome just means the biconditional to be the three-valued material biconditional '$\phi \equiv \psi$' defined as '$(\phi \& \psi) \vee (\neg\phi \& \neg\psi)$', or equivalently as '$(\neg\phi \vee \psi) \& (\neg\psi \vee \phi)$'. But these would produce a version of Leibniz's Law that is much too strong. In the trivial case it would yield:

$$a = a \Rightarrow (Ea \equiv Ea).$$

Since '$a = a$' is logically true, this requires that '$Ea \equiv Ea$' also be logically true. But when 'Ea' lacks truth-value, this (material) biconditional also lacks truth-value.

BROOME $a = b \Rightarrow [(Ea \Rightarrow Eb)\ \&\ (Eb \Rightarrow Ea)]$.

This differs from my own suggested reading, which can be expressed as:

TP $a = b \Rightarrow [(Ea \Rightarrow Eb)\ \&\ (Eb \Rightarrow Ea)]$.

However, in spite of the difference in conditionals in the consequent, it can be shown that these two versions are logically equivalent.[5] I find my own version handier,[6] but there is no difference in content between the views being expressed. (Broome's is the first

---

[5] It is easy to show that TP entails BROOME, since '$\phi \Rightarrow \psi$' entails '$!\phi \Rightarrow \psi$', which is '$\phi \Rightarrow \psi$'. For the other way around, we give a conditional proof. Begin with:

    1. $a = b$ Hypothesis for conditional proof.

The following are all instances of BROOME:

    2. $a = b \Rightarrow [(!Ea \Rightarrow !Eb)\ \&\ (!Eb \Rightarrow !Ea)]$
    3. $a = b \Rightarrow [(!\neg Ea \Rightarrow !\neg Eb)\ \&\ (!\neg Eb \Rightarrow !\neg Ea)]$
    4. $a = b \Rightarrow [(!vEa \Rightarrow !vEb)\ \&\ (!vEb \Rightarrow !vEa)]$

Modus ponens then yields:

    5. $(!Ea \Rightarrow !Eb)\ \&\ (!Eb \Rightarrow !Ea)$
    6. $(!\neg Ea \Rightarrow !\neg Eb)\ \&\ (!\neg Eb \Rightarrow !\neg Ea)$
    7. $(!vEa \Rightarrow !vEb)\ \&\ (!vEb \Rightarrow !vEa)$

Changing '$\phi \Rightarrow \psi$' to '$!\phi \Rightarrow \psi$' turns these into:

    8. $(!!Ea \Rightarrow !Eb)\ \&\ (!!Eb \Rightarrow !Ea)$
    9. $(!!\neg Ea \Rightarrow !\neg Eb)\ \&\ (!!\neg Eb \Rightarrow !\neg Ea)$
  10. $(!!vEa \Rightarrow !vEb)\ \&\ (!!vEb \Rightarrow !vEa)$

Eliminating redundant repetitions of '!' yields:

  11. $(!Ea \Rightarrow !Eb)\ \&\ (!Eb \Rightarrow !Ea)$
  12. $(!\neg Ea \Rightarrow !\neg Eb)\ \&\ (!\neg Eb \Rightarrow !\neg Ea)$
  13. $(!vEa \Rightarrow !vEb)\ \&\ (!vEb \Rightarrow !vEa)$

These can now be reexpressed as biconditionals:

  14. $!Ea \Leftrightarrow !Eb$
  15. $!\neg Ea \Leftrightarrow !\neg Eb$
  16. $!vEa \Leftrightarrow !vEb$

These three together insure that 'Ea' and 'Eb' have exactly the same truth-value status. This is sufficient for the truth of:

  17. $Ea \Leftrightarrow Eb$

Then conditional proof (in its good form) from 1–17 yields:

  18. $!a = b \Rightarrow (Ea \Leftrightarrow Eb)$ QED.

A similar proof can also be given using Broome's first truth-table for 'if then'.

[6] e.g. in the preceding footnote it was trivial to show that TP entails BROOME, but the other way round was complicated.

conditional formulation of Leibniz's Law in the literature that I
know of that is congenial to indeterminacy of identity.)

Johnson (1989) objects strongly to Broome's formulation.
Johnson says that Broome

apparently confuses the object-language symbol for conditionals '⊃', with
a metalinguistic symbol invoking the *truth* of the antecedent and consequent, such that he reads 'P ⊃ Q' as if it symbolized 'if P is true then Q is
true'. One serious consequence of this error is that Broome's truth tables
involve rejection of *modus tollens*; rather than resort to such extremes it
would be better to admit that incoherence of vague identity for which
Evans argues. (1989: 105–6)

(Johnson also objects (1989: 106–7) to my own earlier objections to
Evans's use of abstraction, and of my separation of Leibniz's Law
from its contrapositive.)

I don't see Broome as confusing object-language and metalanguage at all; he merely states in the metalanguage his opinion about
the conditions that are needed for the truth of the conditional in
Leibniz's Law. Does Johnson disagree with these conditions? He
has his own proposal for how to formulate Leibniz's Law as a conditional. He begins his discussion by criticizing this formulation of
the principle:

LL $\forall y \forall z((y = z) \supset [\lambda x(\phi x)(y) \equiv \lambda x(\phi x)(z)])$,

in which he assumes that the conditional is the three-valued ma-
terial conditional, where '$\phi \supset \psi$' is equivalent to '$\neg \phi \vee \psi$', with the
truth-table (Table 6.8) displayed over (and, presumably, the
material biconditional is equivalent to the conjunction of two material conditionals). Johnson agrees that someone who wishes to
attack indeterminate identity will be begging the question by formulating Leibniz's Law in this way, and so he considers ways to
reformulate it. After some discussion, the version of Leibniz's Law
that he finds uncontroversial is the following, which is just like LL
except for the addition of a conditional antecedent making all conjuncts determinate:[7]

LL$_\upsilon$ $\forall y \forall z([\neg \triangledown(y = z) \ \& \ \neg \triangledown \lambda x(\phi x)(y) \ \& \ \neg \triangledown \lambda x(\phi x)(z)] \supset$
$[(y = z) \supset [\lambda x(\phi x)(y) \equiv \lambda x(\phi x)(z)]])$.

---

[7] Johnson uses '$\triangle \phi$' to mean that ϕ is determinate. I have replaced this in his
formula by '$\neg \triangledown \phi$', the equivalent claim that ϕ is not indeterminate.

TABLE 6.8.

ϕ	ψ	$\phi \supset \psi$
T	T	T
T	—	—
T	F	F
—	T	T
—	—	—
—	F	—
F	T	T
F	—	T
F	F	T

It is a straightforward matter to determine (by inspection of truth-tables) that LL_v is logically equivalent to the version of Leibniz's Law proposed by Broome.[8] So Johnson shows how to produce a version of Leibniz's Law that does not disagree with Broome (or myself) on any matter of substance. Does he also avoid what he calls Broome's "resorting to extremes"? Only by looking the other way. The connective that Broome uses for 'if . . . then . . .' is, after all, formulable, as Broome has clearly shown. It is also easily definable using Johnson's own terminology; Broome's '$\phi \rightsquigarrow \psi$' (which is equivalent to '$!\phi \Rightarrow \psi$') is logically equivalent to Johnson's '$\neg \nabla \phi \supset (\phi \supset \psi)$', and one can easily see how this equivalence pattern relates BROOME to LL_v above. And although Johnson avoids Broome's "extreme" conditional, he himself is forced to abandon a conditional formulation of Leibniz's Law in favour of a *conditionalized* conditional version of that law. An acceptable version of the law as a simple conditional will require some conditional very much like Broome's. Note also that if one objects to Broome's conditional because it fails to satisfy *modus tollens*, it is equally objectionable that Johnson's conditional does not satisfy conditional

---

[8] That is, this is easy to establish if we ignore Johnson's use of abstracts. If we do not ignore his use of abstracts, Johnson's version of Leibniz's Law is considerably weaker than Broome's version or mine. They become equivalent if one adopts unrestricted abstraction principles; see Ch. 4.

proof. We have here a deadlock regarding how best to read conditionals, but in the end no difference in the philosophical position being formulated.[9]

The fact that these very different approaches to how to formulate Leibniz's Law as a conditional by myself, Broome, and Johnson turn out to be logically equivalent suggests to me that there is a consensus on the important topic—indeterminacy, and indeterminacy of identity—in spite of differences of instinct about how to treat conditionals.

6.5 WILLIAMSON'S DEFENCE OF THE TARSKI BICONDITIONALS

There are a number of a priori proofs in the literature to establish that there cannot be a failure of bivalence for meaningful declarative sentences. In this section I discuss a recent version using biconditionals that has gained some currency. The argument is from Williamson (1994: §7.2). The argument is put as a *reductio ad absurdum* of any specific claim to the effect that a meaningful declarative utterance is neither true nor false. This is a bold move, since the argument attempts to disprove the existence of truth-value gaps arising from any source, not just those arising from indeterminacy in the world; it attempts, for example, to disprove the existence of truth-value gaps due to semantic indeterminacy, provided only that the utterance in question is a declarative one that succeeds in saying something meaningful.

Williamson is careful to relate his argument to utterances rather than sentences, because context can change the semantics of a sentence, and he is careful to allow that the account will work for utterances of sentences that are not in English. But neither of these is crucial to my discussion, so I simplify by talking as if sentences are at issue, and I stick to English examples. I also avoid marginally meaningful utterances ('The number 2 is green'), ones that are unclear in scope ('Swans are white'), and ethical statements ('The

---

[9] Notice also that Johnson's formulation of Leibniz's Law as LL_v validates the inference rule that I have called Leibniz's Law and fails to validate the inference law that I have called the contrapositive of Leibniz's Law, in spite of Johnson's objections to distinguishing these from one another.

death penalty is immoral'), since these raise special problems of the sort I am not focusing on.

Using Williamson's notation, I suppose that '*P*' abbreviates a sentence of English and that '*u*' is a name of that sentence, e. g. a quotation mark name. For example '*P*' might be:

I am my body,

in which case '*u*' would be:

'I am my body'.

The argument itself is expressed independently of any particular choice for '*P*' and '*u*'. The argument is a short one:

1.	Not: *u* is true or *u* is false	Hypothesis for refutation
2a.	*u* is true iff *P*	Semantic fact
2b.	*u* is false iff not *P*	Semantic fact
3.	Not: *P* or not *P*	Substituting in (1) using (2a) and (2b)
4.	Not *P* and not not *P*.	DeMorgan's Law from (3)

The argument consists of a hypothesis for refutation, two semantic facts, and then two inferences culminating in a contradiction, thus refuting the initial hypothesis. The inference from (3) to (4) is acceptable from my point of view, so I will focus on the earlier lines.

This reasoning is too good to be true. It refutes not only indeterminacy of identity, but indeterminacy of any meaningful declarative utterance, thus demolishing decades of work in the logic and semantics of sentences without truth-value. This is too much to expect. But the reasoning is apparently compelling, and it is certainly incumbent on me to explain where and why the reasoning goes wrong. This is not a simple task, since indeterminacy allows for a number of options regarding what one means and what one says. So there is no avoiding a survey of the options.

The two principal questions that need to be addressed are what one means by the predicates 'true' and 'false', and what one means by the biconditional 'if and only if'. (I take for granted that we agree on the meanings of 'not', 'and', and 'or'. There are options for these as well, but I don't think that Williamson's argument turns on using these differently from the way I do.)

The principal question about the use of 'true' and 'false' is whether they are themselves intended to be used bivalently. I have implicitly adopted a bivalent use for them, in the sense that if a sentence is lacking in truth-value it is determinately not true, as I use 'true' (and it is also determinately not false). Call this the "determinate" use of 'true' and 'false'. There is also another use, explored by several writers on the semantic paradoxes, starting with Martin and Woodruff (1975), and Kripke (1975). Call this the "redundancy" use. On this use, if a sentence lacks truth-value, then so does the claim that it is true or false. So if a sentence lacks truth-value, the claim that it is true is itself indeterminate. This is not my usage here, but it is an important option, so let me deal with it briefly. The important thing to say about it is that holders of such a view will agree with Williamson in rejecting (1), but they will disagree about his claim that (1) is the right way to formulate an assertion of lack of bivalence. Exactly how an assertion of lack of bivalence is to be stated on this view is a matter of some debate, but (1) is certainly not the way to do it. I have discussed elsewhere (in Parsons 1984) how things should go on this option, and it would be too much of a digression to recapitulate it here. It is important to realize that this option exists, partly to be aware that there are other defences of lack of bivalence than the one I will be giving, and to distinguish this alternative approach from my own in this book. But from here on I ignore this option.

Let us settle, then, on the bivalent use of 'true' and 'false', and admit on that view that (1) does correctly formulate a claim of indeterminacy. That then puts the burden on (2a) and (2b). Whether I am willing to endorse (2a) and (2b) depends on how the biconditional is read. There are a number of options here; I focus only on the most relevant ones. One of these, of course, is the biconditional that I have adopted above. I interpret '$\phi \Leftrightarrow \psi$' as being true if ϕ and ψ have exactly the same truth-value status, false if they disagree in truth-value (if one is true and the other false) and otherwise truth-valueless. On this interpretation I would not assert either (2a) or (2b) unless I were sure that P had a truth-value. This is because they would be lacking in truth-value if P were itself lacking in truth-value. For the claim that u is true would be false in that case, and also the claim that u is false. So these would be biconditionals without truth-value:

2a. u is true $\Leftrightarrow P$ No truth-value
2b. u is false $\Leftrightarrow$ not P.   No truth-value

I would thus view Williamson's argument as begging the question by assuming these.

But these are just the old and venerable Tarski biconditionals, unquestioned within a two-valued framework. Certainly they seem to be trying to capture something that is right, and this should not be swept under the rug. What is it about them that is right, and what would I use in their place? A natural option would be the "iff-true" reading of the biconditional. This is a parallel to the "if-true" reading of the conditional, discussed earlier in this chapter. We construe the biconditionals in (2a) and (2b) as conjunctions of the "if-true" conditionals, so that we get:[10]

> 2a. [u is true $\Rightarrow P$] & [$P \Rightarrow u$ is true]
> 2b. [u is false $\Rightarrow$ not P] & [not $P \Rightarrow u$ is false].

These are correct on anybody's view; the only question is whether they say enough. They are also the natural conditional renditions of the following "Tarski biconditional inference schemes", which are also correct on anybody's view:

VALID:	S	'S' is true
	'S' is true	S
VALID:	not S	'S' is false
	'S' is false	not S

Williamson (1994: 300) notes with approval that Evans and McDowell (1976), Machina (1976), and Peacocke (1981) all endorse "disquotational schemas for truth". So do I, in the restricted sense that I regard the inferences above as valid, and the following conditionals as true without exception:

> 'S' is true $\Rightarrow S$ $S \Rightarrow$ 'S' is true.

If we read (2a) and (2b) as indicated, they are true according to the theory I endorse. We thus have (1) as a denial of bivalence, and (2a) and (2b) in forms that I endorse. However, with the versions of (2a) and (2b) just given, (3) no longer follows. For the fact that if 'u is true' is true, so is 'P', and vice versa, does not mean that 'u is true'

---

[10] In the notation originally introduced in Ch. 2, these are:

> 2a. [!(u is true) $\Rightarrow P$] & [!$P \Rightarrow u$ is true]
> 2b. [!(u is false) $\Rightarrow$ not P] & [!(not P) $\Rightarrow u$ is false].

and '*P*' have the same truth-value, since those connections obtain even if '*P*' does not have a truth-value at all and '*u* is true' is false. So without the assumption that '*P*' has a truth-value, the substitution that leads to (3) is not verified. And the assumption that '*P*' has a truth-value is what is at issue.

In summary, there is no doubt that the wording on line (1) of Williamson's proof:

    1. Not: *u* is true or *u* is false   Hypothesis for refutation

can be interpreted so as to deny bivalence. And there is no doubt that the wording on lines (2a) and (2b):

    2a. *u* is true iff *P*   Semantic fact
    2b. *u* is false iff not *P*   Semantic fact

can be interpreted so as to be endorsable by a person who believes in the possibility of non-bivalence. But on these readings, line (3) does not follow.

    3. Not: *P* or not *P*.   Substituting in (1) using (2a) and (2b).

It is also possible to give each of these lines other readings, and on some of these the conclusion does follow, but not in a way that refutes anything that a believer in non-bivalence believes.

    Williamson, of course, is alert to this sort of reply, and so he does not rest content with merely giving the proof. He adds:

It might be replied that if *u* says that *P* and is neither true nor false, then, '*u* is true' is false while '*P*' is neither true nor false, so that the two sides of (2a) do not match in semantic value, and neither (2a) nor (T) is true. A parallel reply might be made to (2b) and (F). The trouble with this objection is that it does nothing to meet the rationale for (T) and (F). It gives no hint, when *u* says that TW is thin, of any way in which *u* could fail to be true, other than by TW failing to be thin, or of any way in which *u* could fail to be false, other than by TW failing to be not thin. (1994: 190)

The principles (T) and (F) that Williamson alludes to are:

    (T) If *u* says that *P*, then *u* is true if and only if *P*.
    (F) If *u* says that *P*, then *u* is false if and only if not *P*.

I do indeed hold that it is possible for the two sides of (2a) not to match in semantic value—the left-hand side might be false when the right has no truth-value at all—so the quoted comment is apt. This shifts the onus of discussion to the rationale for (T) and (F). Williamson states their rationale as follows:

The rationale for (T) and (F) is simple. Given that an utterance says that TW is thin, what it takes for it to be true is just for TW to be thin, and what it takes for it to be false is for TW not to be thin. No more and no less is required. To put the condition for truth or falsity any higher or lower would be to misconceive the nature of truth or falsity. (1994: 190)

I find this rationale completely compelling. The question, however, is whether it validates (T) or (F) on the interpretation that Williamson needs. Notice that (T) and (F) are biconditionals, and the issues discussed above about biconditionals arise here too. If they are given the "iff-true" interpretation, then they are completely acceptable but they are consistent with the view that Williamson is disputing. So suppose that we give them the stronger reading, so that they are false for any meaningful utterance that lacks truth-value. Does the rationale the Williamson gives validate them on that reading? That depends on how the rationale is understood. How are we to interpret, e.g.:

(*) What it takes for 'TW is thin' to be true is just for TW to be thin?

At the very least, we need this to entail that either of these:

'TW is thin' is true
TW is thin

is inferrable from the other; that is, that both of these inferences are valid:

'TW is thin' is true	TW is thin
TW is thin	'TW is thin' is true

.

But they *are* both valid, and that is *not* sufficient in a language with truth-value gaps for the previous argument to be valid. So the *rationale* for (T) and (F) is not sufficient to validate (T) and (F) if they are read so as to entail bivalence.

Then perhaps one wants a stronger rationale. Something like that *can* be provided. I suggest this:

There are three options regarding the state of affairs of TW's being thin: it might determinately hold, it might determinately fail to hold, or neither. It is constitutive of the meaning of the sentence 'TW is thin' that it match these options precisely, so that:

(i) If the state of affairs determinately holds, the sentence must be true.

(ii) If the state of affairs determinately fails to hold, the sentence must be false.

(iii) If neither option is realized, the sentence must be neither true nor false.

This is as strong a rationale as anyone might demand, though it differs from Williamson's. It allows, rather than proscribing, failure of truth-value. No doubt a defender of bivalence will claim that option (iii) cannot be realized, but that is not to say that the rationale is false, it is just to say that it does not rule out lack of bivalence. If more than this is required by Williamson's understanding of the rationale, then the rationale, so understood, is itself far from obvious, and cannot itself be the foundation from which one can argue in a neutral way about bivalence.

My aim here is not to establish that bivalence fails; it is merely to defuse arguments to the effect that it cannot fail. To decide whether it fails, we need to consider whether a hypothesis of lack of truth-value provides a better over-all explanation of the entire set of statements that are prima facie lacking in truth-value, and this cannot be adequately assessed by means of an a priori argument on either side.

7

Understanding Indeterminacy

7.1 "I JUST DON'T UNDERSTAND . . ."

People have told me that they do not understand indeterminate
identity. Sometimes I have told myself the same thing, so it is hard
to discount all the sources of the worry. The point of this chapter
is to see what can be said on this issue.

To begin, we need to divide the question. When someone says
that they do not understand indeterminacy in general, or indeterminate identity in particular, they may be making one of
two kinds of comment. The first is a rejection of indeterminacy,
while the second is merely a confession of lack of understanding.
The first is usually expressed as a comment to the effect that one
does not understand how identity could possibly *be* indeterminate;
the other is merely a report of bewilderment in thinking about
the issue. The first has the effect of a positive assertion rejecting
the claim that identity might be indeterminate, made emphatic by
a comment about understanding. The second is a mere confession
of lack of understanding. These invite different though related
responses.

A claim of the first sort can be put forward from a variety of
rhetorical stances. The most challenging stance is when the intent
is:

> "I don't believe it, because *I can't conceive of its being true.*
> And you can't change my mind about this unless you can show
> me how it is that identity is indeterminate."

The best I can do in response to a challenge of this sort is to point
out what things *would* be like if identity were sometimes indeterminate, e.g. in the classical identity puzzles, and then point out that
things *are* like this, and that alternative explanations have not been

found to be very satisfying. This is true of indeterminacy in general, and of indeterminacy of identity in particular.

The second kind of comment indicates a stance, something like this:

> "I don't believe it, but I'm willing to consider it. But when I ponder it, I feel genuinely bewildered."

This is a very serious challenge, and one that festers inside me as well. It is what has motivated this whole study. I, too, feel the bewilderment (it comes and it goes), and this whole work is devoted to addressing it.

Three things are needed for understanding. The first is to be sure that the terminology being employed is understood; if this is not accomplished, no view will have been presented to be understood or not understood. The second is to address the fact that people need to somehow "conceive of" what it "would be like" for the view to be true. I am not sure what this amounts to, but it has a venerable and influential tradition—including, but not limited to, both empiricist and rationalist theories that require a kind of mental picturing for understanding. The third is to have a kind of working knowledge of the theory; you need to know the sorts of situations in which the view applies to things, and how it is supposed to apply in those cases, and what the consequences are of its not applying in those situations. I address the first two of these in the present chapter; the third is addressed throughout the book. In the next section I discuss the terminology employed in theorizing. After that, I discuss "picturing" what it would be like for the theory to be true.

7.2 UNDERSTANDING THE TERMINOLOGY

I intend my terminology to be completely normal. When I speak of identity, and when I use the sign '=', or use 'is' in the sense of identity, I mean exactly what everyone else means. My definition of identity in Chapter 3 is not meant to confer meaning on the word 'identical'; it is a substantive proposal about when this relationship holds. The same is true of my use of the words 'true' and 'false', and of 'property', 'object', 'refer', 'and', 'or', 'every', and so on. Of course, each of these terms is subject to various interpretations; they are used differently by different people. I have either relied on context to home in on my intended usage, or (e.g. in the case of the truth-table definitions of the connectives) I have explicitly addressed which of the available meanings I had in mind. These accounts are never meant to be stipulative in the sense that I am inventing some new technical meaning from scratch; they are rather meant to be stipulative in the sense that I need to declare which of the several normal uses I intend. If I have not succeeded in doing this in some cases, then that is an error in detail in my exposition—it is a failed attempt to isolate my meaning from a host of familiar ones, not a successful attempt to invent a new idea.

Perhaps the familiar meanings are too corrupt to use; if so, my exposition has failed, along with much of contemporary philosophizing. For example, if Williamson is right, then there is no gap at all between a declarative utterance expressing something meaningful and that utterance being true or false, and so there cannot be a meaningful utterance without truth-value. And, if he and others are right, this is somehow constitutive of the *meaning* of 'true'. And so I cannot possibly say that a meaningful utterance lacks truth-value, meaning by 'true' what others mean by it, while saying something that might be correct. I insist that I do mean what others mean by 'true', and so the challenge must be an assertion that what I have to say is wrong, but not an assertion that what I have to say cannot be understood. If the critics are right, the most they can claim is that what I have to say cannot be believed, because understanding what I mean entails being unable to understand what it would be like for it to be true. But they cannot claim that what I have to say cannot be understood.

With regard to indeterminacy of identity, there are two key notions to understand, 'determinate' and 'identical' as they occur in:

For some object x and some object y, it is not determinate whether x is identical to y.

I have already commented on identity. Determinacy is for me a primitive notion. It can be given more content within certain world-views, such as idealist ones, but I have no transcendent account to give of it. But it is clear, I think, how it is to function in the theory. Of course the displayed statement in which these terms occur involves quantifying into a whether-clause, and this easily invites claims of incoherence. So the stage then shifts to a detailed account of language and the world and the semantical relations between them. Here, plenty of terminology enters, all of it problematic. But none of it is *specially* problematic. Perhaps I am saying things using this terminology that invites special responses in incredulity, but I am not using either terminology or semantical constructions in special ways. And so the issue is either belief, or difficulty of picturing or conceiving of claims that *are* meaningfully expressed.

The question of meaningfulness arises not only when a theory is formulated, but also when it is applied to problematic situations. And I want to emphasize that in all of the applications the terminology I use is normal. In particular, I use words of our native tongue, such as 'person', 'ship', and 'cat'. Here I may be criticized not for using unexplained terminology, but for using familiar terminology that is not sufficiently scientific or philosophically respectable. But in this respect I think the applications described here are superior to approaches that require unexplained technical terminology, such as 'gen-identity', or that suggest that we need completely new terminology to replace ordinary talk of objects, but without providing the new terminology. This issue will be engaged later (in Chapter 10); I raise it now to alert the reader to it and to emphasize that the question of meaningfulness must be addressed with respect to a whole theory including its applications, not just to its theoretical core.

7.3 NON-BIVALENT REASONING

Probably the biggest impediment to understanding indeterminacy of any kind is that it brings with it lack of truth-value, and this affects the kind of logical inferences we can make. There is no mystery about this at all, and the failure of certain inferences we normally take for granted are easy to understand when scrutinized. The problem comes when we do not scrutinize them, but instead take bivalent reasoning for granted. This principally involves what I have called contrapositive reasoning, which is not valid in a non-bivalent setting. I have belaboured this so much elsewhere that it does not make sense to do so again here. But it is important to highlight this phenomenon, since (it seems to me) this is really the root cause of most of our feelings of bewilderment when pondering indeterminacy. I have found that as the instinct to reason contrapositively lessens, the feeling of lack of understanding similarly lessens. This is not a point that can be argued; you need to experience it yourself to get the effect.

7.4 PICTURING INDETERMINATE IDENTITY

The claims that lead to bewilderment are mostly claims to the effect that it is indeterminate whether certain objects have certain properties and/or that certain objects are identical. There is much more to the account than this, but if we can "picture" this part of it, the rest will be easy.

There is a centuries-long tradition of using Venn-like diagrams to picture objects possessing properties and to picture objects being identical or distinct. Many people have found these diagrams conceptually useful; they can be adapted for present purposes as well. In the traditional diagrams, the extensions of properties are pictured by certain subregions of a rectangular figure, and objects are represented by points, as in Figure 7.1. An object represented by a point (such as b) located inside a property-region (such as P) is pictured as having the property in question; a point (such as a) located outside the region represents an object that lacks the property.

Following Parsons and Woodruff (1995), I extend these conventions by representing objects by small shaded regions of the figure. An object-region, a, inside a property-region, P, represents the object's having the property P, one completely outside the property-region, b, represents an object's lacking P, and one lying partially within and partially without the property-region, c, represents its being indeterminate whether the object has P (see Figure 7.2). If a region has no object-images in it, the picture itself is neutral regarding whether there is an object present in it. But if we are told that there are no objects other than the ones pictured, then we know that empty regions represent properties that hold of no objects.

I assume that there is at least one property that holds of no objects. Its representing region can be anywhere in the picture, so

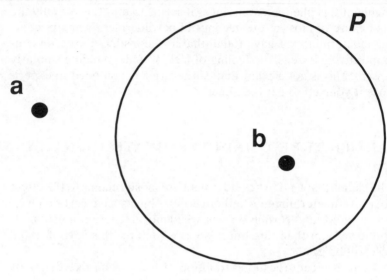

FIG. 7.1

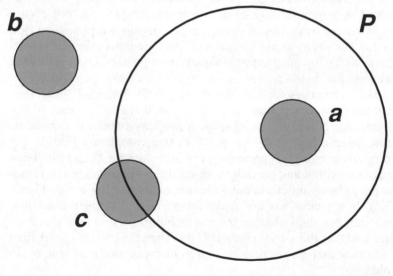

FIG. 7.2

long as it overlaps no object image. For example, if there are only three objects, then the circle labelled '*E*' in Figure 7.3 represents a property determinately not possessed by any object.

These pictures show what things would be like if there is indeterminacy; they do not yet address identity. In the classical picturing, identical objects are represented by coinciding points (or by the same point; there is no difference) and distinct objects are represented by distinct points. I extend this convention by assuming that objects represented by the same regions are represented as being identical, objects represented by disjoint regions are represented as being distinct, and objects represented by partially overlapping regions are represented as being indeterminately identical. Figure 7.4 represents *a* as identical to *b*, and represents both *a* and *b* as distinct from *c*, whereas Figure 7.5 represents *a* as distinct from both *b* and *c*, and represents its being indeterminate whether *b* is *c*. Notice that a partial overlap of object-representatives does not indicate uncertainty as to whether they are identical (we have no means in a picture alone to indicate uncertainty). Partial overlap means that the world is such that it is not determined whether the represented objects are identical.

I require by edict that no object-representatives lie completely inside others, or combinations of others, as pictured in Figure 7.6.

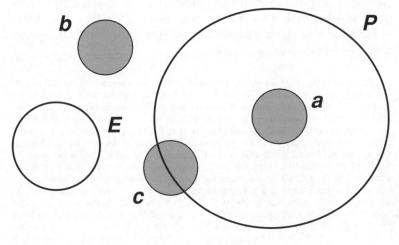

Fig. 7.3

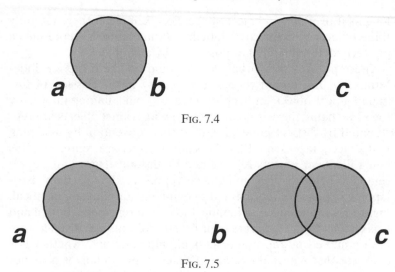

FIG. 7.4

FIG. 7.5

Each object representative gets a bit of its own space in the diagram; that is, part of its region is not shared by any other representative.[1]

Various principles are now built into the picturing conventions. Both symmetry and reflexivity of identity are built in, as is the symmetry and non-reflexivity of indeterminate identity. The transitivity of identity is also built in. It is also built in that transitivity of indeterminate identity fails, for a diagram can look like Figure 7.7.

---

[1] The possibility of making drawings that violate this principle is an artefact of the model, just as is the possibility of drawing different representatives in different colours, or labelling them with different fonts. I disallow such drawings because I think they have no application to worlds such as ours. But the idea is not incoherent. A referee for OUP has suggested that I might determinately possess every property that my body determinately possesses, yet still not be determinately identical with it, and this would be appropriately diagrammable by representing me as a subregion of the region that represents my body. This would require that I be determinately a body, which I do not grant, but certainly someone *could* believe this. My worry about this idea is that it seems to me certain that if I am *a* body, then I am *my* body (I am determinately identical with my body), which this view must disagree with. Similarly, it is determinately true that there is exactly one human body presently in my chair, but this would not be determinately true on the view under consideration. (See Ch. 8 regarding cardinality claims.) The idea is coherent, and is worth exploring, but I do not do so in this work.

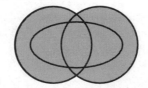

FIG. 7.6

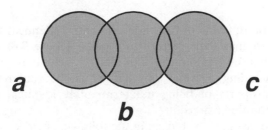

a   *c*

b

FIG. 7.7

Suppose that we require that every region of the diagram repre-sents the extension of some property. Then the ontological version of the Leibnizian definition of identity also results from the pictur-ing conventions: *a* and *b* are represented as identical if and only if their pictures are included in, and are excluded from, and properly overlap, exactly the same property representatives; they are repre-sented as distinct if and only if some property representative includes one of their representatives and excludes the other; and they are represented as being indeterminately identical if and only if some property representative totally includes or excludes one of their representatives while properly overlapping the other.

The pictures are *ontological* in the following sense: the regions in them can be used to represent extensions of properties, but they cannot be presumed to represent the extension of a predicate that does not stand for a property, unless that extension happens to coincide with that of some property. Take for example the Evans pseudo-property of being indeterminately identical to *a*. If there is no indeterminacy of identity at all, or even if there is nothing inde-terminately identical with *a*, then this predicate is coextensive with any null property, and we have decided that *that* has an extension.

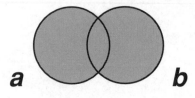

FIG. 7.8

But suppose that *a* is in fact indeterminately identical with some object *b*, so that their picture looks like Figure 7.8. Then it is obvious that no region can completely include *b* while completely excluding *a*, which is what would be required for the (pseudo-)property of being indeterminately identical with *a* to have a picturable extension.

The case just given is typical in the following respect: it is a contingent matter whether there is some property that is coextensive with the predicate 'is indeterminately identical with *a*'. The same goes, for example, for *'being P or indeterminately P'* when '*P*' stands for a property; this is picturable only if its extension and anti-extension happen to coincide with those of some predicate that stands for a property. Figure 7.9 depicts a possible state of affairs, and *'being P or indeterminately P'* cannot stand for a property in this situation. For there would need to be a region that includes all of that of *b* without including any of that of *a*, which is impossible.[2]

---

[2] In Parsons and Woodruff (1995) we considered what abstracts might correspond to properties, and we gave a non-standard interpretation of "ontological abstracts" that guaranteed that they always yield properties. This was artificial, and done for theoretical reasons only. In terms of the diagrams, they worked like this: you take the objects that determinately satisfy the formula of the abstract, and you draw a minimal property-region that includes them; then you declare *this* to be the property represented by the abstract. If the abstract satisfies DDiff, then what you get is exactly right. If not, it is intuitively wrong, but it gives you *some* property-extension as an answer. This is like Frege's idea for insuring that definite descriptions always uniquely refer by requiring that they refer to the right object if there is one, and otherwise letting them refer to a unique "supplied" object. I now don't like our proposal much, not because it is incorrect in any way, or technically flawed, but because of its artificiality. It was done in response to criticisms such as Johnson (1989: 106) about restricting abstraction; the idea was to guarantee that abstracts *always* stand for properties in the world, while—consistent with this—maximizing the extent to which they stand for the "right" property. But its artificiality makes it confusing, and I have abandoned it here.

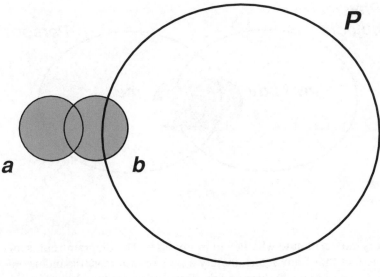

FIG. 7.9

I take it as a thesis of the theory under investigation that if a situation is picturable, then it is metaphysically possible for things in the world to be as the picture represents.[3]

In the next section we look at the intended pictures of the situations in which the paradigm identity puzzles occur.

7.5 REPRESENTING THE PARADIGM PUZZLES

ME AND MY BODY: The first paradigm puzzle presented in Chapter 1 centred around whether I am my body. If this is a case of worldly indeterminacy, then a diagram for the situation should look like Figure 7.10. The overlapping shaded circles represent the fact that

[3] This is not to rule out the fact that it is *de re* impossible for certain objects to have certain configurations. For example, many people think that if $a \neq b$ then necessarily $a \neq b$, and so there is no possible situation represented by overlapping object images *if* those images represent a and b. But there is a possible situation represented by such images if we are neutral about *which* objects they represent.

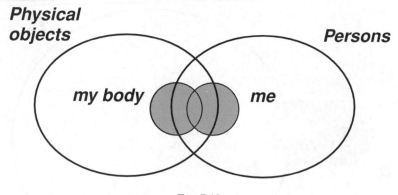

FIG. 7.10

it is indeterminate whether I am my body. The diagram represents the fact that I am determinately a person, whereas it is indeterminate whether my body is, and the fact that my body is determinately a physical object, whereas it is indeterminate whether I am. The diagram takes for granted that being a person is a property, and so is being a physical object.

Figure 7.11 indicates that both I and my body are in my office. In everyday discourse we talk as if I am where my body is, and vice versa, in normal circumstances. (If there literally were such a thing as out-of-body travel, circumstances would not be normal, and I would not be where my body is. If this were to occur, the identity issue would be resolved in the negative.) The diagram is drawn taking this at face value. Some would suggest that there is ambiguity in talk of location of both persons and their bodies; if this is so, the region in the diagram represents the disjunctive property: "being located in my office in the person sense of location, or being located in my office in the physical object sense of location".

THE DISRUPTED PERSON(S): The second paradigm puzzle has a diagram that it isomorphic to the person-body one. Figure 7.12 indicates that person *a* entered the room, though it is indeterminate whether person *b* did, and that person *b* left the room, though it is indeterminate whether person *a* did. It also indicates that both are determinately persons, in the straightforward everyday sense of 'person'. The isomorphism between this diagram and the one for

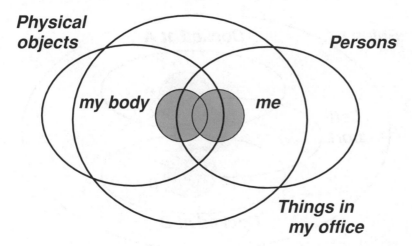

FIG. 7.11

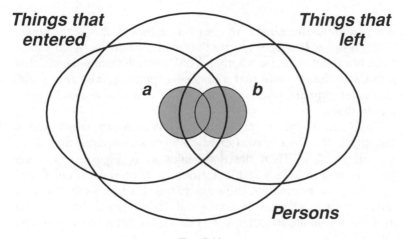

FIG. 7.12

me and my body indicates the lack of relevance of time to the question of indeterminacy of identity.

THE SHIPS: Call the original ship '*o*', the ship with new parts '*p*', and the newly assembled ship '*a*'. Then the diagram for the ships is Figure 7.13. The diagram indicates that it is indeterminate whether

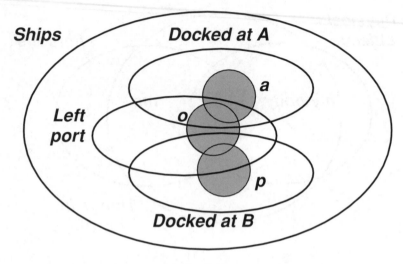

FIG. 7.13

o is *p*, and indeterminate whether *o* is *a*, though it is determinate that *a* is not *p*. It is determinate that *o* left port at such-and-such a time, but indeterminate whether *a* did and indeterminate whether *p* did. It is determinate that *a* docked at place *A*, false that *p* did, and indeterminate whether *o* did. All of *o*, *a*, and *p* are determinately ships.

THE CATS: There are probably millions of p-cats, which makes the picture hard to draw. Let us idealize and assume that there are merely four. Then the diagram is as in Figure 7.14. Each p-cat is determinately distinct from each of the others (since they have determinately different parts). Each is such that it is indeterminate whether it is *the* cat (represented by '*c*'), and also indeterminate whether it is *a* cat. All are determinately on the table.

SOME PILES OF TRASH: None of our paradigm puzzles yield double indeterminacies of identity, but these are clearly possible. Consider a pile of trash p_1 at time t_1, and a pile p_2 at t_2, and a pile p_3 at t_3. Between t_1 and t_2, suppose that pile p_1 has been blown around and had some parts changed, enough to make you genuinely uncertain about whether p_2 is the same pile as p_1. Likewise for p_3 and p_2. It is consistent with this that you might judge that p_3 is genuinely

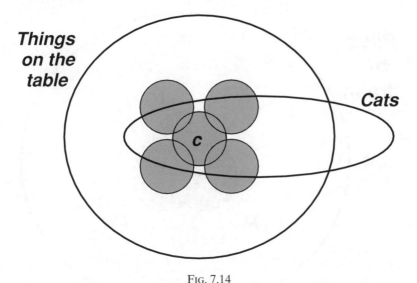

FIG. 7.14

different from p_1, but you also might judge that this is inde-terminate as well. In the latter case, the diagram will look like Figure 7.15.

7.6 PICTURING MADE PRECISE

Pictures are useful conceptual guides, but only if we can trust them to guide us correctly. The discussion of pictures above has been somewhat informal; it needs clarification so as to be clear just what is and what is not a picture, and more discussion is needed about exactly which aspects of pictures are picturing which aspects of the world. The account also needs to be made more rigorous in order to be able to show that it delivers the intended judgements about the world that are being pictured. This is also useful in providing a foundation for the account of worldly resolutions introduced earlier. The remaining sections of this chapter are devoted to working out the technical points that will achieve these goals. (Most of the material in the remaining chapters of this book does not rely on the points discussed here.)

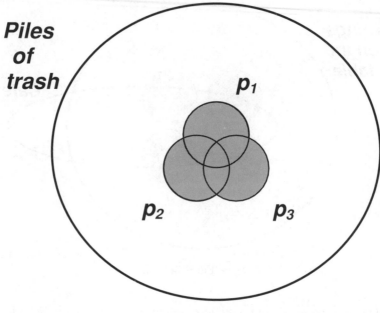

Fig. 7.15

Although we have spoken of our pictures as being two-dimensional, the two-dimensional geometry is not really essential to the representation, nor is the size and shape of the regions. A simple set-theoretical construction can be given which entails the principles discussed informally in the last section. This is simplest if we begin by defining a *robust complete* picture of a world. I call such a picture *robust* because it embodies a principle of plenitude for properties; it is *complete* because it includes images of every object in the world. The diagrams produced above are like snap-shots of some portion of a robust complete picture.

Call the object-images *icons*, and call the regions that represent properties *pictensions*. Then a *robust complete picture* consists of a set O of *points*, a set I of *icons*, which are non-empty subsets of O, and a set P of *pictensions*, which are also subsets of O. What more is required for such a combination to represent the world? All that is required is the right relationship between identity and the possession of properties; that is, what is required is that the icons and pictensions be so related that they portray this relationship properly. It turns out that a single condition will achieve everything we desire. It is that for any two disjoint sets of icons there is a pictension such that the first set of icons represents their objects as determinately having the property represented by that pictension (and no icon not in the first set does this), and the second set of icons represents their objects as being indeterminate whether they have the property represented by p (and no icons not in the second set do this, except for icons that overlap icons in the first set). Given our conventions for representation, this is expressible set-theoretically as:

> [C] For any disjoint sets *s* and *r* of icons, there is a pictension *p* such that:
> any icon *i* is a subset of *p* if and only if it is a member of *s*, and any icon *i* that is not in *s* properly overlaps *p* if and only if *i* is a member of *r* or *i* properly overlaps some member of *s*.

Condition [C] involving *s* and *r* is a kind of principle of plenitude for properties. The condition entails certain of the constraints that were posed above in a seemingly *ad hoc* fashion. For example, it entails that no icon is completely contained inside others. For suppose that icon *i* is completely inside of some other icons. Take the set of those other icons to be *s* in the condition above. Then the first clause of the condition is violated, because no pictension can have exactly those icons as subsets: since *i* is "hidden" by them, it too will be a subset of any set that has all of them as subsets.

As another example, the condition entails that there is a completely empty property (it includes no icons and overlaps no icons); just take both *s* and *r* above to be the empty set.

Most important, the condition yields an analogue of the Leibniz account of identity in terms of properties. Suppose we clarify what it means for an icon and a pictension to represent something about the object and the property they represent as follows:

> DEFINITION: In any picture, if *i* is an icon and *p* is a pictension, then the picture
> (i) *represents i's object as determinately having p's property* iff $i \subseteq p$

(ii) *represents i's object as determinately not having p's property* iff *i* and *p* are disjoint,
(iii) *represents its being indeterminate whether i's object has p's property* iff *i* properly overlaps *p*.

We also clarify what it is for two icons to represent their objects as identical or distinct:

DEFINITION: In any picture, if *i* and *j* are icons, then the picture
(i) *represents i's object as being identical to j's object* iff *i* = *j*
(ii) *represents i's object as being distinct from j's object* iff *i* and *j* are disjoint
(iii) *represents its being indeterminate whether i's object is identical to j's object* iff *i* properly overlaps *j*.

It then follows from condition [C] that in any picture, if *i* and *j* are icons, then the picture[4]

(i) represents *i*'s object as being identical to *j*'s object iff it represents *i* and *j* as determinately having and determinately not having exactly the same properties
(ii) represents *i*'s object as being distinct from *j*'s object iff it represents *i* as determinately having a property that *j* determinately does not have, or vice versa, and
(iii) represents its being indeterminate whether *i*'s object is identical to *j*'s object iff neither (i) nor (ii) of the first definition hold.

An *incomplete* picture is simply one that does not represent every object that there is. This is not an inherent trait of a picture;

---

[4] This is proved as follows.

For (i), the left-to-right argument is trivial. For right-to-left: suppose that the picture represents *i* and *j* as determinately having and determinately not having the same properties; then they are subsets of exactly the same pictensions. If *i* and *j* were not identical, condition [C] applied to {*i*} and the empty set would yield a pictension that includes *i* and does not include *j*, contrary to the supposition.

For (ii): Left-to-right: suppose that *i* represents its object as being distinct from *j*'s object; then they are disjoint. Then, by [C] applied to {*i*} and the empty set, there is a pictension that includes *i* and excludes *j*, and so the picture represents *i*'s object as having a property that *j*'s object does not have. Right-to-left: Suppose the picture represents *i*'s object as having a property that *j*'s object does not have. Then some pictension includes *i* and excludes *j*; and so *i* and *j* are disjoint, and they thus represent their objects as being distinct.

For (iii): this follows from (i) and (ii).

it is a relation between the picture and its intended application. On the other hand, a *non-robust* picture is one that portrays fewer properties than is required by condition [C]. This should be looked at more closely, since condition [C] provides a stronger principle of plenitude for properties than is required by the theory under discussion in this book. In fact, it requires a fairly neat and natural principle. Recall that in §4.5 we discussed the conditions under which an abstract '$\lambda x[\phi x]$' *might* stand for a property. The condition is that DDiff be satisfied for ϕ:

$$\neg \exists x \exists y [!\phi x \ \& \ !\neg\phi y \ \& \ \triangledown x = y].$$

Suppose we have a complete and robust picture of the world, and ϕ satisfies DDiff. Let s be the set of icons that represents objects that determinately satisfy ϕ, and let r be the set of icons that represents objects that indeterminately satisfy ϕ. Sets s and r are disjoint. If condition [C] obtains, there is a pictension p that represents a property P that is determinately possessed by all and only objects that are pictured by the icons in s, and is indeterminately possessed by all and only the objects pictured by the icons in r. Then ϕ expresses that property P, in the sense that it is determinately satisfied by exactly the objects that determinately possess P (namely, those depicted by an icon in s), and it is determinately dissatisfied by exactly the objects that dispossess P (namely, those that are not represented by any icon in s or r). So condition [C] turns the DDiff condition from a test for whether a formula ϕ *may* express a property, into a test for whether ϕ *does* express a property. This gives concrete form to the linkage between what is true in the language and what properties there are in the world.

For those who want to get along with fewer properties, we can ignore robustness and define a (general) *picture* as we did above, replacing [C] by this weaker condition:

[Weak C] (i) Icons i and j properly overlap if and only if some pictension properly overlaps i and either totally includes or totally excludes j, or vice versa.

(ii) Icons i and j are disjoint if and only if some pictension totally includes i and totally excludes j, or vice versa.

(iii) No icon is totally included in the union of any set of icons not containing it.

This condition entails the Leibniz definition of identity in terms of properties while positing the bare minimum of properties for this to hold.

Most of the figures in this book do not themselves satisfy either of the conditions [C] or [Weak C]; this is because the diagrams are intended to picture a *portion* of a world. They are to be taken as partial pictures which can be fleshed out to a picture that satisfies at least [Weak C], and that contains icons for the rest of the objects that there are in the world, and contains pictensions for the rest of the properties.

7.7 PICTURING RESOLUTIONS

Suppose we say that a picture is *identity-determinate* if none of its icons properly overlaps. An identity-determinate picture represents a situation with no indeterminacy of identity among the objects represented, and an identity-determinate picture of the whole world represents a world with no indeterminacy of identity at all. Suppose we say that a picture is *precise* if each icon consists of exactly one point. A precise picture represents a situation with no indeterminacy of any kind, and a precise picture of the whole world represents a completely determinate world.

There are precise pictures, and there are pictures that are not precise but are identity-determinate, and there are pictures that are neither. This corresponds to the idea that the world might be completely determinate, and it might be indeterminate but contain no indeterminacy of identity, and it might be indeterminate and also contain indeterminacy of identity.

In §5.4 we introduced the notion of a *resolution* of a world. If a picture satisfies a certain condition (if it "covers all the options"), it is straightforward to produce from it a picture of a resolution of the world that the original picture represents. If a picture does not cover all the options, it is equivalent to one that does. The remainder of this section characterizes how to turn any picture into one that covers all the options, and how to turn a picture that covers all the options into a "fully refined" picture, which will represent a resolved world.

Say that a picture *P covers all the options* if and only if this is satisfied:

> For any set *s* of icons in *P* for which any two members of s properly overlap each other, there is a non-empty region *r* (a set of points) that is a subset of each icon in *s* and is disjoint from every icon not in *s*.

In pictorial terms, this means that when objects properly overlap, they produce as many overlapping regions as possible. When only two icons overlap, this condition is automatically satisfied, but if there are three or more, it may or may not hold. For example, if *a*, *b*, and *c* all properly overlap each other, then Figure 7.16 covers all the options, and Figures 7.17 and 7.18 pictures do not cover all the

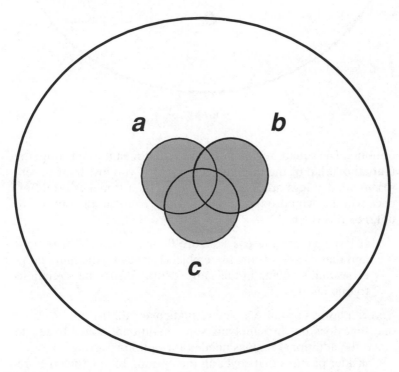

FIG. 7.16

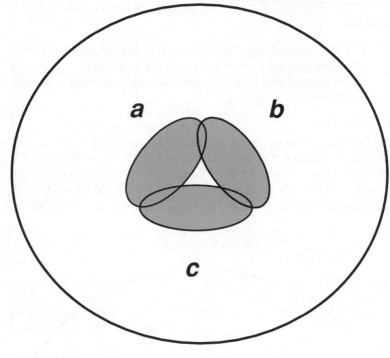

F<small>IG</small>. 7.17

options. (The square region in Figure 7.18 is meant to illustrate the mutual overlap of the three object icons.) If you just want to represent what things are like in the world, then it makes no difference whether you produce a picture that covers all the options or not. For this is true:

> If *P* is a picture, there is a picture *P'* that covers all the options and that represents the same objects as having the same properties and standing in the same identity/distinctness relations to one another.

You can always produce a picture that covers all the options from one that does not by supplying some additional points to use to make the additional regions needed for option-covering.

Consider pictures that cover all the options. In any such picture, each icon is partitioned into cells by its overlap with other icons: if

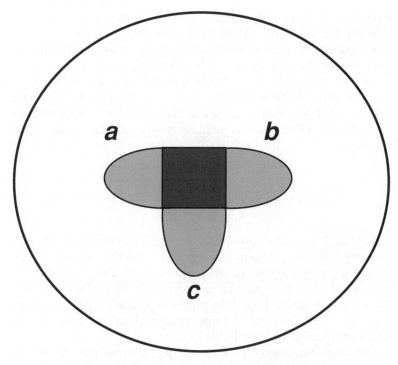

FIG. 7.18

it overlaps no other icon, it consists of one cell, if it overlaps one other icon it consists of two cells, if it overlaps two other icons it consists of three cells or four, depending on whether the other icons overlap each other. And so on. Given a picture P that covers all the options, an *identity-refinement* results from P by replacing each icon in P with one of its cells. Notice that icons always become more determinate, not less, in an identity-refinement, and that identities all become completely determinate. Given an identity-refinement of P, a *full refinement* is produced by replacing each icon in the identity-refinement by the unit set of one of the points in it. In a full refinement, there is no indeterminacy of any kind.

Recall the resolutions of the world that were discussed in Chapter 2. The full refinements of a picture correspond exactly to the resolutions of the world represented by the picture. That is, given a world and a picture that represents it, an object has a property in a resolution of that world if and only if its icon is a subset of the pictension representing that property in the corresponding full refinement of the picture of the world.

So you can easily see what is true in every resolution of a pictorial situation by expanding the picture (if necessary) to one that covers all the options, and then examining every refinement of that picture. (Refinements are discussed further in the next chapter.)

7.8 PICTURING COMPLEX PROPERTIES

Little has been said above about complex properties, because metaphysical issues about indeterminate identity do not appear to depend on what view is taken about them. The following discussion concerns how pictures that explicitly represent properties (by circled regions) implicitly represent complex properties by geometric combinations of those regions. This discussion is not relied on elsewhere in the book.

There are two ways in which our pictures are metaphysically neutral, and this should be kept in mind lest some significance be attributed to the pictures that our picturing conventions do not embody. First, suppose we have a picture with two distinct but coextensive pictensions p and q. That is, p and q are distinct sets of points, but they include and exclude exactly the same object icons. Condition [C] requires that there be a "complement" to p and q, a pictension r that includes the icons that p and q exclude and excludes the icons that p and q include. Suppose that there is only one such pictension, r. Then p and q can represent distinct properties not both of which have a unique negation (if property negation obeys the principle that the negation of the negation of a property is that property itself). We can picture a situation in which p has a unique negation, r, but q has no negation: there is no property whose negation is q, even though there is a property (namely, r) which is coextensive with the negation q would have if q had a negation. As a consequence of this, it is possible to have a pictension, q, whose complement (the set of points not in q) is not itself a pictension. In terms of our two-dimensional diagrams, this means that if we have a circle in the diagram representing q, we may not assume that the region outside the circle itself represents the extension of a property—though some region that includes and excludes exactly the same object images as that region does, does represent a property. For the latter reason, it is harmless for most purposes to assume that the region outside a circle represents a property.

But the issue is more serious when we consider conjunctions and disjunctions of properties. Consider the Figure 7.19. If all the objects that exist are already pictured in this diagram, then it is harmless to assume that the region enclosed by the two circles together (the union of the circles) represents the disjunction of p and q. After all, we know by condition [C] that there is some region that encloses (excludes) exactly the same object images as are enclosed (excluded) by the p region or the q region, and the union of p and q does this. But the union of two property regions does not *automatically* do this. For suppose we have instead Figure 7.20. Here, the object pictured is totally included in the union of the two property regions, but it is *not* included in either

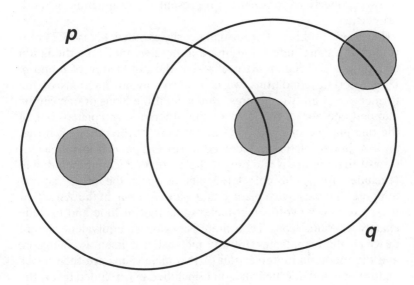

Fig. 7.19

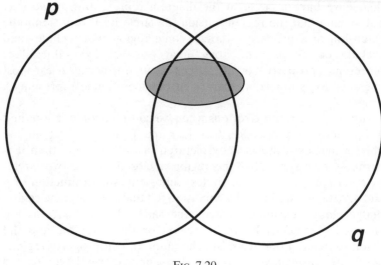

Fig. 7.20

region *p* or region *q* or both. So this is a diagram in which the union of two property regions cannot represent the disjunction of those properties.

Diagrams of this sort are usually easily avoided. Figure 7.21 represents the same states of affairs, and here we *may* take the union of region *p* and region *q* to represent the disjunction of *p* and *q*. Under certain conditions, we can always avoid diagrams of the former sort. Call two pictures *equivalent* if the icons of one can be mapped one-one to the icons of the other, and the pictensions of the one may be mapped one-one to those of the other, such that an icon in one picture is included in (or excluded from) a pictension of that picture if and only if the correlated icon is included in (excluded from) the correlated pictension in the other picture. Suppose that we have a picture that is *extensional*, in the sense that there are never two distinct pictensions that include and exclude exactly the same icons. Then there is always an equivalent picture in which the complement of any pictension is itself a pictension, and the union and intersection of two pictensions are themselves pictensions, and in which an icon is included in (excluded from) the intersection of two pictensions if and only if it is included in

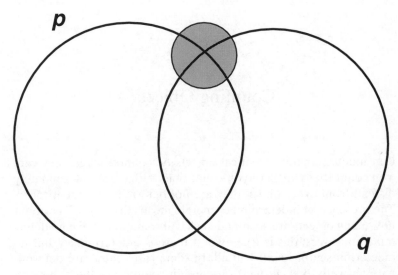

FIG. 7.21

(excluded from) each pictension, and an icon is included in (excluded from) the union of two pictensions if and only if it is included in (excluded from) at least one of the pictensions.

Similar results hold under certain natural conditions on non-extensional pictures, but a further investigation of this phenomenon is of no apparent direct interest to our general metaphysical enterprise, so it will not be discussed further.

8

Counting Objects

Can indeterminately identical objects be counted? Yes, they can. You count them just like you count objects that are determinately distinct from every object they are not determinately identical to. The presence of indeterminacy merely means that questions about how many objects are such-and-such will sometimes have no determinate answers; this is true even if there is indeterminacy, but no indeterminacy of identity at all. In some cases there are determinate answers to such questions, and in some cases there are not. Which cases are which? That is hard to sum up in the abstract. But in most cases we find that we have pretty solid judgements about how many objects are such-and-such, or we judge that there ought not to be an answer. A good theory should agree with these judgements, or it should give us reason to revise them. The theory under consideration reveals different ways to interpret the claims at issue; in every case, one of the ways makes the theory agree with the judgements we are inclined to make.

8.1 TWO SOURCES OF INDETERMINACY IN COUNTING

There are two ways in which indeterminacy complicates the process of answering the question 'How many ϕ's are there?' One complication arises when some of the ϕ's are indeterminately identical to others, so you don't know whether to count them as one or as more than one. Another complication arises when there are things which are indeterminately ϕ; thus it is indeterminate whether you should count them at all. These two complications are different from one another, and they need to be addressed differently.

Begin with the complication due to indeterminacy of identity.

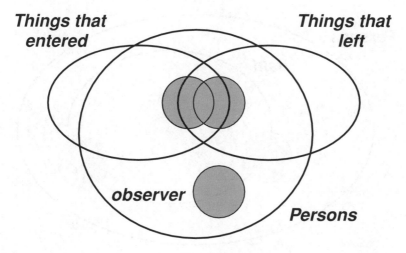

FIG. 8.1

Consider the case of the disrupted person, and imagine that there is one person looking on, as in Figure 8.1. Suppose you are asked how many people there are all told. You point to the observer, and say "one". You point to the person entering, and say "two". You wait a while, then you point to the person leaving, and you . . . what? The problem is that you must not count this person if you have already counted them, but you must count him/her if you haven't counted him/her yet. Since it is indeterminate whether the person leaving is the person who entered, it is indeterminate whether this is a person you have already counted. Thus it is indeterminate whether you are to count them now. It follows that the question of how many persons there are all told has no correct answer. We are not in complete ignorance, of course. We know that any answer less than "two" is incorrect, since you haven't counted everyone, and we know that any answer more than "three" is incorrect, since you must have counted someone twice. There are an infinite number of incorrect answers, two indeterminate ones, and no correct ones. This is disconcerting, perhaps, but fairly straightforward. In fact, in this case it seems clear that these are the right things to say: any answer less than two or more than three is wrong, and either "two" or "three" is such that it is indeterminate whether it is correct.

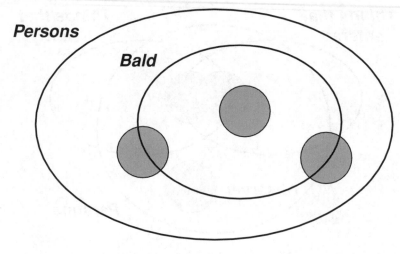

FIG. 8.2

Now consider a different kind of case: indeterminacy due to predication. Suppose there are three people, one of whom is determinately bald and two of whom are such that it is indeterminate whether they are bald (Figure 8.2). You decide to count the people who are bald. You point to the person who is determinately bald, and you say "one", and then what? It appears that in this case any answer less than one or more than three is definitely wrong, but the answers "one", "two", or "three" should all have indeterminate truth-value.

Now let us consider a case of predicational indeterminacy combined with indeterminacy of identity. Recall the ships and what they are like; they are pictured in Figure 8.3. Suppose we ask here how many ships left port? The structure of the situation is like that of the bald persons above, and so there apparently should be no determinate answer. But then what about the judgement, which I earlier took to be part of the extended data, that exactly one ship left port? Something like that is correct, but how can it be? I suggest that we can either count ships that *left port*, or ships that *determinately left port*. In normal circumstances we take determinacy for granted, and there is no relevant difference in our assertions between 'ϕ' and 'determinately ϕ'. Also, since we aim to assert what

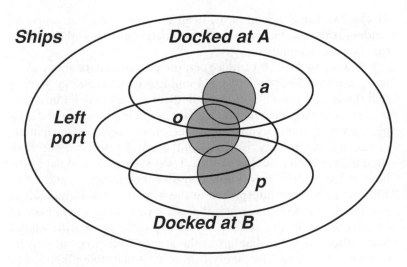

FIG. 8.3

is (determinately) true, there is no difference between asserting 'S' and asserting 'determinately S'. But when a clause is embedded inside an assertion, and when there is a possibility of indeterminacy, then we need to distinguish whether we mean 'determinately ϕ' or just 'ϕ'. This is the case when we assert 'there are n ϕ's' in a situation of indeterminacy. In the case at hand, there is a difference between counting the *ships that left port*, or the *ships that determinately left port*. The considerations raised above seem to show that if we ask the first question, assuming that we do not intend the qualifier 'determinately',[1] then there is no answer. But if we mean the second, we get an answer. This is because we point at the ship leaving port and say "one"—because it is determinately leaving port—and we do not count the other ships because we know that they are not determinately ships that left port. A natural language assertion may thus be interpreted either austerely, without an assumption of determinacy, or with determinacy qualifying any of

---

[1] Using 'entered' without a determinacy modifier is not the same as saying 'determinately or indeterminately entered'. The bare predicate 'entered' is neither true nor false of certain things, and that is why there is a problem in counting; the predicate 'either determinately or indeterminately entered' is either true or false of each thing, and it raises no such problem.

its otherwise unqualified parts. I call the former the "unadorned" reading (the reading unadorned with determinacy) and the latter the adorned reading.

It follows that when I catalogued the extended data about identity puzzles in Chapter 1, I used ambiguous terminology, hoping that the reader would interpret it in the way I intended. I intended to classify as data the fact that exactly one thing is determinately a person who entered. In my experience, most people will have interpreted me in this way. But some others will not have, and they should have been troubled by what I was saying there. What I now hope is that everyone will now consider the ambiguity, and agree with the data when interpreted in the way in which I intended. It will turn out below that when there is a case of indeterminacy of identity, a cardinality statement will typically agree with what I have called the data when given the adorned reading, but not the unadorned reading. The theory is thus most plausible if applied to ordinary judgements with the adorned reading being the default reading in cases where the theory posits indeterminacy of identity. I will assume this hereafter. (The baldness case above is not one of these, and so it is not subject to this default.)

This discussion has taken place at a somewhat informal level. We need to be precise about whether our language actually works as I have just said, and there are various interpretations to be surveyed. The following sections spell this out.

8.2 ANALYSING CARDINALITY CLAIMS

There are standard techniques for representing finite numerical claims in terms of quantifiers, connectives, and identity. The simplest and least controversial are judgements of the form 'there are at least n ϕ's'. These are analysable as follows:

There is at least one ϕ:	$\exists x \phi x$
There are at least two ϕ's:	$\exists x \exists y (x \neq y \,\&\, \phi x \,\&\, \phi y)$
There are at least three ϕ's:	$\exists x \exists y \exists z (x \neq y \,\&\, x \neq z \,\&\, y \neq z$ $\&\, \phi x \,\&\, \phi y \,\&\, \phi z)$

What about 'there are at most n ϕ's'? The usual formulation of this is roughly that any $n + 1$ ϕ's are such that some of them are identical. That is, we have these analyses:

There is at most one φ: $\forall x \forall y(\phi x \ \& \ \phi y \Rightarrow x = y)$

There are at most two φ's: $\forall x \forall y \forall z(\phi x \ \& \ \phi y \ \& \ \phi x \Rightarrow x = y \lor y = z \lor x = z)$

. . .

'There are exactly *n* φ's' is equivalent to the conjunction: 'there are at least *n* φ's *and* there are at most *n* φ's'. Combining this with the above analyses yields:

There is exactly one φ: $\exists x \phi x \ \& \ \forall x \forall y(\phi x \ \& \ \phi y \Rightarrow x = y)$

There are exactly two φ's: $\exists x \exists y(x \neq y \ \& \ \phi x \ \& \ \phi y) \ \& \ \forall x \forall y \forall z(\phi x \ \& \ \phi y \ \& \ \phi x \Rightarrow x = y \lor y = z \lor x = z)$

These analyses are natural hypotheses about the meaning of cardinality claims. If we use them, then the theory under consideration gives the right answers when they exist, and correctly entails that there are no answers in the other cases. I detail this below. We will also need to look at alternative formulations that give slightly different results.

8.3 COUNTING ALL THE SHIPS

Consider the puzzling ships. Our naïve judgement is that exactly one ship left port and exactly two ships docked. But how many ships were there all told? Not fewer than two, since two ships docked, and not more than three, since there are none under consideration except for the one that left port and the two that docked. So any answer that is less than two or more than three should be definitely wrong. Were there exactly two? That seems impossible to answer; since the world does not see fit to determine whether either of the later ships are the original ship, there should be no answer. (If your instinct tells you that the right answer should be "exactly two", see §8.5 for a possible account of that instinct.) Were there exactly three? Same response. Were there two *or* three? Here is where the idiosyncrasies of disjunction creep in. In one sense, if it is wrong to say there were two, and wrong to say there were three, then it is wrong to say that there were two or three. In another sense, we seem to want to say this is right. At least, we want to say something like "two-to-three is the right *range* of answers". This, too, will be addressed in §8.5.

Setting aside disjunctions, the theory confirms our naïve judgements about cardinalities. That is, it confirms them on the assumption that it is indeterminate whether the original ship is the newly assembled ship, and indeterminate whether it is the ship with new parts, and determinate that the newly assembled ship is distinct from the ship with new parts.

I begin with the question of how many ships there are all told. The answer according to the theory is whatever we get by feeding the extended data into the numerical formulas above. Here are the relevant data. Let o be the original ship, a the newly assembled ship, and p the ship with new parts. First, o, a, and p *are* ships under consideration:

> D1 $So \;\&\; Sa \;\&\; Sp.$

And these are *determinately all* the ships that are under consideration:

> D2 $\forall x(Sx \Rightarrow !x = o \lor !x = a \lor !x = p).$

Ship a is not ship p, and it is indeterminate whether o is either of them:

> D3 $\neg(a = p)$
> $\triangledown o = a$
> $\triangledown o = p.$

D1–D3 then generate the answers to the "how many" question. (The arguments that follow are elementary but a bit lengthy. They are not much longer, however, than the same sorts of arguments that are needed when there is no indeterminacy at all.)

Exactly one? It is false that there is exactly one ship, since it is false that there is at most one. If it were not false that there is at most one, this would not be false:

> $\forall x \forall y(Sx \;\&\; Sy \Rightarrow x = y).$

So every instance of it would not be false, including this one:

> $Sa \;\&\; Sp \Rightarrow a = p.$

But by D1, these are true:

> $Sa \;\&\; Sp.$

This entails that '$a = p$' is not false, contrary to D3.

Exactly two? It is indeterminate whether there are exactly two, since it is true that there are at least two (infer '$\neg(a = p)$ & Sa & Sp' from D1 and D3 and existentially generalize it), and indeterminate whether there are at most two. We can show that it is indeterminate whether there are at most two by refuting the other two options: that it is true that there are at most two, and that it is false that there are at most two.

Suppose it is true that there are at most two ships. That is, this is true:

$$\forall x \forall y \forall z (Sx \text{ & } Sy \text{ & } Sx \Rightarrow x = y \vee y = z \vee x = z).$$

This, together with D1 lets us infer that this is true:

$$o = a \vee a = p \vee o = p.$$

But D3 rules out the possibility that any of the disjuncts are true.

Suppose on the other hand that it is false that there are at most two ships; this is false:

$$\forall x \forall y \forall z (Sx \text{ & } Sy \text{ & } Sz \Rightarrow x = y \vee x = z \vee y = z).$$

Then some instance is false. So there are entities e, f, and g, such that this is true:

$$Se \text{ & } Sf \text{ & } Sg \text{ & } e \neq f \text{ & } e \neq g \text{ & } f \neq g.$$

From this and D2 we infer each of:

$$e = o \vee e = a \vee e = p$$
$$f = o \vee f = a \vee f = p$$
$$g = o \vee g = a \vee g = p.$$

These yield six cases to consider (actually, twenty-seven cases, but twenty-one are immediately ruled out by the non-identities above), with each of them contradicting D3. For example, one of the cases is:

$$e = o \text{ & } f = a \text{ & } g = p.$$

This, with '$e \neq f$' from the above six-part conjunction, entails that this is true:

$$o \neq a$$

contradicting:

$$\nabla o = a$$

from D3. The other five cases are parallel.

Exactly three? It is indeterminate whether there are exactly three, since it is indeterminate whether there are at least three (this proof is similar to the proof that it is indeterminate whether there are at most two) and true that there are at most four (proof left to reader).

Exactly four? It is easily shown (using D3) that it is false that there are at least four ships, and this is sufficient to refute the claims that there are exactly four, exactly five, etc.

8.4 COUNTING THE SHIPS THAT LEFT PORT

When we counted ships above, we assigned a cardinality to the extension of a predicate, 'ship', that is determinately true or determinately false of each thing. As discussed earlier, new complications enter when this condition is not met. Suppose we ask how many ships left port. Certainly the original ship left port; that is determinately true. Since it is indeterminate whether the ship with new parts is the original ship, it is indeterminate whether the ship with new parts left port; likewise for the newly assembled ship. (These inferences presume that leaving port is, or is equivalent to, a property; they also presume that if either of the ships that docked had left port, that ship would *be* the original ship. Each of these is an additional assumption that may be questioned.) It appears then that there might be no determinate answer regarding how many ships left port. But I suggested above that exactly one ship left port. Which is right?

On the analysis that we have so far, exactly one ship *determinately* left port. But there is no answer to the "unadorned" question of how many ships left port. To verify these claims we need additional data about which ships left port. As indicated earlier, I assume that o left port, and it is indeterminate whether a or p did:

D4 Lo & $\triangledown La$ & $\triangledown Lp$.

To show that exactly one ship determinately left port we need to show that this is true:[2]

---

[2] By D4 it is determinate for each entity under discussion whether or not it is a ship. Thus 'Sx' and '$!Sx$' are equivalent, and we need only consider one version; I use the simpler.

$\exists x!(Sx \ \& \ Lx) \ \& \ \forall x \forall y (!(Sx \ \& \ !Lx) \ \& \ !(Sy \ \& \ !Ly) \Rightarrow x = y).$

The first conjunct is easy since D1 and D4 yield that this is true:

$So \ \& \ Lo.$

Since it is true, we can add the required '!', and existentially general-ize to get the first conjunct. To see that the second conjunct is true, we need to show that any instance that has a true antecedent also has a true consequent, and that any instance that has an indetermi-nate antecedent has a true or indeterminate consequent. Suppose, first, that we have an instance where the antecedent is true:

$!(Se \ \& \ !Le) \ \& \ !(Sf \& !Lf).$

By D2 we have both of:

$e = o \lor e = a \lor e = p$
$f = o \lor f = a \lor f = p.$

We can rule out any of these disjuncts being true except the first on each line, because any of the others, by Leibniz's Law, would lead from the displayed conjunction to theses that contradict D4. But the first disjuncts taken together entail '$e = f$', which makes the consequent of the conditional true. It remains to show that any instance that has an indeterminate antecedent has a true or inde-terminate consequent. This is vacuously true, since the antecedent cannot be indeterminate:

$!(Se \ \& \ !Le) \ \& \ !(Sf \& !Lf).$

This is determinate in virtue of its form (because of the determi-nate-truth connective).

If we interpret the question as how many ships left port, *omitting* the determinacy modifier, then the proof would go the same right up to the last step. But at that point the antecedent would be indeter-minate if $e = a$ and $f = p$; in that case the consequent is false, and so the whole conditional is indeterminate. So on this reading it is inde-terminate whether exactly one ship left port. This is the kind of case that rationalizes the decision in §8.1 to take the adorned reading (the one that includes the determinacy modifier) as the default reading for claims involving indeterminate identity.[3]

---

[3] See the appendix to this chapter for a comparison of these results with the ones one would get on a classical analysis of the situation using supervaluations.

8.5 VARIANT ANALYSES

In bivalent logic there are many different equivalent formulations of cardinality claims. It is important to note that some of these are not equivalent in a non-bivalent setting. In fact, there is a fairly natural way to formulate 'there is exactly one φ' which is plainly wrong. It is the formulation that says 'something is φ, and any φ is it':

$$\exists x[\phi x \ \& \ \forall y(\phi y \Rightarrow x = y)].$$

To see that this is wrong, notice that in the ship case this tells us that it is indeterminate whether there is exactly one ship. The formula that says there is exactly one ship is nonfalse because there is something—the original ship—which is determinately a ship, and such that every ship is either determinately or indeterminately identical with it. But it is plainly false that there is exactly one ship, since two distinct ships docked at the end of the trip. So this seemingly natural formulation that is equivalent in bivalent logic to the one we have used above is not equivalent in non-bivalent logic.[4] This will be important in assessing how definite descriptions work in the next chapter.

8.6 SUPER-RESOLUTIONAL READINGS

There is no correct answer to the question about how many ships there are all told; all answers except 'two' and 'three' are false, and those are indeterminate. Thus this is also indeterminate:

There are two *or* three ships.

---

[4] The equivalence in bivalent logic depends on the transitivity of identity. In the present application, this turns into a case of the transitivity of indeterminate identity. But indeterminate identity is not transitive. The ship case refutes the transitivity of indeterminate identity, since one of the later ships is indeterminately identical to the original ship, which is indeterminately identical to the other later ship, but the later ships are distinct from one another.

But some of us have some inclination to endorse this claim. This appears to be a matter of interpreting the disjunction in accord with the super-resolutional reading discussed in Chapters 3 and 5. Consider all ways of making properties more determinate; then a list of options is correct on the resolutional reading if and only if each option is made true on some resolution, and every resolution does make one of the options true. In the case of the ships, any resolution identifies ship *o* with ship *a*, or with ship *p*, or with neither; the first two options produce two ships, and the last produces three. So this kind of reading validates the assertion that there are two or three ships, while leaving each disjunct indeterminate.

There are people whose instincts tell them that there should be *exactly* two ships all told. When asked to explain why they think this, they tend to answer that however things go, the original ship must be identical to one of the resulting ships; it is indeterminate which it is identical to, but there can be no third option where the original ship just ceases to exist. I have not taken this to be part of the extended data (because I think it is false), and the theory alone does not yield this as an option. But it is possible to accommodate it. If indeed it *is* genuinely impossible for the original ship to cease to exist while being replaced by two distinct completely new ships, then the resolution that turns out that way is not a possible way the world could go. If that is so, it should not be one of the resolutions that we count when evaluating the truth of a claim on all resolutions. If it is ruled out as a resolution, then the super-resolutional reading does indeed say that there are exactly two ships overall. This is an automatic product of the theory sketched here coupled with the claim that it is impossible for the original ship to cease to exist and be replaced by two others. I don't agree with that claim about what the possibilities are, but if I did, I would say that the theory correctly accommodates my view on the super-resolutional reading.[5]

---

[5] A similar point applies to the question of how many ships left port. The super-resolutional reading by itself leaves this indeterminate between one, two, and three. But the answer is determinately one if you add that it is impossible for either of the later ships to leave port while being distinct from the original ship.

8.7 PERSONS, CATS, AND PILES
OF TRASH, ETC.

The material discussed above carries over straightforwardly to the other paradigm puzzles. The results are:

> Me and my body: Suppose it is determinate that both I and my body are in the office, and nothing else is there. Then there are not less than one nor more than two things in the office; it is indeterminate whether there is one and indeterminate whether there is two. In the super-resolutional reading, there are either one or two. For the unadorned reading of how many persons there are in the office, we get the same answer, but for the determinate-person reading we get the answer "exactly one".

> The disrupted person(s): Exactly one person entered the room in either the determinacy or the unadorned sense. It is false that there were less than one or more than two persons, but both 'one' and 'two' are indeterminate as answers. On the resolved reading there are either one or two.

> The cat: There is exactly one cat on the table in the determinacy sense, which is what I consider to be the default case; there is no answer on the unadorned reading.

> The piles of trash: There is not less than one pile of trash nor more than three; there is no determinate literal answer, but in the resolved sense there are between one and three piles of trash.

A more complicated case: Suppose there are two similar ships, a and b, afloat near one another. Each ship has its planks replaced with planks from the other, until the planks are completely interchanged, and we end up with a ship c whose location is continuous with that of a's, which consists entirely of the planks from b, and a ship d whose location is continuous with that of b's, which consists entirely of the planks from a. One might want to argue that there is no fact of the matter whether a is identical with c or with d, and likewise for b. The picture would look like Figure 8.4. There are at least two ships here, and not more than four, but it is indeterminate whether there are two and indeterminate whether there are three and indeterminate whether there are four. On the resolved

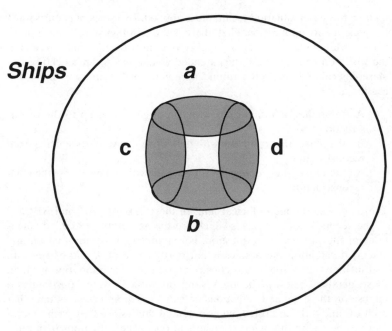

Ships

a

c

d

b

FIG. 8.4

reading there are either two or three or four. (One might want to argue on the basis of the symmetry of the example, that the resolution into three is impossible. If we impose a constraint on the resolutions that they be symmetrical, then we would conclude that there are at least two ships, and not more then four, and not exactly three; it would be indeterminate whether there are two and indeterminate whether there are four.)

Appendix: A Classical Analysis Using Supervaluations

A referee for OUP has suggested a comparison of these results with the ones one would get on a classical analysis of the situation using supervaluations. The answer is that a variety of answers are obtainable, depending

on how the supervaluation technique is applied. Two sorts of choices must
be made in any application. First, there is the ontological one: since there
is no worldly indeterminacy of identity, one must decide what there is in
the world on which to base the extended valuations. A typical choice is a
mereological one, where the atomic ingredients of the situation under discussion are:

> A: the object that coincides with the original ship up to the recon-
> struction
> B: the object that coincides with the ship with new parts starting from
> reconstruction
> C: the object that coincides with the ship with old parts starting from
> reconstruction

There are also the mereological sums of these: AB, AC, BC, and ABC.

The second choice involves which are the acceptable extended valuations of the predicates in question. For simplicity, I assume that on any
extended valuation the predicate 'left port' is true of A and of any sum
that includes A. (Without this constraint, we get many more options than
those detailed below.) The interesting question is what constraints to
impose on the extended valuations of 'ship'. For simplicity, I assume that
both BC and ABC are ruled out as potential ships, since they each require
there to be a ship that is in two places at once. The valuations then must
be chosen from among the following as possible extensions for 'ship':

> ϕ, {A}, {B}, {C}, {AB}, {AC}, {A, B}, {A, C}, {A, AB}, {A, AC}, {B, C},
> {B, AB}, {B, AC}, {C, AB}, {C, BC}, {AB, AC}, {A, B, C}, {A, B, AB}, {A,
> B, AC}, {A, C, AB}, {A, C, BC}, {A, AB, BC}, {B, C, AB}, {B, C, BC},
> {B, AB, AC}, {C, AB, BC}, {A, B, C, AB}, {A, B, C, BC}, {A, B, AB, BC},
> {A, C, AB, BC}, {B, C, AB, BC}, {A, B, C, AB, BC}

If all of these are allowed (an implausible application) then each exact cardinality judgement for ships leaving port from zero to five is superindeterminate, and those from six up are superfalse. A more plausible option
is to require that some ship left port, and that at least two docked; this
reduces the possible extended valuations of 'ship' to:

> {C, AB}, {B, AC}, {AB, AC}, {A, B, C}, {A, B, AC}, {A, C, AB}, {A, C,
> BC}, {A, AB, BC}, {B, C, AB}, {B, AB, AC}, {C, AB, BC}, {A, B, C, AB},
> {A, B, C, BC}, {A, B, AB, BC}, {A, C, AB, BC}, {B, C, AB, BC}, {A, B,
> C, AB, BC}

With these options it is superfalse that no ship left port, and each exact
cardinality judgement for ships leaving port from one to five is superindeterminate. One might wish to also insist that on any extended valuation no
two ships ever overlap. This would reduce the extended valuations to:

{A, B, C}, {AB, C}, {AC, B}

Now it is supertrue that exactly one ship left port.

Instead of the above choices, one might allow ships to overlap but insist that no ship that left port ceases to exist midway in the voyage; if this is added to the edict that no ship is ever in two places, the possible extended valuations are:

{AB, C}, {AC, B}, {AB, AC}

On this option it is superfalse that no ship left port, superindeterminate whether one, or whether two, left port, and superfalse that three or more left port.

(I suppose that one should not really rule out the option that there was never more than one ship, namely, ABC. That leaves the last two options just discussed unchanged for the question of how many ships left port, though it would change the results for the judgement about how many ships docked.)

9

Denoting Objects

9.1 THE ISSUE

Suppose it is indeterminate whether a is identical to b. Can we then refer to a without, in some sense, also referring to b? If not, since reference is supposed to be unique, can we refer to a at all? This sort of issue arises regularly in the literature. There are two dimensions to the worry. The first is that if indeterminacy of identity prevents unique reference, we may not be able to make determinate claims about any object at all if it is indeterminately identical with some object. The second is that if indeterminacy of identity automatically brings with it indeterminacy of reference, it would seem difficult to claim that there is indeterminacy in the world, as opposed to it being an illusion generated by vagaries in the semantical relations between language and the world. In this chapter I address the question of how we may refer determinately to objects that are indeterminately identical to "other" objects. In the next chapter I examine the proposal that all indeterminacy of identity is an illusion based on semantic indeterminacy.

It is easy to generate worries about denotation when objects are indeterminately identical. Here is an example from Burgess (1990) about a mountain Aphla which is (allegedly) indeterminately identical with a mountain Ateb. He suggests that it is wrong to hold that the singular term 'Aphla' can denote a unique object in such a case. He argues as follows:

If there is something with which Aphla is indefinitely identical, then there is no (unique) thing which Aphla is. We cannot gloss "'Aphla' denotes Aphla" as "'Aphla' denotes Aphla, whatever it may be", we should have to say "'Aphla' denotes Aphla, whatever unique thing it may *become*". This gives the game away, implying as it does, that there is no unique thing which Aphla is already. If there is no unique thing which Aphla is already, then the sense of 'Aphla' is not yet sufficiently definite to determine a unique object for Aphla to be. That the sense of the name could be modified to overcome this difficulty is no excuse for holding that we can regard this task as already having been accomplished. The prolepsis involved in the manœuvre is unintelligible. (1990: 271)

If Aphla is indeterminately identical with Ateb, then apparently there is no unique thing that we denote by 'Aphla'. A similar point is also articulated by van Inwagen (1988):

[I]f identity is indeed vague, then the semantical relation between name and thing named must also be vague. If, for example, 'Alpha' definitely names x, and it is neither definitely true nor definitely false that $x = y$, then it seems inevitable to suppose that it is neither definitely true nor definitely false that 'Alpha' names y. Our semantics must somehow reflect this consequence of vague identity for the naming relation. (1988: 259)

Cowles (1994) goes further; in commenting on this passage from Van Inwagen he says:

I think that van Inwagen is wrong to suggest that 'Alpha' could *definitely* name x even when it is neither definitely true nor definitely false that $x = y$. (1994: 147)

Determinate reference presupposes determinate individuation. The case of Alpha/Omega [the disrupted person(s)], however, is a case in which determinate individuation is *ex hypothesi* absent. (ibid. 153)

Stalnaker (1988) makes a related point. Commenting on Salmon's argument against indeterminate identity (Chapters 4 and 11), he says:

[T]he argument shows that if it is indeterminate whether $a = b$, then it is indeterminate what 'a' refers to, or what 'b' refers to. (1988: 354)

These comments raise severe questions about what objects we are talking about when we use singular terms. The questions need to be addressed.

9.2 NAMES

Suppose we see a ship leave port on Tuesday, and we dub it 'Samantha's Pride'. On Wednesday we see a ship dock, and we dub it 'Kim4Ever'. (We also see another ship dock, which we dub something else.) Then we discover that in between there occurred the sort of repair/assembly that leads us to conclude that there is no fact of the matter about whether Samantha's Pride is Kim4Ever. Suppose that we try to explain part of the situation by saying that it is indeterminate whether Kim4Ever left port on Tuesday. Are we then speaking indeterminately about Samantha's Pride? If so, what are we saying about it? Are we saying indeterminately that it is indeterminate whether Samantha's Pride left port on Tuesday? But it is determinate that Samantha's Pride left port. It seems wrong to say of Samantha's Pride, even indeterminately, that it is indeterminate whether it left port on Tuesday. Is it then indeterminate whether we have said something wrong? I hope not. I think that I can say that it is determinate that Samantha's Pride left port on Tuesday, and indeterminate whether Kim4Ever left port on Tuesday, without even being indeterminately wrong.

The key question is this: If it is indeterminate whether Kim4Ever is Samantha's Pride, have I indeterminately dubbed Samantha's Pride 'Kim4Ever' when I dub Kim4Ever 'Kim4Ever'? I don't think so. I have dubbed Kim4Ever 'Kim4Ever', and as a result the name 'Kim4Ever' as used by me determinately refers to Kim4Ever and determinately does not refer to Samantha's Pride. And so I am not speaking of Samantha's Pride at all, even indeterminately.

At least this is how I think I use the name. This is in spite of an obvious argument to the contrary. Suppose that I (determinately) use the name 'Kim4Ever' to refer to Kim4Ever, and (determinately) do not use the name to refer to Samantha's Pride. Then it seems that by Leibniz's Law, Kim4Ever and Samantha's Pride are distinct, in spite of the fact that it is indeterminate (by hypothesis) whether they are identical. Fortunately, this does not follow. This is reasoning not by Leibniz's Law, but by a contrapositive version of it. The contrapositive version holds only for contexts in which the predicates stand for properties. But conceptual or semantic predicates do not necessarily stand for worldly properties; such predicates instead characterize parts of our conceptual apparatus for representing the world. 'N refers to x' is a paradigm case of a predicate that does not stand for a property of x.

What about the question raised by Burgess: Is there a unique thing which Kim4Ever is, and which we denote by 'Kim4Ever'? What does it mean to ask if there is a "unique thing"? A thing is unique in some respect or other. Apparently what is being addressed here are the following two questions about uniqueness:

Is there a unique thing which is Kim4Ever? That is, is there exactly one thing which has the property, *being Kim4Ever*?

Is there a unique thing which is denoted by 'Kim4Ever'? That is, is there exactly one thing *which is denoted by 'Kim4Ever'*?

The answers to these are implicit in the results of the last chapter. There are two ways to read questions like these: unadorned, and with the determinacy interpretation. On the unadorned reading, the question sometimes has no answer; it has no answer *because* it is indeterminate whether Kim4Ever is identical with Samantha's Pride. On the determinacy reading it is answered yes. There is exactly one thing which is determinately Kim4Ever.

As I use the name, the second question can also be answered "yes". There is exactly one thing denoted by the name 'Kim4Ever'; it is the exactly-one-thing that answers to the determinacy reading of the first question. You can reason otherwise by using a fallacious contrapositive version of Leibniz's Law, but not otherwise.

This is also the reply to Van Inwagen's comments. If 'Kim4Ever' definitely names Kim4Ever, and if it is indeterminate whether Kim4Ever is Samantha's Pride, then it does not follow that it is indeterminate whether 'Kim4Ever' names Samantha's Pride. Not only does it not follow, it is not true.

The position I take here is a consistent one, but hardly one that will convince someone who is wedded to the opposite view. Can I do anything to win over such a person? Perhaps not if we discuss only proper names. The semantics of proper names is controversial, partly because the facts are so undetermined. The names themselves have no semantic structure at all, and so we need to look at our usage and our intent. And in the area of indeterminacy, these give us little uncontroversial guidance. Perhaps we can do better by looking at something with more structure? With this hope, I turn to a consideration of definite descriptions.

9.3 DEFINITE DESCRIPTIONS

Theories of definite descriptions fall into roughly two categories. One, endorsed by Russell, is that definite descriptions are not semantical units in themselves, and so they have no semantic

Denoting Objects

analysis. Instead, one analyses sentences that paraphrase the descriptions; instead of trying to analyse 'the present queen of England' in 'The present queen of England is old' one merely analyses 'There is exactly one queen of England, and she is old.' It is clear from the discussion of the preceding chapter that sentences of this sort will often be determinately true if given the determinacy interpretation even if the queen of England has previously undergone a disruption that makes her indeterminately identical with the former princess. That is, in the circumstances described, this may be true:

$$\exists x[!(x \text{ is QE}) \text{ \& } \forall x \forall y[!(x \text{ is QE}) \text{ \& } !(y \text{ is QE}) \Rightarrow x = y] \text{ \& } x \text{ is old}].$$

However, it may be worth discussing also those views that take definite descriptions to be genuine semantical units, since this is the area in which the discussion of semantic indeterminacy is often located. There are dozens of theories of this sort, but they almost all agree on the condition under which a definite description denotes something, and what it denotes. The condition is:[1]

[D]: '$\iota x[\phi x]$' denotes o if and only if o is ϕ and at most one thing is ϕ.

In this condition, the 'if and only if' is to be read strongly (it is to be read as our '$\Leftrightarrow$'), in the sense that this is true, or false, or neither true nor false:

'$\iota x[\phi x]$' denotes o

if and only if this is true, or false, or neither true nor false respectively:

$$\phi o \text{ \& } \forall x \forall y[\phi x \text{ \& } \phi y \Rightarrow x = y].$$

For definiteness in discussing how this works, I focus on the case of the disrupted person(s), and the definite description 'the person who entered'. The metaphysical situation is the one pictured in Figure 9.1. The question is whether the description 'the person who entered' denotes a determinately, or indeterminately, and in either case whether it also denotes b indeterminately. As in the previous

---

[1] The second condition uses 'at most one thing is ϕ' instead of 'exactly one thing is ϕ' because the former is simpler, and they are equivalent when conjoined with 'o is ϕ'. It also avoids the natural but wrong analysis discussed in §8.5.

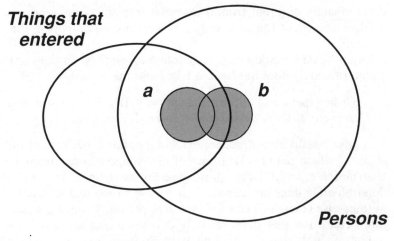

Things that entered

a b

Persons

FIG. 9.1

chapter, there are two interpretations to consider: the unadorned reading, and 'the thing that is determinately a person who entered'. Between them they seem to capture the things people want to say about cases of this sort.

9.3.1 Determinate denotation of a without indeterminate denotation of b

First, consider the determinacy reading of 'the person who entered':

ιx!(x is a person & x entered).

I say that this determinately denotes person a in Figure 9.1. It denotes person a because this is true:

!(a is a person & a entered) & ∀x∀y[!(x is a person & x entered) & !(y is a person & y entered) ⇒ x = y].

The first conjunct is true since both 'a is a person' and 'a entered' are determinately true. The second conjunct is true because it is a universally quantified conditional with all true instances. Instantiating both variables with a validates both antecedent and consequent. Instantiating either variable with b or with anything determinately different from *a* makes it true since this produces a false antecedent (because only *a* is *determinately* a person that entered).

Does the definite description denote *b* as well? No, it does not. It determinately does not denote *b* because this is false:

!(*b* is a person & *b* entered) & ∀*x*∀*y*[!(!(*x* is a person & *x* entered) & !(*y* is a person & *y* entered) ⇒ *x* = *y*].

It is false because the first conjunct is false; this is because of the initial '!' which requires that both of the component conjuncts be true, and '*b* entered' lacks truth-value. So the definite description determinately does not denote *b*. It is easy to see that it denotes nothing else (except *a*) too, for the same reason. So here is a definite description that determinately denotes *a* and that does not indeterminately denote anything at all. So there is such a thing as determinate denotation unaffected by indeterminate denotation even when the term determinately denotes a thing that is indeterminately identical to something.

So indeterminate denotation is not forced on us by every term denoting a thing that is indeterminately identical with something. But there *is* indeterminate denotation as well.

9.3.2 Determinate denotation of a with indeterminate denotation of b

On the unadorned reading, 'the person who entered' determinately denotes *a* but *also* indeterminately denotes *b*, just as the critics say. Consider first *a*. The truth-value status of:

'ιx[*x* is a person & *x* entered]' denotes *a*

is the same as the truth-value status of:

[*a* is a person & *a* entered] & ∀*x*∀*y*[*x* is a person & *x* entered & *y* is a person & *y* entered ⇒ *x* = *y*].

The first conjunct of this is true, so consider the second. This is a universal claim, and it requires all of its instances to be true for it to be true. Clearly it is true if we instantiate the same thing for both

variables, since this makes the consequent true. Likewise it is true
for any instantiation other than a or b, since all such instances make
the antecedent false. The remaining option is to instantiate a for
one variable and b for the other; this makes the conditional true
since it makes both antecedent and consequent indeterminate, and
the '$\Rightarrow$' connective is true in such a case. (So this is an instance in
which our formulation of condition [D] may be controversial; see
below.) Thus the definite description determinately denotes a.

The description indeterminately denotes b. This is because this
is indeterminate in truth-value:

[b is a person & b entered] & $\forall x \forall y[x$ is a person & x entered
& y is a person & y entered $\Rightarrow x = y]$.

The first conjunct is indeterminate because it is indeterminate
whether b entered. The second is true as argued above. So the
whole is without truth-value; it is indeterminate whether the definite description denotes b.

It is easy to show that the definite description determinately does
not denote anything other than a or b. So the definite description
determinately denotes a, indeterminately denotes b, and denotes
nothing else.

This conclusion is dependent on a particular reading of condition [D], one that employs our '$\Rightarrow$' connective to symbolize 'nothing
other than z is ϕ'. Clearly, this might be symbolized differently; for
example, it could be symbolized with the material conditional
(using '$\phi \supset \psi$' for '$\neg \phi \vee \psi$'):

[a is a person & a entered] & $\forall x \forall y[x$ is a person & x entered
& y is a person & y entered $\supset x = y]$.

If this is used in condition [D] then it alters the judgement of how
the definite description with the unadorned reading denotes a. It
now denotes a indeterminately instead of determinately, because
when the second conjunct is instantiated so as to yield a conditional
whose antecedent and consequent are both indeterminate, the
whole material conditional lacks truth-value. With this change
it turns out that the definite description indeterminately denotes
both a and b. (This change has no effect on the determinacy
reading, where the definite description is '$\iota x![x$ is a person & x
entered]'.)

There thus appear to be three reasonable ways to interpret the English phrase 'the person who entered the room'. On one interpretation it determinately denotes *a* and does not denote anything indeterminately. On a second interpretation it determinately denotes *a* and indeterminately denotes *b*. On a third interpretation it indeterminately denotes both *a* and *b*.

9.4 SUMMARY OF THE VIEW BEING DEFENDED

We have seen that there are clear cases in which a definite description determinately denotes an object x and determinately does not denote an object y even though it is indeterminate whether x is y. There are also cases in which indeterminacy of identity leads to indeterminacy of what is denoted, perhaps—or perhaps not—even indeterminacy coupled with determinacy. This has been shown by considering definite descriptions; proper names are harder to draw clear conclusions about, but I see no reason why they cannot do what the definite descriptions do. (None of the examples I considered had to do with scope distinctions or with modalities, which are the two main areas in which names and descriptions are alleged to behave essentially differently.)

I take this to vindicate my own policy in *formulating* the theory of indeterminate identity. I have presumed that each of the singular terms in the theory I formulate determinately denotes something, and does not indeterminately denote anything. I have assumed this so that I could present the metaphysical issues without becoming entangled in issues of *semantic* indeterminacy. Since it *is* possible for singular terms to behave in this way, I am justified in presuming that mine do. I will continue with this policy.

It would be fascinating to pursue a study of the logic and semantics of indeterminate denotation, expanding the language introduced in Chapter 2 to include singular terms that do not denote determinately. However, this would be an exercise in semantics or logic that is distinct from the metaphysical issues addressed in this book. Our issues are difficult enough already without these additional complications. For this reason, I will not introduce indeter-

10

Alternatives to Indeterminate Identity

Perhaps the most popular view about indeterminacy of identity is that it is an illusion generated by inexactness in our language, or in the system of concepts embodied in our language. The world appears indeterminate because our linguistic/conceptual apparatus does not yield determinate judgements, but the lack of determinacy lies in the apparatus itself, not in the world it purports to articulate. The point of this chapter is to investigate such ideas.

Proposals of this sort are often stated, and even more often endorsed, but they are rarely implemented in any detail. In my experience, they sound more plausible in the abstract than in the concrete. It is a central theme of our heritage of work in twentieth-century analytic philosophy that questions apparently about reality are to be reconstrued as questions about the language with which we describe such reality, and so a proposal to do that has great instinctive appeal. But in any given case, such a proposal is still merely a hypothesis, not a given fact, and it deserves to be examined like any other hypothesis. That is the point of this chapter.

It takes little reflection to see that some work needs to be done in order to have a view worth examining. There needs to be a positive doctrine spelled out about how our language works, and then about how it applies to the problematic situations. Further, it needs to either account for the (extended) data with which we begin, or show us how those data are wrong. For the latter purpose, it can't just be an announcement that the opinions with which we begin are naïve and inherently untrustworthy. The opinions with which we begin are our own; they are the principles upon which we base all our decisions, and if we are to reject some of them it must be on the basis of others of them, not on the basis of a general charge of naïvety. But then the work needs to be done to show which are which.

The theme of this chapter will be that theories that account for minate denotation into the official language of the theory, and I will not speak of it any more.

There remains the question of how to interpret data that is formulated in natural language. When we report on puzzling cases, we use wordings that come naturally to us. And when we consider that some statements lack truth-value, we may do so pre-theoretically, without being certain about why. So in considering the "data" I may not be certain that the singular terms used in its formulation uniquely refer. I do think that it is justifiable to assume this prima facie, at least if there is no reason to believe otherwise, and this is the policy I have followed so far. In the next chapter, I consider some challenges to this policy.

the traditional identity puzzles in terms of the nature of language, or of concepts, are not compelling in their present forms. Of course, there are identity statements that lack truth-value because of the nature of language, but the identities in the traditional puzzle cases are not of this sort. I will not attempt to prove that one could not give a plausible account of this sort, because I cannot. My goal is instead to establish the present absence of settled accounts of this kind. Such accounts should be developed further in the face of criticisms raised here, but it is appropriate that such development be undertaken by those who believe in them. I will not try to carry this out myself.

The available pieces of language that need clarifying are singular terms, the identity predicate itself, and general terms with which the identity puzzles are stated. I consider them in that order. In each case we need to see how it is that our use of language can account for the data that lead to the identity puzzles, and how understanding that language dissolves the puzzles while preserving the data that lead to them.

10.1 CLARIFYING DENOTATION WITH SUPERVALUATIONS

A view that seems quite natural to many writers supposes that indeterminacy of identity is an illusion fostered by the fact that one or both of the singular terms composing the identity statement has more than one potential referent. There is at least one thing that is a potential referent of both the terms in common, and at least one that is a potential referent of one term but not of the other. Since at least one singular term lacks a unique referent, the identity statement itself is essentially ambiguous, and it has no unique reading which could yield a single truth-value. The statements that articulate the data are affected in this way too, because of the lack of unique reference of their terms, but if they are given supervaluational readings, they come out true. They come out true because they are true no matter how the references of the terms are clarified. This is not so for the identity statement; some valuations (some ways of singling out unique referents for the terms from among their multiple potential referents) make it true and some make it false, and so it lacks supervaluational truth-value. Thus we have a truth-value gap for an identity statement, but without any indeterminacy of identity in the world; the truth-value gap is simply a consequence of semantic variation in the potential reference of the terms.

Here is an illustration of how this might work in a transparent case. Suppose that Old Ivy Lodge, which is on Main Street, and Structuralist Manor, which is around the corner on Cedar Avenue, have been incorporated into a much larger structure, PostModern Hulk, which occupies the corner of Main and Cedar. But tradition is strong, and the old designations are still in use. Suppose that Smith has an office in Old Ivy Lodge (and therefore in PostModern Hulk) and Jones has an office in Structuralist Manor (and thus in PostModern Hulk). We are naturally inclined to assent to the claim that the building in which Smith has her office is on Main Street, and to the claim that the building in which Jones has his office is on Cedar Avenue, but it seems that there is no answer to the question whether the building in which Smith has her office is the building in which Jones has his office.

The supervaluation approach to singular terms accounts for these judgements as follows. Let 'S' abbreviate 'the building in which Smith has her office' and 'J' abbreviate 'the building in which Jones has his office'. Then both 'S' and 'J' have multiple potential referents; the former potentially refers both to Old Ivy Lodge and to PostModern Hulk, and the latter potentially refers both to Structuralist Manor and to PostModern Hulk. We treat the statement 'S is on Main Street' as true because it is supervaluationally true. It is supervaluationally true because there are two valuations, one for each potential referent of 'S', and both make the statement true. For parallel reasons, 'J is on Cedar Avenue' is supervaluationally true. But 'S is J' lacks supervaluational truth-value, because there are four valuations for it, corresponding to the various combinations of the potential referents of the terms; three of these are false and one is true, so there is no consensus among them, and there is no supervaluational truth-value.

This seems to me to be a nice analysis of the situation,[1] but this pattern of analysis does not necessarily carry over neatly to the

---

[1] Nice, but not compelling. I prefer to see the statements as all contextually ambiguous. The fact that certain of them come out true no matter how the ambiguity is analysed explains why we may not bother to raise the issue of ambiguity in a practical situation, not why the sentence *has* a definite truth-value.

identity puzzles. Let us consider one of them: the case of me and my body. A diagnosis of this case would go as follows: both 'this person' and 'this body' have multiple potential referents. They share a potential referent; call this '*a*'. There is also a potential referent of 'this person' which is not a potential referent of 'this body'; call it '*p*'. And there is a potential referent of 'this body' which is not a potential referent of 'this person'; call it '*b*'. In evaluating the identity statement 'this person = this body' some classical valuations assign *a* to both terms, yielding a classical valuation that is true, and some assign different things to the terms (e.g. one valuation assigns *p* to 'this person' and *a* or *b* to 'this body'), yielding a classical valuation that is false. As a result, the identity statement is assessed as supertruthvalueless. Further, any allowable classical valuation to both 'person' and 'this person' makes the former true of the latter, so 'This person is a person' is supertrue; likewise for 'This body is a body'. But some allowable classical valuations to both 'this person' and 'this body' assign *a* to 'this person' and a set containing both *a* and *b* to 'body' (making 'This person is a body' true), whereas some other allowable valuations do not assign either *a* or *p* to the extension of 'body'; so 'This person is a body' is supertruthvalueless, and likewise for 'This body is a person'. As a result, one gets the required extended data.

This procedure is formally adequate.[2] My worry about it is not

---

[2] In a draft MS I argued—mistakenly—that there is a formal difficulty with this solution; I am indebted to a referee for OUP for pointing this out. The mistaken objection goes as follows:

> Since 'This person is a person' must come out supertrue, every potential referent of 'this person' must be in the extension of 'person', including entity *a*. For a parallel reason, *a* must also be in the extension of 'body'. It then follows that some entity, namely, *a*, is in the extension of both 'person' and 'body', and so at least some bodies are determinately persons.

The mistake is to speak of "*the* extension of 'person'" as if this is a fixed thing. Instead, the predicate 'person' has multiple potential extensions, and which one is selected for a valuation can be made to depend on which potential referent is selected for 'this person'. (Cf. Fine (1975) on penumbral connections.) So whenever there is an assignment to the pair 'person' and 'this person', the thing assigned to the latter can be in the extension assigned to the former. But this permits an assignment of *p* to 'this person' together with an assignment of an extension to 'person' which includes *p* but excludes *a*. Because of such assignments it will not be supertrue that *a* is a person.

(I believe that there are difficulties in explaining *how* these assignments to multiple pieces of language are jointly allowable; these reservations are implicit in the discussion in §§10.4–7.)

logical, but rather metaphysical. The procedure requires me to be uncertain as to which of two things I refer to with 'this person' (that is, with 'me') and equally uncertain as to which of two things I refer to with 'this body'. The solution in fact requires (at least) three entities to be the potential referents of the two singular terms. But I can locate no such entities. I don't believe that there are any such entities. When I consider what the world is actually like, I can find at most two entities that are relevant to the puzzle: me and my body. Perhaps these are not two entities, but only one; that is at issue. But there certainly are not three candidates that I am choosing among. At least, that is what I think. That is, I believe that this situation is not at all like the building case above. There, I am certain that there are multiple buildings in question, some of them parts of others. I believe that there are at least three of them, and that there is at least some kind of uncertainty about which of them are denoted by phrases like 'the building in which Smith has her office'. But when I consider the case of myself and my body, I am not able to convince myself that there are here three distinct entities I am choosing among.

Others, of course, will disagree. Anyone who accepts an old and once well-established view of the nature of persons would disagree. On that view, there are three things to consider: two substances and a composite of the two. One substance, the analogue of p above, is my soul; the other substance, the analogue of b above is that material object typically called (perhaps unclearly) my body. In addition to these two substances, there is their combination, which corresponds to a above. The notion of a person is unclear between whether it applies to souls or to combinations of souls with bodies, and the notion of a human body is unclear between whether it refers merely to the material substance or to the combination, to the body-informed-by-a-soul. On such a view, the supervaluational account works perfectly. And it is easy to find more plausible, modern views that also have the same structure. For example: p is a person considered in abstraction from the matter that contingently makes it up, b is that mereological (three-dimensional) sum of matter that "constitutes" the person, and a is the constituted person. My problem is that I do not believe in such theories. I see at most two things that are at all relevant to the puzzle—me and my body—and I am unsure whether they are the same or not. I just don't see anything else. Rather, I see plenty of other things, such as a certain set of molecules, but I am convinced that these other things are neither me nor my body, *and the problem of the identity of me and my body remains.*

I don't expect all others to share this perspective. It remains possible for some others to patiently explain to me that there really are three or more entities relevant to the issue, and that I am just not sufficiently aware of the way in which the semantics of my own language works. I suspect, however, that there are many such explanations, and although they will all show that I am wrong, they are not likely to agree with one another. This, then, is the weakness I see in holding that the identity puzzles are to be dissolved by an application of the technique of supervaluations; there is not at present any particular application that will command general assent.

10.2 CLARIFYING THE IDENTITY PREDICATE

I am not aware of any viable proposals for solutions to the identity puzzles that result from clarifying the identity predicate itself. However, there is an idea in Lewis (1993) that one might try to tailor for this purpose. Lewis does not propose it for the purpose of solving the identity puzzles, so this is entirely my own invention, and it is probably a straw man. But it caught my interest, and so I describe it here.

Lewis explores the case of the cat and the p-cats. He has a supervaluational solution, which will be discussed later; he also has a non-supervaluational solution, which I discuss here. Recall that none of the p-cats is in exactly the same place as any other, for each determinately differs from another with respect to the having of some part. They all mostly overlap, but not quite. Lewis will not acknowledge the existence of a cat which is indeterminately identical with each p-cat, for he does not believe in indeterminate identity, nor will he acknowledge a cat without determinate location. His solution is to suppose that the p-cats are all that there are, and that we need to account for talk of the cat in terms of talk of the p-cats. The difficulty comes when we ask which of these entities is a cat. Lewis suggests that each p-cat is literally a cat:

The constituters are cat-like in size, shape, weight, inner structure, and motion. They vibrate and set the air in motion—in short, they purr (especially when you pat them). Any way a cat can be at a moment, cat-constituters also can be; anything a cat can do at a moment, cat-constituters also can do. They are all too cat-like not to be cats.[3] (1993: 26)

Since each p-cat is determinately distinct from each of the others, there turn out to be millions of distinct things on the table, each of which is a cat. This validates the statement 'There are millions of cats on the table', and falsifies 'There is exactly one cat on the table.' Lewis concludes that this is correct, and that he literally has many pets.

It is easy to defuse certain objections to this view. For example, the many cats are not difficult to feed, because you feed them all at once. The difficulty is not a practical one, but a theoretical one. The theory yields hosts of consequences that contradict conventional wisdom; in each case the conclusion is that conventional wisdom is wrong, but harmlessly so. The many cats are, in a sense, as cheap to feed as a single cat, even though the reasons that led us to posit many cats also leads us to posit many bowls of food. So they cost a great deal to feed, but that is no worry since you pay with a single ten-dollar bill. Actually, the bill itself is multiple, so you indeed pay a great deal of money, but this is money you already possess. This does not make you wealthy, since you also have such high expenses. And so on.

Does this mean rejecting the data? In a sense yes, and in a sense no. Lewis explains that although there are many cats, it is *almost* the case that there is only one, and you *almost* feed them only one bowl of food, from a bag that *almost* costs a moderate amount of money, etc. Thus our initial data are incorrect, but are *almost* correct. The reason it is almost correct, Lewis suggests, is that when we count cats, we do not do so using identity, we do so using spatial coincidence, and the cats all *almost* coincide. That is, when we say that there is exactly one cat on the table we do not mean:

A cat is on the table, and any cats x and y on the table are such that $x = y$.

---

[3] Lewis calls the p-cats "constituters" in this quote since he is here arguing against the theory which says that there is one cat which the p-cats all constitute.

We mean:

> A cat is on the table, and any cats x and y on the table are such that x coincides with y.

In everyday talk about cats the 'coincides' becomes 'almost coincides', and that is good enough for practical purposes. The identity puzzle about the cat is thus explained as a confusion about senses of 'exactly one'. If we use true identity in counting cats, we conclude, paradoxically, that there are many cats on the table. But when we make ordinary everyday judgements about how many things there are, we do not mean this. Instead, we mean something that is analysable in terms not of identity but of coincidence, and in this sense there is exactly one cat on the table. Well, not *exactly* exactly one, but *almost* exactly one.

Before examining this theory we should distinguish two versions of it. We have explained p-cats in terms of their present near-coincidence with the cat, but we have not discussed their histories. There are broad p-cats and narrow p-cats. A narrow p-cat is a thing with determinate parts that almost coincides with the cat for its entire existence; a broad p-cat may, but need not, do this; a broad p-cat almost coincides with the cat right now, but may diverge widely from it in the past or the future. So there is a version of the account in which we construe p-cats narrowly, and one in which we construe them broadly, and these accounts differ substantially. Lewis intends the broad construal. The quote above continues as follows:

They are all too cat-like not to be cats. Indeed, they may have had unfeline pasts and futures, but that doesn't show that they are never cats; it only shows that they do not remain cats for very long. (1993: 26)

This version of the theory is a reformist view that is not well suited for explaining the apparent data as being almost correct. For there are hosts of things that we say about cats that are not even almost true if cats are p-cats in the broad sense. Cats tend to have a lifetime of over ten years, they habitually return if you feed them, they grow larger for much of their life, etc. None of these generalizations is even almost true of most broad p-cats. Further, not only do I think that there is exactly one cat on the table; I think that there is exactly one cat on the table that I got at the pound, but although the former is almost true, the latter is not.[4] So the broad construal of p-cat, coupled with the claim that p-cats *are* (now) cats, is straightforwardly inconsistent with many of our common beliefs. (One could imagine it being made consistent by a massive project of reinterpreting our ordinary sentences. One way to do this might be as follows. We call something a *maximal cat* if it is a cat throughout its existence and if it does not ever almost coincide with something that is also a cat throughout its existence and exists longer. Then 'Cats usually live over ten years' might be interpreted as 'Maximal cats almost always live over ten years, and each cat, whenever it is a cat, almost coincides with a maximal cat.' But maximal cats are then our narrow p-cats, and this is really a theory of narrow p-cats, with the broad ones thrown in as epicycles.)

In order to return to the task of this chapter—which is to explain the data, not to reform them—I focus on the version of the theory that appeals to narrow p-cats.

I will not take issue with whether an almost-right solution is good enough to be a solution; *if* we have a solution that explains how the data in question is almost right, that is pretty good—it is almost good enough, and perhaps fully good enough. I have two other worries about this solution. The first is that it is not almost correct as it stands; the second is that even if it is almost correct, it does not generalize to the other identity puzzles.

The reason the solution is problematic as it stands is that it supplies a way to construe the data that almost validates that data, without giving us any reason not to also construe the data in equally good ways, where it does not do this. Suppose that we sometimes interpret claims about how many things there are by substituting coincidence for identity. This does not mean that we always do this. In some cases, we cannot, for we make plenty of assertions about how many things there are where spatial coincidence is not applicable: "There are two prime numbers between 3 and 9", "Three theorems were formulated by McGuillicutty", "Four electronic payments failed to reach the bank". When coincidence and identity coincide, we can also use coincidence. But when it is absolutely clear and uncontroversial that near-coincidence diverges from actual coincidence, in a situation in which actual coincidence coin-

---

[4] This sort of fact will raise difficulties for any account of definite descriptions based on this view.

cides with identity, identity rules, or it is at the very least a natural option. This is easy enough to illustrate by focusing on the p-cats themselves, setting aside the question of whether they are cats. How many p-cats are there on the table? Presumably, millions, and there is no sense at all in which there is exactly one p-cat; that claim is not in any sense almost true, even though the p-cats almost coincide. If p-cats are under discussion, we count them using real identity, and this is the only available interpretation. But the p-cats *are* cats, and the cats *are* p-cats; there is no difference at all between cats and p-cats on this view. So there are exactly as many cats as p-cats. So there can be no difference in the answer to the question "how many are there?".

This is perhaps a bit too facile as a refutation. The response will be, of course, that there can be a difference in the answer, if the interpretation of the question is sensitive to the vocabulary used in it. Perhaps 'cat' suggests an ordinary context in which we count with near-coincidence, and 'p-cat' suggests a technical context in which we count with identity. Then there are two ways to construe the question, and Lewis has made the natural choice.

This *is* true about popular usage in some related cases. For example, in popular usage, there may be "nothing" in a room, when we know there is air, dust, wallpaper, and so on. But we can clarify our usage, making clear for example whether we are going to count air molecules as things, or only larger solid entities, and when we do this there are two interpretations of the question, with two different answers. We can do the same for the question about cats, making clear whether by 'exactly one' we mean *one that doesn't differ much from the others* or *one, and there are no others*. When I do this, I don't get any interpretation of the question that yields a plausible answer that there are actually millions of cats on the table. But this is not a point amenable to argument, since this is the point at which we will disagree about the data. Lewis has made it clear that once the question is clarified, he believes that there are literally many p-cats on the table, and since each p-cat is too cat-like not to be a cat, it is only in a loose and popular sense that there is only one cat there. I think that there is only one cat no matter how strict we are in our wording.

A distinct question is whether this solution, if it is a solution, generalizes to other identity puzzles. Recall that Lewis does not say that it does, and I think it does not. Consider the case of the disrupted person. The supervaluational approach to the person case is similar to the cat case, in that we are driven to suppose that there are several persons in the same place at the same time. But in the many-person case, the persons are not in *almost* the same place; they are in *exactly* the same place. We find this problematic since we are forced to say there are many with no differences at all among them. So what if we replace the multiple persons in exactly the same place by multiple p-persons in almost the same place? That solves the problem of distinguishing them, since they all occupy slightly different places. But distinguishing the p-persons will not solve the puzzle. We would have a solution to the puzzle if some p-persons persisted through the change and some did not. But there is no reason to expect the disruption to cleave along the lines that distinguish p-persons. For example, if the disruption consists of a partial brain transplant, then all of the p-brain portions get transplanted or none does. It is not that some do and some do not. (Or, if that is what happens, it is unrelated to the issue of identity.) So an appeal to p-persons does not solve this problem, nor any of the other paradigm puzzles that we have discussed.[5] We need some different approach.

10.3 INDEFINITE CONCEPTS

It is natural to hold that the concepts expressed by our words are imprecise. Since the concepts associated with our words determine the propositions that get expressed, and since the truth of these propositions determines the truth of the sentences that express them, if the concepts are imprecise, this may produce propositions with no truth-value. Perhaps this is what is to blame for identity puzzles with no answers. A solution to the puzzles might be to consider how we imagine replacing our imprecise concepts by more precise ones.

---

[5] One might try to create an analogue to the cat case by considering the p-persons at time t to be the temporal parts of the person that exist at t. A supervaluational reading then tells you that there is one person here now, and there was one person there then, but there is no answer to the question whether the person who is here now is the person who was there then. However, this result follows even if there is no disruption at all; thus there would be no answer to the question of whether *anyone* now is the person born previously at a given time and place.

Of course, more needs to be said than this. Holding that our concepts are imprecise does not, by itself, explain why they nonetheless allow us to express a great deal of exact information. The ship
puzzles arise not because we have no idea how many ships there
were originally, and finally, but because we think there was originally one and finally two. Somehow our concepts are good enough
for determinate judgements about these matters. So what is needed
is an explanation of how imprecise concepts sometimes do, and
sometimes do not, yield determinate judgements, and how some
appeal to precise concepts might shed light on this.

Here is one explanation. Our concept, say, of *person* is imprecise.
Ideally, it would be replaced by a more refined concept. But that
takes time, effort, and work, and we have other priorities. So we
use the word 'person' without refining the concept associated with
it, but with the understanding that there are indeed ways to refine
it, and we know a fair amount about what would result. In ordinary
everyday situations we don't bother to consider these refinements,
because there is no particular way to refine the concept that is
importantly different from any other way. This is because, for the
purpose of the judgement at hand, any refinement would produce
the same result. For example, when we say that one ship left port,
we know that there are many ways to refine the notion of a *ship*,
and that *any* way of doing this will validate the claim that one *ship**
left port, where '*ship**' expresses the resulting refinement of the
unrefined concept of *ship*. We don't bother refining on the spot
because it wouldn't make any difference to the correctness of the
claim at issue. The identity puzzles are unusual cases in which it
does make a difference how we refine things. If we refine *ship* in
one way, it is correct to conclude that the original $ship_1$ is identical
with the $ship_1$ with new parts, where '$ship_1$' expresses one particular refined version of the concept *ship*, and if we refine in some
other way, it is correct to conclude that the original $ship_2$ is identical with the $ship_2$ with new parts. Refining yet a third way lets us
conclude that the original $ship_3$ ceased to exist, and was replaced
with two new $ship_3$'s. Since how we refine makes a difference to the
correctness of the identity judgement, there is no unique answer to
the original (unrefined) question.

This proposal is an application of supervaluations. A *valuation* of
a general term results from its coming to express a refined version
of the concept that it actually expresses. (If the term occurs twice,

we must be sure that the same valuation is used for each occurrence.) Then a judgement is intuitively true (and, so, part of our extended data) if and only if it is supervaluationally true on this account. In the ship case, the claim that exactly one ship left port is supervaluationally true, since it is true no matter how the concept *ship* is refined; likewise the claim that exactly two ships docked. But any of the problematic identity judgements lack supervaluational truth-value, since they come out true on some valuations (some refinements) and false on others.

In §10.1, I argued that no supervaluational assessment will solve the problem of me and my body. However, the person/body puzzle is a special one, and this may be too narrow a point to reject supervaluational solutions in general. So it is worth looking more closely at an intuitively motivated theory of this sort. An example of this approach is proposed in Stalnaker (1988). Stalnaker considers a puzzle about restaurants that is isomorphic (with respect to identities) with the ship puzzle. A restaurant is started called 'Bookbinders'. At some later date, there are two rival restaurants with almost the same name, each claiming to be the original Bookbinders, and with a history posited that makes each identity claim as plausible as the other. Stalnaker (1988: 353) supposes that "the concept of restaurant is indeterminate in that it is indeterminate what counts as the same restaurant at different times." On some ways of arbitrarily refining our concept, the original "restaurant" will become one later "restaurant", on other ways it will become the other, and on yet others it will cease to exist, to be succeeded by two new "restaurants". This creates indeterminacy in the term 'the original restaurant', but no indeterminacy in the world.

For this solution to be plausible it is important to emphasize that we do not ordinarily think of ourselves as seeking a common content of multiple precisifications of our imprecise concepts. Rather, we use our imprecise concepts as they stand. The use of supervaluations of precise versions is an analysis of how we *would* rationalize our use of the imprecise concepts, if such rationalization were called for. We would rationalize our use of the imprecise concepts by granting that we are using imprecise concepts, and granting that we are using them in situations in which it is not relevant to our present concerns how to make them more precise— it is not relevant because it doesn't matter how this is done, for the same answer would result no matter how we do it consistent with our intentions. What makes the identity puzzles special is that they are cases in which identity statements can be made for which it *does* matter how we make our concepts more precise. And the instinctive recognition that making them precise in different ways would yield divergent answers is what underlies our bewilderment when confronting them.

That is the view. But why should we think that it works? How can we be sure, for example, that it is true on any refinement that exactly one ship left port? There is nothing about the view as it is sketched to guarantee this. The theory must be fleshed out so as to guarantee it. The theory needs to specify *how* to refine concepts, perhaps something like this: Whenever we refine our sortal terms, we do so in such a way that if a sortal term is true of extended spatio-temporal objects, then nothing counts as a refinement of the concept that it expresses unless the refined concept is never true of two spatially coincident things in normal circumstances. (The 'in normal circumstances' is there to avoid, for example, science-fiction cases in which techniques have been developed to let objects pass through one another, so that two of them might momentarily coincide.) If it does this, then any refinement of the concept *ship* will let you stand at a dock and know that there is exactly one *refined-ship* in front of you no matter how you refine *ship*.

However, this proposal, all by itself, is not adequate. This is because so few guidelines are given for refining our concepts. In any particular case, this seems outright impossible to do.[6] To refine the notion of *ship* we need to explain how to tell if there is a ship present (or several ships present) in a given situation, and we need to explain how to tell for any such refinement whether any given refined-ship *a* is identical with any refined-ship *b*. If this is not accomplished, there remains a set of identity puzzles for refined-ships that are not solved by the technique. But concept refinement needs to be implemented with the resources at our disposal. Since the conceptual resources at our disposal consist entirely of unrefined concepts, it is difficult to see how to go about this task. It is

---

[6] Criticism of this sort appears in Woodruff and Parsons (1997) and Parsons (forthcoming) in somewhat primitive form. (Because of the "fest-conference" in which it originated, the tone of writing in the latter was meant to be "festive"; no disrespect was meant to the views criticized there.)

conceivable, but unlikely, that combinations of imprecise concepts can in all cases yield precise ones. It is even more difficult to have confidence that the end result will yield the hoped-for patterns needed to solve the identity puzzles.

There is, however, an answer to this challenge. Recall that the view is not that we already grasp and use a multiplicity of refined concepts when we speak; we only need to be confident that our concepts *could* be refined on demand. But even this is perhaps not necessary. The view could be that we do not ever have to *be able* to produce the refined concepts, we just speak *as if* we are expressing precise concepts; we do this in the knowledge that all *attainable* concepts are imprecise, but we have in mind, at least vaguely, ways they might be made *more* precise, and we suppose that there exist concepts which are *precise enough*, even though they are perhaps in principle ungraspable by us. We have in mind *ideals* of completely precise concepts. When we use a word, it is to be taken *as if* it were expressing a precise concept, one which is a refinement of the imprecise one we actually express. Generally, it won't matter which refinement of our imprecise concept we use, because in everyday matters they all will validate what we are saying. But for applications far removed from present-day concerns, it may matter. The identity puzzles are of this sort, which is why they lack answers.

But, again, why assume that this will work as advertised? If we consider the most obvious ways of refining our concepts, it will not work at all. Suppose that the refined concepts work like this. Instead of the imprecise notion of *ship* wherein it is often unclear whether a ship survives replacement of its parts, or whether it survives disassembly and reassembly, we have various refined notions of *ship*. Some of these permit their denotata to have many of their parts replaced and go on existing, and some of them rule that if their denotata lose parts, they thereby cease to exist, even if the parts are replaced. Likewise for disassembly and reassembly. Some refined notions of *ship* rule that their denotata come into existence upon assembly, regardless of whether the parts were previously parts of a refined-ship before being separated. And so on. These various combinations of criteria for identity through time are embodied in various refined notions of *ship*, the only requirement being that none of them permits any indeterminacy in the question of whether one of its denotata exists at a time and place that a ship-like thing exists, or in whether one of its denotata existing at one time and place is identical with one of its denotata existing at some other time and place. However, if *these* are what refinements are like, then the proposal is in trouble. For although it produces the correct answer in the ship-puzzle case, it produces wrong answers in apparently non-problematic cases. It produces indeterminacy where we do not want it. Consider Queen X's ship that is buried with her under her pyramid; this was the royal barge on which she held court during her reign. When she died it was transported to her burial chamber, where it lies available for her afterlife journey. We would like to say that she held court on exactly one ship during her reign, and that one ship is buried with her, and that the ship on which she held court *is* the ship that is buried with her. But, unfortunately, they had to take it apart to get it into the burial chamber, where they reassembled it. And so the theory under consideration agrees that she held court on one ship, and it agrees that one ship is buried with her, but it holds that it is indeterminate whether the ship that is buried with her is the ship on which she held court. This is because on some refinements of the notion of *ship* the ship on which she held court was transported to the burial chamber (by disassembly and reassembly), and on other refinements it ceased to exist upon disassembly and a new ship was assembled from its parts. And so by the supervaluational approach, there is no truth-value for the claim that the ship on which she held court is the ship buried with her. But this is just plain wrong. And the wrongness extends to a host of everyday cases. If I had to disassemble my desk to get it into my study when I moved, there is now exactly one desk in my study, but the proposal says that there is no truth-value for the claim that the desk in my study was originally purchased at a thrift shop—for this is true on some refinements of the concept of *desk* but not on others. So this natural implementation of the refined-concept view yields the wrong answers in cases in which identity puzzles should not arise.

Obviously, we are working with too crude a notion of concept refinement. We need to refine our notion of *refinement*. It was apparently a mistake to suggest that there is a refined notion of *ship* on which a ship survives disassembly and reassembly, and one on which it does not. This is an overly simplistic proposal for what a refined concept should be. Instead, we need to say that there is a refinement of *ship* on which a ship survives disassembly and reassembly *when another ship continuous with and resembling the original gets new parts*, and another on which a ship ceases to exist upon disassembly *when another one continuous with it and resembling it gets new parts*. Or something like this. This appears to be an *ad hoc* move, and it is not at all clear how to generalize it. But we must be careful not to be too hasty with charges of *ad hocness* if the resulting account gets the answers right. The *ad hocness* of an account that gets the right answers might be the outer appearance of a natural account that we have not yet been able to articulate. So let us proceed with this idea: that our everyday judgements are all to be assessed in terms of supervaluational readings, where the extended valuations are produced by refining our concepts in *whatever* way it takes to get the desired answers. This may make the theory too abstract to evaluate, but we won't know if we don't try.

Here is a second objection. It applies to all of the puzzles, but I will discuss it in application to the refinements of the sortal notion of a person. It goes as follows:

No matter how the notion of a *person* is refined, a person had better be something that thinks, feels, plans, and makes commitments to other people—otherwise the proposal will end up attributing lack of truth-value to truisms such as that (normal) people think, feel, plan, and make commitments. Now consider the judgement in the disruption case:

The person who entered is the person who left.

This needs to turn out to lack truth-value. On the supervaluational approach, this can happen only if the refinements in the concept of *person* result in multiple potential referents for 'the person who entered' and/or 'the person who left'. So for this to be a solution, there need to be divergent refinements of *person* such that 'the person who entered' ends up with divergent potential referents, at least one of which left, and at least one of which did not. Now let us call any object that is truly characterized by some refinement of the concept of *person* a "refined-person".[7] Then there were two refined-people in the same place at the same time before entering. So there were two thinking, feeling, beings there at the same time.

---

[7] This is a technical notion. A refined-person is not a person who is refined. An entity x is a refined-person if and only if there is a refinement of the concept of *person* such that, under that refinement, a is a person.

But this is just as objectionable as the traditional solution to the puzzle which held that there were two ordinary persons in the same place at the same time. How can I reassure my wife by telling her she is the only person I love, if she knows that I love many refined-persons, that is, many female, thinking, feeling beings, and that I feel committed to each of them? (Of course, I speak loosely of "my wife", since that is unrefined talk, but I do have a *refined*-wife; in fact, I may have several of them. What will *they* think?) The point is that the solution at hand demands an expanded ontology, and one expanded with things that give rise to the original puzzle all over again. The identity puzzles all reappear with 'person' replaced by 'thing that thinks, loves, plans, owes money on a mortgage, etc.'. We are thus in danger of having a version of the traditional "many persons in the same place" solution, with a slight change of vocabulary (with 'person' replaced by an elaborate explanation of what all refined-persons have in common).

There is a natural way to escape that objection.[8] The proposal under discussion says that we need to consider refining our concepts, but we have really only considered refining our sortal concepts. Since the difficulties above involve reconstructing identity puzzles with non-sortal concepts (*thinking being*, instead of *person*), one obvious option is to consider refining these as well. At first glance, this merely enhances the difficulty. Consider the person standing in that doorway, and consider the female being standing in that doorway. We would like to say that the female being standing in the doorway *is* the person standing in the doorway. But now we appear to have (at least) two different unrefined concepts to work with: *female* and *person*. If each of them resolves into many refined concepts, we get twice-many combinations of them. Some such combinations may render true the statement:

the female being in the doorway = the person in the doorway

but many will not. That is, given that there are many different refined-persons standing in the doorway, corresponding to each of them will be many different refined-female beings. But most of them will not correspond. In general, if the person$_{14}$ is identical with

[8] I am indebted to Calvin Normore for helpful conversation regarding the material in the remainder of this chapter.

the female being$_{14}$ and distinct from the person$_{22}$, then one resolution will be:

the female being$_{14}$ in the doorway = the person$_{14}$ in the doorway

but another will be:

the female being$_{14}$ in the doorway = the person$_{22}$ in the doorway.

Since the first of these is true, the second is false, and the supervaluational reading with the refinements providing the valuations will lack truth-value. Thus the apparent data is not preserved.

There is, however, a way to try to get this to work out. It is sometimes speculated that any use of a non-sortal word as a noun in language presupposes some underlying sortal. So if you say 'red thing', you must have in mind some sortal concept to flesh out 'thing'. This is controversial, but it has some credence. So suppose that our uses of a word like 'female' are coordinated with a sortal concept, such as *person*. Then we just need to rule that in evaluating our utterances in terms of supervaluations, we must limit the valuations to the "coordinated" ones. For example, we need to suppose that 'the female being in the doorway' means 'the female *person* in the doorway'. Then we go back to just refining the sortals, as we did before, but we refine the implicit ones along with the explicit ones. If we do this, the underlying structure of our problem example is:

the female person in the doorway = the person in the doorway.

We also need to assume that a refined-person is female at a time if and only if every refined-person that coincides with it then is also female then. Now we can refine *person* any way we like; so long as we refine uniformly, the above statement will come out supervaluationally true. For although there are many refined-people in the doorway, on any given refinement there is only one. Likewise, if we also coordinate the refinements of 'think', 'feel', and so on, there is only one thinking thing in the doorway, and that thinking thing *is* the female there.

The catch lies in the constraint we need to impose on 'female' so as to make the account work. When do we impose a constraint of this sort, and how do we tell exactly which constraint to apply? I am not sure how to do this. The category analysis is still only a sketch of a solution. This becomes even clearer if we consider how entities of different categories are to interact. Consider Stalnaker's restaurant case, and imagine that I am a server in the original restaurant, before the problematic split. There are at least two refined-restaurants that employ me. There must be two refined-restaurants here in order for the identity claims to be indeterminate between the original restaurant and the later ones, and I must work for each of them, for otherwise 'I work for the restaurant on the corner of Main and Elm' will not be true. Now when I file my income taxes, I need to submit a W2 form for each of my employers. It thus appears that I must fill out (at least) two W2 forms. This is because each refined-restaurant does literally employ me, and they are literally distinct from one another. Coordinating categories does not reduce the number in this case since the category of *person* under which I fall is not coordinated with the category of *restaurant* under which they fall. So we conclude incorrectly that I need to fill out two W2 forms.

Or do I? Perhaps 'W2 form' needs refinement, and perhaps *it* is coordinated with the category of *restaurant*. Of course, there would not be a direct coordination of *W2 form* and *restaurant*, but there might be a coordination of *W2 form* with *employer*, and perhaps the category of *restaurant* is to be analysed as *employer that serves food*. Then I fill out one W2 form, because the requirement to fill out one per employer is fulfilled no matter how we refine both *W2 form* and *employer*, so long as we coordinate the refinements. However, it is not reasonable to analyse *restaurant* as a subcategory of *employer*, for there are other equally good categories under which it fits: *purchaser, sales-tax collector, retail establishment*, etc.

10.4 LEFT IN LIMBO . . .

Ideally, I would now be able to say that I have refuted the linguistic/semantic alternatives to the hypothesis that there is indeterminacy in the world. But clearly I have not; I have only raised problems for how to work out various versions of alternative views, without any solid conclusions in principle about how they might be altered and developed so as to take account of the problems. And so we are left in limbo. But I hope to have shown that there does not yet exist an alternative view about which we can be confident. And so the worldly indeterminacy of identity view is deserving of close consideration.

11

Sets and Properties with Indeterminate Identity

11.1 IDENTITY CONDITIONS FOR SETS

Sets, whatever else they are like, are the sorts of things that can be said to be identical to or distinct from one another. So they are subject to all of the logical principles involving identity discussed elsewhere in this work. But they are also subject to an additional principle. What is most distinctive about sets—which distinguishes them from other sorts of things—is that their identity is determined by their membership. This is meant in the strongest possible sense, in that:

> (i) if everything that is determinately a member of set A is determinately a member of set B, and vice versa, and everything that is determinately not a member of set A is determinately not a member of set B, and vice versa, then A is determinately identical with B;
> (ii) if something is determinately a member of set A but determinately not a member of set B, or vice versa, then A and B are determinately distinct;
> (iii) otherwise it is indeterminate whether set A is identical to set B.

This is a spelling out of a point that can be put more simply by saying that if A and B are sets, then the truth-value status of the claim that they are identical:

$$A = B$$

should be exactly the same as the truth-value status of the claim that they have exactly the same members:

$\forall x(x \in A \Leftrightarrow x \in B)$.

In terms of a single principle, this equivalence is true:

[Set Essence] $A = B \Leftrightarrow \forall x(x \in A \Leftrightarrow x \in B)$.

I assume that any non-bivalent theory of sets will adopt this as a basic axiom. A particular theory of sets will result by adding to [Set Essence] some principles that say which sets exist, usually by stating which conditions have sets corresponding to them.

11.2 DDIFF FOR SET MEMBERSHIP

Before considering which sets exist, we have another question to consider. This is whether sets are to be thought of as robust constituents of the world, or whether they are merely part of the conceptual apparatus in terms of which we view that world. We can formulate theories about either sort of entity, but we need to be clear about the choice when developing the theory. The difference between these two conceptions of set is whether being a member of a set is itself a worldly property that a thing has, or whether talk of a thing being a member of a set is just about a kind of conceptual classification. If the former, then we can expect that membership in a given set is one of the worldly properties in terms of which we characterize worldly identity. If the latter, then we make no such assumption. In the first case, I speak of *worldly sets*, and in the second, *conceptual sets*. I postpone a consideration of conceptual sets to §11.9, and consider worldly sets here.

Worldly sets obey the principle that if some thing x is determinately a member of such a set, and if y is determinately not a member of that set, then x is distinct from y. The principle is:

$!x \in Z$ & $!\neg y \in Z \Rightarrow \neg x = y$.

This is equivalent to the claim that membership in a given set satisfies principle DDiff from Chapter 4. So I give it that title:

[DDiff for $\in$ Set] $!x \in Z$ & $!\neg y \in Z \Rightarrow \neg x = y$.

11.3 SETS OF OBJECTS

Suppose we wish to formulate a theory of objects and sets of objects, with the understanding that sets do not themselves contain sets as members. Such a theory is formulable by the adoption of the two principles discussed above together with a principle of set comprehension which says that any formula with a free variable over objects determines a set if it satisfies DDiff for set membership. Suppose that we temporarily use small letters for variables over objects (and not over sets) and capital letters for variables over sets (and not over objects). We assume the logical laws of identity for the identity sign between any size letters, along with the following axioms (with the understanding that they are all implicitly universally quantified):

[Set Essence] $X = Y \Leftrightarrow \forall z(z \in X \Leftrightarrow z \in Y)$.

[DDiff for $\in$ Set] $!x \in Z \ \& \ !\neg y \in Z \Rightarrow !\neg x = y$.

[Comprehension] $\exists X \forall z(z \in X \Leftrightarrow \phi z)$ where ϕ is any formula satisfying DDiff and not containing 'X' free.

[Sets aren't Objects] $\forall x \forall Y \neg(x = Y)$.

These assumptions all strike me as defensible for a theory of sets of objects.

11.4 INDETERMINATE IDENTITY FOR SETS

If one wishes to combine such a set theory with a theory encompassing indeterminacy, then one must allow sets to be indeterminately identical to one another even if there is no indeterminacy of identity of individuals at all. This is because one can devise distinct defining conditions for sets such that it is indeterminate whether the defining conditions specify the same members or not; [Set Essence] then entails that it is indeterminate whether the sets defined from those conditions are the same. Here is a sketch of a proof that addresses this phenomenon.

Suppose there is no indeterminacy of identity among objects at all, but there is *some* indeterminacy; i.e. there is a formula ϕx true only of individuals and such that it is indeterminate whether ϕa is true:

$\nabla \phi a$

Since there is no indeterminacy of identity of individuals, both 'ϕx' and '$\phi x \vee x = a$' satisfy DDiff. Applying [Comprehension], there are sets A and B such that:

$\forall x(x \in A \Leftrightarrow \phi x)$
$\forall x(x \in B \Leftrightarrow \phi x \vee x = a)$

It is easy to show that $a \in B$. Then we may show that it is indeterminate whether $A = B$ by refuting both the claim that $A = B$ and the claim that $\neg A = B$. For, assuming the first claim ($A = B$), we can show that $a \in A$, and thus ϕa, contradicting $\nabla \phi a$. And assuming the second claim ($\neg A = B$) lets us infer that there is some determinate member of B that is determinately not a member of A; this can only be a, and thus $\neg \phi a$, again contradicting $\nabla \phi a$. As a result, the identity '$A = B$' is indeterminate.

Thus, the mere existence of indeterminacy among objects generates indeterminate identities among sets, even if no objects are indeterminately identical at all. This is because any indeterminacy can be used to provide conditions to define set membership, as in the proof just given.

Of course, indeterminate identity among objects also leads to indeterminate identity of sets. Suppose that it is indeterminate whether $a = b$. Our axioms entail the existence of the "unit set" of a, call it $\{a\}$, the set yielded by [Comprehension] applied to the formula '$z = a$'. This set has a as a determinate member and it has everything determinately distinct from a as a determinate non-member; anything that is indeterminately identical with a is such that it is indeterminate whether that thing is a member of $\{a\}$. In particular it is indeterminate whether $b \in \{a\}$. There is also a "pair set" of a and b, call it '$\{a,b\}$', yielded by [Comprehension] applied to the formula '$z = a \vee z = b$'. This set has both a and b as determi-

nate members. It is easy to see that there is nothing that is determinately a member of one of these sets:

$\{a\}$

$\{a,b\}$

that is determinately not a member of the other. So they are not
determinately distinct. But they are also not determinately the
same, since b is determinately a member of the second, but not of
the first. So it is indeterminate whether they are the same:

$\triangledown(\{a\} = \{a,b\})$.

So if there is any indeterminacy at all there will be sets that are
indeterminately identical, whether individual objects are indeterminately identical or not.

Let us now review Salmon's argument to the effect that set
theory is incompatible with indeterminacy of identity of individuals. Changing ordered to unordered pairs (to pair-sets), the argument is:

(1) $\triangledown(a = b)$	Hypothesis to be disproved	
(2) $\neg\triangledown(a = a)$	Truism	
(3) $\neg(\{a,b\} = \{a,a\})$	From (1) and (2)	[No!]
(4) $\neg(a = b)$	From (3), by [Set Essence]	
(5) $\neg\triangledown(a = b)$	From (4)	

There is no way to derive (3) from (1) and (2). In order to derive
step (3) from [Set Essence], we would need to show that there is
some member of $\{a,b\}$ that is not a member of $\{a,a\}$, or vice versa,
but there is no way to do that. Instead, we can show, using comprehension, that it is indeterminate whether $\{a,b\} = \{a,a\}$, as we did
above.

11.5 A ZERMELO–FRAENKEL-LIKE
HIERARCHY OF SETS

The logical power of set theory comes when we admit not only sets
of objects, but also sets of sets, and sets of those sets, and so on

without limit. The following theory is adapted from Woodruff and Parsons (forthcoming). In it we suppose that sets are built up in stages from objects, which in the spirit of set theory are here called "individuals". At stage 0 are sets whose members are only individuals. At stage 1 are sets whose members are themselves sets of individuals, perhaps along with some individuals. At each stage, sets contain as members or indeterminate members only those things that exist at earlier stages. Assumptions are made that yield a transfinite series of such stages, just as in Zermelo–Fraenkel set theory. There are two constraints on this process that are automatic in the bivalent formulation of classical Zermelo–Fraenkel but that need articulating in our framework. One is the DDiff condition for sets: if y is determinately a member of X and z is determinately not a member of X, then it is determinate that $y \neq z$. The other is that a set may not contain indeterminate members with ranks higher than the ranks of all of its determinate members. The theory that results from these assumptions is "neat", in that sets fall into ranks determined by the stage at which they are constructed, and it is determinate whether a given set is a member of a given rank. Further, if it is indeterminate whether $X = Y$, then X and Y will be determinately of the same rank, and if it is indeterminate whether $X \in Y$, then it is determinate that X falls into a rank immediately below that of Y. Other sorts of assumptions might be made, but they are not considered here.[1]

Our vocabulary includes at least the primitive two-place predicates '$\in$' and '$=$'. We assume a primitive name 'I' for the set of individuals and '$\varnothing$' for the set with no determinate or indeterminate members. Hereafter we understand small letters to range over everything (over individuals and sets) and capital letters to be variables restricted to sets (to non-individuals); so '$\forall X[\ldots X \ldots]$' is short for '$\forall x[\neg x \in I \Rightarrow \ldots x \ldots]$'. In order to formulate the rank restriction it is convenient to have a primitive two-place predicate 'ranks', where 'α ranks x' means that the ordinal α is the rank of entity x. The two axioms above, [Set Essence] and [DDIFF for

---

[1] The "neat" falling into definite ranks is a consequence of the principle that a set may not contain indeterminate members with ranks higher than the ranks of all of its determinate members. Relaxing this constraint has far-reaching consequences, such as unit sets that are two or more ranks above their members (see Woodruff and Parsons forthcoming: §2). I do not know how to develop a systematic theory of worldly sets without such a constraint.

∈ Set], along with the following are our axioms for IZFU ("Indeterminate Zermelo–Fraenkel set theory with Ur-elements").

I present the remaining axioms beginning with things of the lowest rank.

[Bivalence of Individualness] $\quad x \in I \lor \neg x \in I$

[Individuals Lack Members][2] $\quad x \in I \Rightarrow \neg \exists y y \in x$

[Empty Sets] $\quad \neg \exists y! \phi y \Rightarrow \exists S \forall y [y \in S \Leftrightarrow y \in I \,\&\, \phi y]$

[Empty Sets] generates sets with no determinate members and with arbitrary sets of individuals as indeterminate members. Selecting 'ϕy' to be '$\neg y = y$' entails the usual empty set axiom of ZF:

$$\exists S \forall y \neg y \in S.$$

This yields an "emptiest set", $\varnothing$, a set with no determinate *or* indeterminate members:

[Emptiest Set] $\quad \neg \varnothing \in I \,\&\, \forall y \neg y \in \varnothing.$

If there are any individuals at all, there will be sets indeterminately identical to $\varnothing$; they, unlike $\varnothing$, have indeterminate (individual) members.

The following structural axioms are straightforward from classical set theory.

The pair set of x and y, denoted by '$\{x,y\}$', is the set whose determinate members are exactly x and y, and whose indeterminate members are those things that are not determinately identical to x or to y but are indeterminately identical to x or to y:

[Pairs] $\quad \exists S \forall u [u \in S \Leftrightarrow u = x \lor u = y].$

The union of a set of sets is the set whose members are members of one of those sets:

[Union] $\quad \exists S \forall z [z \in S \Leftrightarrow \exists u (z \in u \,\&\, u \in X)].$

The power set of a set is the set of subsets of that set. Define "subset" as follows:

$$x \subseteq y =_{\text{df}} \neg x \in I \,\&\, \neg y \in I \,\&\, \forall u (u \in x \Rightarrow u \in y).$$

Then the power set axiom is:

[Power Set] $\exists S \forall z [z \in S \Leftrightarrow z \subseteq X].$

---

[2] This axiom together with the previous one entail that I is a set (a non-individual): $\neg I \in I$.

The usual ZF axiom of infinity assumes that there is a set containing $\varnothing$ and containing the "successor" of any of its members, where the successor of Y is the set whose members are the members of Y along with Y itself:

[Infinity] $\exists S[\varnothing \in S \ \& \ \forall Y(!Y \in S \Rightarrow \exists Z[Z \in S \ \& \ \forall U(U \in Z \Leftrightarrow U = Y \vee U \in Y)])]$.

As discussed above, our Replacement scheme requires rank restrictions. To formulate the rank restrictions, we first define the ordinals. As a preliminary, we call a set 'tight' if its indeterminate members are limited to those things that are indeterminately identical to some determinate member of the set:

$\text{Tight}(x) =_{df} \neg x \in I \ \& \ \forall y[\triangledown y \in x \Rightarrow \exists z(!z \in x \ \& \ \triangledown y = z)]$.

Transitive sets are ones whose determinate members are determinate subsets:

$\text{Transitive}(x) =_{df} \neg x \in I \ \& \ \forall y(!y \in x \Rightarrow !y \subseteq x)$.

Ordinals are then defined as tight transitive sets whose determinate members are all tight and transitive:

$\text{Ord}(x) =_{df} \text{Tight}(x) \ \& \ \text{Trans}(x) \ \&$
         $\forall y[!y \in x \Rightarrow \text{Tight}(y) \ \& \ \text{Trans}(y)]$.

So-defined, being an ordinal is a bivalent condition:

THEOREM: $\text{Ord}(x) \vee \neg\text{Ord}(x)$.

To express ordinal comparison, we define:

$x < y =_{df} \text{Ord}(x) \ \& \ \text{Ord}(y) \ \& \ x \in y$.

$x \leq y =_{df} x < y \vee x = y$.

In order for the ordinals to be well ordered we take this as an axiom:

[Least Ordinal] $\exists x[\text{Ord}(x) \ \& \ !x \in S] \Rightarrow \exists x[\text{Ord}(x) \ \& \ !x \in S \ \& \ \forall y[\text{Ord}(y) \ \& \ !y \in S \Rightarrow x \leq y]]$.

Hereafter we use small Greek letters to range over the ordinals. To complete the structuring of the ordinals we adopt:

[Ordinal Non-Self-$\in$] $\neg\alpha \in \alpha$.

The following axioms constrain rankings. The first two resemble parts of a familiar definition of ranking by recursion, but they are stated here as axioms because 'ranks' is primitive notation:

[Individuals are Not Ranked] $x \in I \Rightarrow \neg y$ ranks x.

[Ranking for Sets] z ranks $X \Leftrightarrow z$ is the least ordinal such that $\forall y[\exists x(!x \in X \ \& \ y$ ranks $x) \Rightarrow y < z]$.

As discussed earlier, we posit that no indeterminate member of a set exceeds all the determinate members in rank:

[Rank Limitation of Indeterminate Members]
$\neg!\neg x \in X \ \& \ \alpha$ ranks $x \Rightarrow \exists y \exists \beta[!y \in X \ \& \ \beta$ ranks $y \ \& \ \alpha \leq \beta]$.

Our final axiom scheme is [Replacement]. Suppose we have (i) a bivalent relational formula $x\psi y$ which (ii) is functional on a set S, and suppose that $x\psi y$ "projects" from S a condition satisfying (iii) the rank constraint and (iv) DDIFF for set membership. Then its range for domain S is a set:

[Replacement]
If:
 (i) $u\psi y \vee \neg u\psi y$
 (ii) $\neg!\neg u \in S \ \& \ \neg!\neg v \in S \ \& \ u\psi y \ \& \ v\psi z \ \& \ u = v \Rightarrow y = z$
 (iii) $\neg!\neg u \in S \ \& \ u\psi Y \Rightarrow \exists v \exists z[!v \in S \ \& \ v\psi z \ \& \ \exists \alpha \exists \beta[\alpha$ ranks $Y \ \& \ \beta$ ranks $z \ \& \ \alpha \leq \beta]]$
 (iv) $!\exists x(x \in S \ \& \ x\psi u) \ \& \ !\neg \exists y(y \in S \ \& \ y\psi v) \Rightarrow \neg u = v$
Then:
$\exists X \forall y[y \in X \Leftrightarrow \exists z[z \in S \ \& \ z\psi y]]$.

In Woodruff and Parsons (forthcoming) the above axioms are shown to be consistent if classical bivalent Zermelo–Fraenkel set theory with ur-elements is consistent.

Theorems. The following are some useful theorems.
THEOREM: $\exists \alpha[\alpha$ ranks $X]$
THEOREM: x ranks $y \vee \neg x$ ranks y
THEOREM: α ranks $x \ \& \ \beta$ ranks $x \Rightarrow \alpha = \beta$.
THEOREM: $Y \in X \Rightarrow \exists \alpha \exists \beta[\alpha$ ranks $Y \ \& \ \beta$ ranks $X \ \& \ \alpha < \beta]$.
THEOREM: $\neg!\neg X = Y \Rightarrow \exists \alpha[\alpha$ ranks $X \ \& \ \alpha$ ranks $Y]$

[Separation] follows from [Replacement]. Given a set S and formula ϕ, a separated set exists if ϕ satisfies DDIFF with respect to the members of S and if the appropriate rank constraint is satisfied:

THEOREM: [Separation]
If (i) $!(x \in Z \& \phi x) \& !\neg(y \in Z \& \phi y) \Rightarrow \neg x = y$
(ii) $\neg!\neg(Y \in Z \& \phi Y) \Rightarrow \exists x[!(x \in Z \& \phi x) \& \exists\alpha\exists\beta[\alpha$ ranks $x \& \beta$ ranks $Y \& \alpha \geq \beta]]$,
then $\exists S\forall x[x \in S \Leftrightarrow x \in Z \& \phi x]$.

[Foundation] holds in the following form:
THEOREM: $\exists yy \in X \Rightarrow \exists y[\neg!\neg y \in X \& \neg\exists z(z \in y \& z \in X)]$.

Determinate tight separation: [Separation] is restricted by the DDIFF and rank constraints, which can be irksome in practice. If we want a separated set and we care only about getting a set with a certain determinate membership, then the constraints may be ignored. For any set S and formula ϕ we have:

THEOREM: [Determinate Tight Separation]: $\exists X[\text{Tight}(X) \& \forall z[!z \in X \Leftrightarrow !(z \in S \& \phi z)]]$.

(Proof: Let the 'ϕx' in [Separation] be '$\exists y[!(y \in S \& \phi y) \& x = y]$'.)

Tightenings: As a corollary, every set S has a "tightening":
THEOREM: $\exists X[\text{Tight}(X) \& \forall z[!z \in X \Leftrightarrow !z \in S]]$.

11.6 RECOVERING CLASSICAL ZF

The above is the full general theory, designed to accommodate both objects and sets that may be indeterminately identical. There are complications, such as the constraints on Separation and Replacement, but for familiar purposes, familiar techniques remain valid. For example, for considering the foundations of classical mathematics, one usually works with a pure version of ZF. Classical ZF is equivalent to a subtheory of IZFU. That is, within IZFU one can define the *hereditarily pure tight sets*, which correspond to the pure sets of ZF. Define a hereditarily pure tight set of rank α as follows.

$HPT_\alpha(x) \Leftrightarrow Tight(x) \,\& \,\forall y[!y \in x \Rightarrow \exists \beta[\beta < \alpha \,\& \,HPT_\beta(y)]].$

The hereditarily pure tight sets are then given by:

$HPT(x) =_{df} \exists \alpha : HPT_\alpha(x).$

The HPT sets resemble the usual ones from ZF; the first few are:

One of rank 0:	$\varnothing$
One of rank 1:	$\{\varnothing\}$
Two of rank 2:	$\{\varnothing\}, \{\varnothing, \{\varnothing\}\}$
Four of rank 3:	$\{\varnothing, \{\varnothing\}, \{\varnothing, \{\varnothing\}\}\}, \{\varnothing, \{\varnothing, \{\varnothing\}\}\}, \{\{\varnothing\}, \{\varnothing,$ $\{\varnothing\}\}\}, \{\{\varnothing, \{\varnothing\}\}\}$
etc.	

One can easily establish by induction that both identity and membership are bivalent relations between HPT sets. Further, suppose that our primitive predicates are limited to '∈', '=', and 'ranks'. Then if all quantifiers are relativized to HPT sets, the axioms given above all hold, and yield HPT sets. For example, if '$x \subseteq y$' is redefined as '$\forall z(HTP(z) \Rightarrow (z \in x \Rightarrow z \in y))$' then the power set axiom holds, and yields an HPT set. Most importantly, the restrictions on [Separation] and [Replacement] concerning DDIFF and ranks vanish. So one can simply take over all classical results of ZF into this theory.

11.7 RELATIONS

In set theory, relations are usually represented as sets of ordered pairs. We can do the same here, so long as we have the right construal of ordered pairs. The usual account is to represent the ordered pair $\langle x, y \rangle$ as follows:

$\langle x, y \rangle = \{\{x\}, \{x, y\}\}.$

However, in our bivalent framework, this does not satisfy the basic identity conditions for ordered pairs, given by:

$\langle a, b \rangle = \langle c, d \rangle \Leftrightarrow a = c \,\& \,b = d.$

This fails when we have $\nabla a = b \,\& \,\nabla c = b \,\& \,!\neg a = c$. For then it follows that $\nabla a \in \{b, c\}$ and $\nabla c \in \{b, a\}$, and so [Set Essence] entails that $\triangledown\{a,b\} = \{c,b\}$. Another application of [Set Essence] then yields that $\triangledown\{\{b\},\{a,b\}\} = \{\{b\},\{c,b\}\}$. But by the proposed definition of ordered pairs we could then infer that $\triangledown(\langle b,a\rangle = \langle b,c\rangle)$. This is wrong, since $!\neg a = c$.

A solution is to use a slightly more complicated definition of ordered pairs:

$$\langle x,y\rangle =_{df} \{x, y, \{x,\{y\}\}\}.$$

On this construction, the identity conditions for ordered pairs are satisfied.

In §3.1 we assumed that if r is any relation and x any object, there is a property got by "plugging up" r with x: the property of bearing r to x. This is validated in our framework for relations among individuals. To show this, we need some additional definitions:

$$OP(x) =_{df} \exists y\exists z[x = \langle y,z\rangle]$$

$$Reln(r) =_{df} \forall x[x \in r \Rightarrow !OP(x)]$$

$$Domain(r,x) =_{df} !Reln(r) \;\&\; \forall z[z \in x \Leftrightarrow \exists y(\langle z,y\rangle \in r)]$$

$$Range(r,x) =_{df} !Reln(r) \;\&\; \forall z[z \in x \Leftrightarrow \exists y(\langle y,z\rangle \in r)]$$

We can then prove:

Thm: $!Reln(r) \Rightarrow \exists X Domain(r,X)$

Thm: $!Reln(r) \Rightarrow \exists X Range(r,X)$

In the set theory developed here it is not always possible to produce a set from a relation by "plugging up" one of its places with an individual or a set; that is, if r is a relation and x an individual or set then there may be no set whose elements are defined as being those things y such that $\langle x,y\rangle \in r$. This is because such a putative set may violate the condition called [Rank Limitation of Indeterminate Members]. However, if r is a relation limited entirely to individuals, it is impossible to violate this condition, and so we may always produce a set from a relation in the described manner. So we do have:

Thm: $!Reln(r) \;\&\; \forall x\forall y[\langle x,y\rangle \in r \Rightarrow x \in I \;\&\; y \in I] \Rightarrow \exists S\forall z[z \in S \Leftrightarrow \langle x,z\rangle \in r]$.

This is the principle that was appealed to in §3.1.

11.8 CONCEPTUAL SETS

We postponed the treatment of conceptual sets from §11.2. Their theory is a simple variation of the theory of worldly sets. In particular, since membership in them is not expected to make a difference to the identity of their members, we can eliminate [DDiff ∈ Set] from the set of axioms governing them. This then lets us eliminate the restriction in [Comprehension] (in the theory of objects and sets) or in [Replacement] (in the full theory of the hierarchy of sets) requiring that φ satisfy DDIFF. If we do this, then these sets cannot play the role of properties in the Leibnizian account of identity. They may, however, be identified with the conceptual properties mentioned in §4.4.

11.9 SETS AS PROPERTIES?

Suppose that we think that worldly properties are extensional, in the sense that if properties p and q determinately hold of exactly the same objects, and determinately do not hold of exactly the same objects, they are identical. (And if one of them determinately holds of an object that the other determinately does not hold of, they are distinct. And otherwise, it is indeterminate whether they are identical.) People usually do not consider properties to be extensional in this sense, but that may be because they are thinking of conceptual properties. If we distinguish between conceptual properties and worldly properties, then I am not aware of any compelling argument to the effect that worldly properties are not extensional. Suppose that they are, and let us temporarily use the notation '$x \in Y$' to mean that the individual object x *has* the property Y. Then the theory developed above is a theory of objects and their properties. It is a formalization of the framework of the world put forth in Chapters 2 and 3, with the additional thesis that properties are identical if they are possessed by the same objects. (This is in addition to the principle that properties are identical if they themselves have the same properties.) It also assumes the principle of plenitude for properties discussed in Chapter 7.

If properties are not extensional, then the set theory described above can be weakened to a theory of properties by changing the major connective of Set Essence from a biconditional into a conditional. So far as I can see, none of the earlier discussion turns on the question of whether or not properties are extensional.

12

Higher-Order Indeterminacy

12.1 WHAT IS HIGHER-ORDER INDETERMINACY?

Is there such a thing as "higher-order" indeterminacy? In the context of the present book, the question arises in the following form: Some identity puzzles have answers, and some do not: each answer to a puzzle of the latter kind ("true", "false") is such that it is indeterminate whether it is correct. So indeterminacy arises because of questions that have no answers. Now are there identity puzzles of which we wish to say that it is indeterminate *whether* they have answers (i.e. whether any of "true", "false", or "indeterminate" is correct)? If so, this seems to be a kind of higher-order indeterminacy; it is indeterminacy *about* indeterminacy.

Of course there are puzzles in which we are confused about whether or not they have answers. But this may be only epistemic uncertainty, not metaphysical indeterminacy. Is there any persuasive case to be made for meaningful questions of identity such that it is *metaphysically* unsettled whether they have answers? I see no natural application of this idea to certain of the questions discussed earlier, such as whether I am or am not identical with my body. But certain of the others seem to turn on matters of degree, and one might want to appeal to higher-order indeterminacy here. Suppose that in the ship case you are sure that if the ship with new parts very much resembles the old ship, and if 95 per cent of the old planks were used to construct the newly assembled ship, then there is no answer regarding which later ship is identical to the original ship. But suppose, instead, that 10 per cent of the planks are retained in the ship with (mostly) new parts, and suppose that the newly assembled ship is made of 80 per cent of the original planks, with the other 10 per cent thrown away. Then perhaps you will be uncertain whether or not this is a case in which there is no answer. If you think that no additional information will help, you *might* think that this is because of how the world is (or is not). And so the same sort of consideration that drove us originally to think that sometimes there are no answers to identity questions might lead us to think that sometimes no answer is determined as to *whether* we have an example of that sort.

One thing is clear: if we are driven in this way to second-order indeterminacy, then third-order indeterminacy will follow as well, with only increasing bewilderment to cloud our minds to this consequence. And fourth-order, and so on, without limit. So we will then have arbitrarily high levels of indeterminacy.

I suspect that there is no such thing as higher-order indeterminacy. Where there appears to be higher-order indeterminacy, there is instead epistemic uncertainty about whether there is determinacy—or else we may be dealing with a case of linguistic vagueness (which is a quite different phenomenon, and one that I see as much more difficult to address than indeterminacy). However it is hard to be certain about this, so it is worth investigating what higher-order indeterminacy would be like. In this chapter I explore how to extend the theory of the previous chapters to include higher-order indeterminacy.

First, there is a conceptual dilemma that needs to be addressed. Suppose that we have a case in which we are tempted to say that it is indeterminate *whether* S is true, false, or indeterminate. If it is indeterminate whether S is true, false, or indeterminate, then it seems to follow that it is indeterminate whether S is true or false, and thus it seems to follow that S *is* (simply) *indeterminate*. So higher-order indeterminacy collapses to ordinary indeterminacy, and there is no additional higher-order indeterminacy after all. Although I suspect that this may be the right answer, our task here is to make sense of second-order indeterminacy, not to dispute its existence. So we need to examine ways around this "collapse".

In particular, we must decide what status to attribute to a proposition such that it is indeterminate whether it is true, or false, or indeterminate. It seems that this status cannot be simple indeterminacy, because then there is no higher-order indeterminacy, as argued above. So there must be some *additional* status in addition to: *true, false*, and *indeterminate*. Let me distinguish this additional status with the term 'unsettledness'. A proposition is *unsettled* if there is no answer to the question whether it is true, or false, or indeterminate, and so a proposition which is unsettled is thereby *not* either true, or false, or (simply) indeterminate. This idea is explored in the next section.

An alternative might be to see second-order indeterminacy as *compatible* with first-order determinacy (or indeterminacy). That is, one might hold that it is indeterminate whether there is an answer to the question, though perhaps there *is* (or *is not*) an answer to the question. Again, using 'unsettledness' for second-order indeterminacy, a proposition may be unsettled and also have any one of the statuses true, false, or indeterminate. This alternative seems odd to me, but it is a coherent one. I discuss it in the second section following.

12.2 UNSETTLEDNESS AS A STATUS DISJOINT FROM TRUTH, FALSEHOOD, AND INDETERMINACY

To keep the first-order and second-order notions separate, let me continue to speak of the world determining (or not determining) whether a state of affairs holds or not, and let me speak of it being settled or not settled in each given case whether the world does or does not determine whether a state of affairs holds. If the relevant state of affairs is settled, then a proposition describing it will be true, or false, or indeterminate; otherwise it is unsettled. (We can no longer consider simple indeterminacy a case of having no truth-value, since that exhausts the options and leaves no room for levels of indeterminacy. Our old indeterminacy must now be a status such as "definite indeterminacy", with unsettledness a kind of "indefinite indeterminacy".) There are now, in effect, four mutually exclusive truth-statuses (though perhaps 'truth-status' is no longer appropriate; there are now simply four *statuses*):

> *true*
> *false*
> *undetermined*
> *unsettled*

A proposition is *second-order undetermined* iff it is unsettled.

Our notation now needs to have its meaning extended so as to address the new status. I suppose that if a proposition is settled, then our language works as before. If it is unsettled, we need to specify what status its negation has, and so on. There is a certain arbitrariness of formulation here; for the sake of definiteness I make some particular choices about notation. In parallel with previous notation, I will use '§S' to mean that it is settled that S is true, with the intent that '§S' is false if S is unsettled. Then we use our determinacy notation: '!S' to mean that S is determinately true, but with the intent that '!S' is unsettled if S itself is unsettled. With these two notions we can express the other natural options. Using 'u' for the unsettled status, some relevant truth-conditions are given in Table 12.1.

Let us say that our other connectives (conjunction, disjunction, and negation) retain their old values when their constituents have settled statuses (when they have statuses other than u), and that the negation of an unsettled sentence is itself unsettled, and that a conjunction (disjunction) with an unsettled part is false (true) if the other part is false (true), and indeterminate (has status '−') if the other part is indeterminate, and otherwise unsettled. The quantifiers will again be generalizations of conjunction and disjunction. I skip discussing conditionals for the reasons given earlier: they introduce complexity without addressing any new metaphysical issues.

Identity must now mean coincidence in all respects. We must assume that there are more ways in which properties are had by objects, and say:

TABLE 12.1.

S	determinate truth !S	settled truth §S	indeterminacy ▽S	settledness §S ∨ §¬S ∨ §▽S
T	T	T	F	T
—	F	F	T	T
F	F	F	F	T
u	u	F	u	F

Object a is (definitely) identical to object b iff for any
property P:
it is true that a possesses P iff it is true that b possesses P
it is false that a possesses P iff it is false that b possesses P
it is indeterminate whether a possesses P iff it is indeterminate
whether b possesses P
it is unsettled whether a possesses P iff it is unsettled whether
b possesses P

Object a is (definitely) not identical to object b iff for some
property P:
it is true that a possesses P and it is false that b possesses P, or
vice versa

It is indeterminate whether object a is identical to object b iff
a is neither (definitely) identical with b nor (definitely) not
identical with b, and for any property P, it is settled whether a
possesses P iff it is settled whether b possesses P

It is unsettled whether object a is identical to object b iff for
any property P:
it is neither true nor false nor indeterminate whether a is
identical with b.

We now have a logic that incorporates second-order indeterminacy (i.e. unsettledness). Since assertion is still assertion of truth,
most of our natural inferences from premises are unaffected by
the introduction of unsettledness. For example, $A \vee B$ together
with $\neg A$ still entails B, and so on. Indirect proof, naturally,
needs revising. But if you add premises to the effect that all
sentences used in the proof are settled, (are true or false or indeterminate), then our old argumentation is totally unaltered. Whatever you do, Leibniz's Law is still valid, and contrapositive versions
of it are not generally valid. So although some material of the
preceding chapters now needs fine-tuning, none of the major theses
is lost as a result of admitting higher-order indeterminacy in the
form of unsettledness. (Of course, if there are interesting identity
puzzles that turn on unsettledness, they need to be addressed from
scratch.)

This approach can be generalized to a theory with any number
n of levels of indeterminacy. One needs to have n truth-value
statuses in addition to T and F; call these $u_1, \ldots, u_n$, with u_1 being
the same as our earlier $-$, and u_2 the same as u above. Introduce n

determinate-truth connectives $\S_1, \ldots, \S_n$, with $\S_1 = !$ and $\S_2 = \S$ from above. Each $\S_k$ maps

> T to T,
> F to F,
> u_i to itself if $i > k$,
> u_i to F if $i \leq k$.

If $n = \omega$, then there can be indeterminacy of every finite level.

12.3 UNSETTLEDNESS AS COMPATIBLE WITH OTHER STATUSES

It will help if we have an intuitive picture for a kind of unsettledness that is compatible, for example, with definite truth. Suppose that we believe in indeterminacy because we are idealists: some kind of mind (perhaps our own, or perhaps God's or . . .) makes some things true, other things false, and leaves the rest open (indeterminate). Can we raise the question of its being indeterminate whether something, S, is made determinate, independent of whether or not S is indeterminate? Yes, we easily can, if we presume a superior mind which, for each proposition p, either decides that p is to be true, or decides that p is to be false (by deciding that its negation is to be true), or decides to let the primary mind determine whether or not p is to be true, or false, or neither. In the latter case it is second-order indeterminate whether p is determinate. In particular, suppose that the superior mind produces a (possibly) partially indeterminate world, as discussed in earlier chapters. Then the primary mind gets to produce a *partial* resolution of that world, as discussed in §5.4; that is, the primary mind gets to make determinate some (or all) of the states of affairs left indeterminate by the superior mind. (So a partial resolution differs from a "resolution" in that not all states of affairs need to be made determinate.) We call a proposition unsettled if it does not have a truth-value in the first world, and indeterminate if it lacks a truth-value in the second world.

To keep the first-order and second-order notions separate, let me continue to speak of the primary mind (or world) determining (or not determining) whether a state of affairs holds or not, and let me speak of the superior mind bestowing *pre-emptive truth* or *pre-emptive falsehood* on propositions. There are now, in effect, five truth-statuses:

Pre-emptive status:

pre-emptive truth	the superior being decrees truth
pre-emptive falsehood	the superior being decrees falsehood

Non-pre-emptive status:

(non-pre-emptive) truth	the subordinate being decrees truth
(non-pre-emptive) falsehood	the subordinate being decrees falsehood
no value	the subordinate being does not decide

A proposition is second-order undetermined iff it is neither pre-emptively true nor false. Such a proposition may be true, or false, or indeterminate.

Notation for the five statuses:

pre-emptive truth:	pT
pre-emptive falsehood:	pF
ordinary truth:	T
ordinary falsehood:	F
lack of truth-value:	–

Our linguistic notation needs to have its meaning extended. I will introduce '$\wp$' for 'it is pre-emptively true that', and I shall interpret determinate truth as either truth or pre-emptive truth. The truth-conditions will then be as in Table 12.2.

It is natural to say that a conjunction is pre-emptively true if both its parts are pre-emptively true, and pre-emptively false if either part is pre-emptively false. If neither of these conditions apply, it is non-pre-emptively true if each part is true or pre-emptively true, and false if at least one part is false. A disjunction is pre-emptively true if either part is pre-emptively true, and pre-emptively false if both parts are pre-emptively false. Otherwise it is non-pre-emptively true if either part is non-pre-emtively true, and pre-emptively false if both parts are true (pre-emptively or non-pre-emptively). The quantifiers are to be the natural

TABLE 12.2.

S	pre-emptive truth ℘S	determinate truth !S	pre-emptiveness ℘S ∨ ℘¬S	determinacy !S ∨ !¬S	negation ¬S
pT	pT	pT	pT	pT	pF
pF	pF	pF	pT	pT	pT
T	pF	T	pF	T	F
F	pF	F	pF	T	T
—	pF	F	pF	F	—

generalizations of conjunction and disjunction. Again, I skip discussing conditionals.

We must now characterize identity. The most natural treatment is to do so in a fashion parallel to that of the last section, so that identity means complete coincidence of statuses of possession of properties. But now that we have two kinds of truth, we will have two kinds of complete coincidence: pre-emptive complete coincidence, and non-pre-emptive complete coincidence. Informally, an identity will be pre-emptively true iff for each property P, either P pre-emptively holds of both a and b, or it pre-emptively fails to hold of either. Truth in general (pre-emptive or non-pre-emptive) will mean that for each property P, the status of whether P holds of a is the same as the status of whether P holds of b. The remaining conditions should parallel those of the last section.

We again have a logic that incorporates second-order indeterminacy (lack of pre-emptiveness). If assertion is still assertion of some kind of truth, (pre-emptive or non-pre-emptive) most of our natural inferences from premises are unaffected by the introduction of the new level. For example, $A \lor B$ together with $\neg A$ still entails B, and so on. Indirect proof naturally needs revising. But if you add premises to the effect that all sentences used in the proof are true or false or indeterminate, then the old argumentation is recovered unaltered.

Leibniz's Law is still valid, and contrapositive versions of it are not generally valid.

As in the preceding section, although some material of earlier chapters now needs fine-tuning, none of the major theses is lost as a result of admitting higher-order indeterminacy in the form of lack of pre-emptive determinacy. (Also, if there are interesting identity puzzles that turn on lack of pre-emptive determinacy, they need to be addressed from scratch.)

To generalize this account to a theory with any number n of levels of indeterminacy one needs n levels of pre-emptive truth and falsehood; call these $T_1, \ldots, T_n$ and $F_1, \ldots, F_n$, where, for example, $T_1 = T$ above and $T_2 = pT$ above. And we add n pre-emptive-truth connectives $\wp_1, \ldots, \wp_n$, with $\wp_1 = !$ and $\wp_2 = \wp$ from above. Each $\wp_k$ maps

- to F_k,
T_i to itself if $i \geq k$, and likewise for F_i
T_i to F_k if $i < k$, and likewise for F_i.

12.4 CONCLUSION

I hope at least to have made a case that the possibility of higher-order indeterminacy does not threaten the theorizing of the rest of this book. This is because if there is no higher-order indeterminacy, then the theory is unaffected, and if there is, the theory may be adapted in one of the ways given above.

APPENDIX

Evans on Indeterminacy:
An Unorthodox Interpretation

In Chapter 4, I indicated that Evans (1978) is subject to various interpretations, including ones irrelevant to the topic of this book. The purpose of this appendix is to describe such an interpretation and explain why it is plausible that this is what Evans had in mind.[1]

1. THE ISSUE

Evans (1978) proposed to refute the claim:

$$\triangledown(a = b),$$

which he reads metalinguistically as "the identity statement '$a = b$' is of indeterminate truth value". Most commentators[2] have understood this to be a claim that the identity statement '$a = b$' has *no* truth-value (or has some value distinct from truth or falsity); the sentential operator '$\triangledown$' combines with a sentence to produce a larger sentence that is true if the ingredient sentence lacks truth-value, and false otherwise. So the truth of '$\triangledown(a = b)$' amounts to the lack of truth-value of '$a = b$', and Evans meant to argue that this cannot happen if the terms 'a' and 'b' actually refer to objects. I will call this the "standard interpretation" of Evans's paper.

The "non-standard" interpretation was first suggested to me by David Wiggins.[3] It is not much endorsed in print.[4] On this interpretation, inde-

---

[1] I am indebted here to Peter Woodruff (as usual), and to Peter Smith and an anonymous referee for *Analysis* for criticisms of an earlier flawed account of these matters.

[2] Including, among others: Broome (1984), Cook (1986), Cowles (1994), Garrett (1988), Johnson (1989), Keefe (1995), Lewis (1988), Noonan (1990), Parsons (1987), Parsons and Woodruff (1995), Thomasson (1982), van Inwagen (1988), Woodruff and Parsons (1997). Several authors have written commentaries that do not address this issue specifically. Pelletier (1989: 482) considers the possibility that indeterminacy might be consistent with having a truth-value, but rejects this as a reasonable option (ibid. 485–6).

[3] Personal communication, 1987.

[4] Gibbons (1982) interprets Evans in this way, and concludes that the resulting view is "strange". Pelletier (1989) quotes David Lewis as reporting a communica-

terminacy is not a lack of truth-value; indeterminate truths are a subset of the truths. To take an illustration wholly unrelated to identity, one might hold that it is not determinate whether it is raining, without thereby denying that it is either true that it is raining or false that it is raining. (If indeterminacy is contingency, this is a claim that many have found plausible; likewise if indeterminacy means lack of knowledge.) On this interpretation '$\triangledown S$' means that S is neither definitely true nor definitely false,[5] though it *is* either true or false.

Recall the central argument that occupied us in Chapter 4. It is a *reductio* in five steps:

(1)	$\triangledown(a = b)$	The hypothesis to be refuted
(2)	$\lambda x[\triangledown(a = x)]b$	Abstraction from (1)
(3)	$\neg\triangledown(a = a)$	Truism
(4)	$\neg\lambda x[\triangledown(a = x)]a$	Reverse abstraction from (3)
(5)	$\neg(a = b)$	(2), (4) by Leibniz's Law

The point of this proof is that from the assumption that it is indeterminate whether $a = b$, we conclude that $\neg(a = b)$. According to Evans we thereby "[contradict] the assumption from which we began". But how? Since line (5) does not *explicitly* contradict (1), Evans explains how to go on to complete the proof. He says:

> If 'Indefinitely' and its dual 'Definitely' ('$\triangle$') generate a modal logic as strong as S5, (1)–(4) and, presumably, Leibniz's Law, may each be strengthened with a 'Definitely' prefix, enabling us to derive
> (5′) $\triangle\neg(a = b)$
> which is straightforwardly inconsistent with (1).

These remarks have puzzled almost everyone who has read them. They seem to suggest that Evans finds plausible the modal principles of system S5 of modal logic with '$\triangle$' playing the role of necessity and '$\triangledown$' the role of possibility. But then consider line (3):

(3) $\neg\triangledown(a = a)$ Truism

This "truism" asserts the analogue of "it is not possible that $a = a$". This is not a truism, it's the opposite of one. Further, if '$\triangledown$' were the dual of '$\triangle$' then we could replace '$\triangledown$' by '$\neg\triangle\neg$' in (3), getting:

tion from Evans saying that he intended his signs for determinacy and indeterminacy as modal ones; Pelletier argues that this option is, in essence, an error on Evans's part.

[5] Evans uses 'definitely' and 'determinately' as synonyms.

(3′) ¬¬ᴀ¬$(a = a)$

or

(3″) ᴀ¬$(a = a)$.

And if 'ᴀ' plays the role of necessity in modal logic, this would entail

(3‴) ¬$(a = a)$

and we could derive this absurdity from a truism alone, without even using the hypothesis that is supposed to be refuted. Clearly something is wrong here.

The explanation is simply that Evans made a slip. Several commentators have speculated that this is so, and Evans confirmed it himself later.[6] But exactly what slip? He seems to have replaced an appeal to '*it is determinate that* S' with '*it is determinate whether* S'. The latter is the dual of the connective '∇', but the former is what is needed for his remarks to make sense. What he intended appears to be this, using a sideways triangle for 'definitely';

> If '*not definitely not*' and its dual '*Definitely*' ('▷') generate a modal logic as strong as S5, (1)–(4) and, presumably, Leibniz's Law, may each be strengthened with a 'Definitely' prefix, enabling us to derive
>
> (5′) ▷¬$(a = b)$
>
> which is straightforwardly inconsistent with (1).

Evans then supposes a modal logic in which definite truth (symbolized with '▷') plays the role of necessary truth. The rightwards triangle '▷' for 'definitely' is analogous to our determinately true connective '!', except that Evans's symbol is a modal operator that, unlike '!', combines with a sentence *having* truth-value, making a true sentence with some of these and a false one with others.

Indeterminacy is definable in this logic as:

$$\nabla S =_{df} \neg{\triangleright} S \ \& \ \neg{\triangleright}\neg S$$

Indeterminacy is thus an analogue of contingency, not of possibility.

Why is this interpretation better than the standard one? Because it makes the argumentation of the article make better sense than on the standard reading. Of course, Evans may have been confused, in which case an interpretation making good sense of the article may falsify it. Let us take that possibility for granted; it is still of interest to see if there is an interpretation that makes good sense.

---

[6] In a letter to David Lewis, reported in Pelletier (1989: 482).

2. DIFFICULTIES WITH THE STANDARD INTERPRETATION

There are four difficulties with the standard interpretation. The first difficulty is that Evans cites Leibniz's Law while using a contrapositive version of it. On the standard interpretation, he is reasoning within a non-bivalent framework in which it is a fallacy to appeal to a principle to justify a contrapositive application of it.

The second difficulty is the unjustified assumption (emphasized in Chapter 4) that the abstracts introduced in the proof stand for properties that obey the abstraction principles and also stand for the real sorts of properties in terms of which identity is defined.

The third difficulty is that, on the standard interpretation, there is a very simple extension of the proof from step (5) to a step that completes the *reductio*: infer '$\triangleright\neg(a = b)$' from (5). But Evans does *not* do this, and he writes as if to do so is *problematic*; he implies that a more complex justification is needed, one that appeals to a fairly elaborate set of modal principles, including the reduction principles of S5. Why?

The fourth difficulty is that Evans appeals to a modal extension of the proof by alluding to a modal logic "as strong as S5". This clearly assumes that the reader will know what S5 is. But on the standard interpretation, the proof is given in a non-bivalent language, and thus one needs to know what a formulation of S5 *in non-bivalent logic* is. This is hardly something that any writer would expect readers to be familiar with.

(There is a fifth difficulty, perhaps already implicit in the fourth. Evans stated later[7] that he intended the indeterminacy symbols in the original argument as modal operators. A typical modal operator combines with truth-valued sentences to produce truth-valued sentences, not with sentences that lack truth-value altogether. And a typical modal operator will combine with some true sentences to produce truths and with others to produce falsehoods. But the determinacy connective, on the standard interpretation, does not do this.)

3. SOLUTIONS TO THE DIFFICULTIES

The non-standard interpretation avoids these difficulties. First, on the non-standard interpretation, the language that Evans is using is bivalent.

[7] According to Pelletier (1989).

Indeterminacy is not lack of truth-value, it is possession of truth-value but in a certain way. In a bivalent logic, if a principle is valid, so is its contrapositive. So even though Evans does cite Leibniz's Law while using a contrapositive version of it, in bivalent logic the contrapositive version *is* entailed by the Law itself. If this is an error at all, it is a minor infelicity in exposition—there is no *logical* error at all.

Second, what about the abstracts? On the non-standard interpretation, the abstraction steps are redundant; they could be skipped completely so long as Leibniz's Law itself is thought to apply to all singular terms. For (5) can be inferred directly from (1) and (3) by the (valid) contrapositive version of Leibniz's Law. So why are the abstracts there at all? Answer: They are there to make explicit that Leibniz's Law does indeed apply to the terms in question. This can be done in one of two ways, and I am not sure which Evans had in mind. First, the point of the reformulation could be to show (claim) that it is not relevant that the names are within the scopes of modal operators. Since the names are supposed to be rigid, and occur *de re*, being within the scope of a modal operator is irrelevant to the appeal to Leibniz's Law later on; the abstraction steps show this by *removing* the names from the scopes of the operators. On this interpretation, the question of whether the abstracts refer to properties is not germane; the abstraction is rather intended to give an equivalent form in which the names in question occur in overtly extensional contexts. The second option to suppose that Evans had in mind the kind of property called *conceptual* in Chapter 4. If this is so, then the abstraction steps are completely justified (as argued in Chapter 4). And since the logic is now bivalent, the use of Leibniz's Law does not depend on *what* kind of property the abstracts stand for, so there is no fallacy.

Third, why not infer '$\triangleright\neg(a = b)$' from '$\neg(a = b)$' and be done with it? Well, recall that the reason for inferring '$!\neg(a = b)$' from '$\neg(a = b)$' in Chapter 4 depended on interpreting '!' as the determinate-truth connective, which combines truly with *any* true sentence. But Evans's determinacy operator, '$\triangleright$', does *not* combine truly with *any* true sentence; it combines truly with some and falsely with others. So Evans does *not* have available this rule of inference:

$$\frac{S}{\triangleright S}.$$

This is because the form '$S \ \& \ \neg\triangleright S$' is consistent in his logic. Then why does he say that line (5) contradicts line (1)? Because it does! But not because any old sentence of the form 'S' contradicts '$\neg\triangleright S$'; line (5) is a special case of this pattern, and has a special role in the proof. For this reason, it is going to take some explanation of *why* the proof shows that line (5) contradicts line (1). And that is why Evans gives such an explanation, couched in terms of a sketch of how to expand the original proof so as to show this. In fact, a correct proof *can* be given along the lines he sketches, using a modal logic with the principles of S5. (That is, it is completely correct as a proof; we will return in §3 to question whether it is reasonable for him to presume that the S5 principles hold.) The proof is within a bivalent logic, which thus avoids the fourth difficulty mentioned above.

The proof is supposed to show that step (5) contradicts step (1). The idea behind the proof is easy to explain with an analogy from modal logic. Suppose we start with an assumption that '*S* is possible', and then we derive '¬*S*' from this. Does that or does it not refute the possibility of '*S*'? It does, but for a subtle reason, since '¬*S*' does not *in general* contradict '◊*S*'. Indeed, '¬*S* & ◊*S*' is generally a consistent form. But if you *derive* '¬*S*' from '◊*S*', using only principles of modal logic, that *does* refute '◊*S*'. If the possibility of S *entails* the falsehood of '*S*', then '*S*' is not possible. At least this is so in the modal system S5. And that is Evans's strategy in his proof. The proof does not show that (5) contradicts (1) because of the way their operators relate to one another; it shows that (5) contradicts (1) because (5) must contradict (1) *if it logically follows from* (1), and the proof already given in (1)–(5) has shown precisely that.

The reasoning just sketched is not obvious, and so Evans shows how to prove it from more basic principles. He doesn't give the proof, but he sketches the strategy; it involves prefixing "definitely" operators to the lines of the original proof. His technique works fine if one takes for granted certain derived principles of S5, substituting 'definitely' for 'necessarily'. They are these:

Principles from S5:

[Interchange] Definite equivalents may be interchanged anywhere.

[Definition] '▽*S*' is (definitely) equivalent by definition to '¬▷*S* & ¬▷¬*S*'

[S5-Reduction] Every sentence that begins with an operator (or the negation of such a sentence) is definitely equivalent to the result of prefixing that sentence with '▷'. E.g. '▽*S*' is equivalent to '▷▽*S*', and '¬▽*S*' is equivalent to '▷¬▽*S*'.

[Necessitation] If '*S*' is proved from logical principles alone, you may infer '▷*S*'.

[Rule-Necessitation] If '*A*' follows logically from '*B*' and '*C*', then '▷*A*' follows logically from '▷*B*' and '▷*C*'.

Here is a proof that results by following Evans's directions. It is slightly simpler than what he suggests, because I have eliminated the abstraction steps; this assumes that Leibniz's Law applies in an unrestricted manner to precise rigid names, and that '*a*' and '*b*' are examples of such names.

1. $\triangledown(a = b)$ The hypothesis to be refuted
2. $\triangleright\triangledown(a = b)$ From 1 by S5-Reduction
3. $a = a$ Logically true
4. $\triangleright(a = a)$ Necessitation from 3.
5. $\neg\triangledown(a = a)$ From 4 by definition of '$\triangledown$' and propositional logic
6. $\triangleright\neg\triangledown(a = a)$ From 5 by necessitation
7. $\triangleright\neg(a = b)$ From 2 and 6 by the rule-necessitation of the contrapositive of Leibniz's Law[8]
8. $\neg\triangleright(a = b)$ & $\neg\triangleright\neg(a = b)$ From 1 by definition of '$\triangledown$'.
9. $\triangleright\neg(a = b)$ & $\neg\triangleright\neg\ (a = b)$ From 7 and 8 by propositional logic

The original steps (1) and (3) are retained here, and the new steps 2, 4, and 6 are, as Evans says, the results of prefixing the old (1), (3), and (5) by the 'definitely' operator. The additional steps just spell out some of the additional details. So this proof is an implementation of the sketch that Evans gives, and it does reach a full *reductio* by employing principles taken directly from S5.

4. WHAT DOES THIS ACCOMPLISH?

What does Evans's paper show if it is interpreted as above? Clearly, it provides a formal refutation of any view that accepts the premises and rules of proof that are used. But which views do this?

---

[8] In case this step looks fishy, here is how to get it from Leibniz's Law alone, without appeal to any derived principles, by using the S5 principle for conditionals:

$\triangleright[A \supset B] \supset [\triangleright A \supset \triangleright B]$.

We have:

2. $\triangleright\triangledown(a = b)$
6. $\triangleright\neg\triangledown(a = a)$

We get to 7 as follows:

6a. $a = b \supset [\triangledown(a = b) \supset \triangledown(a = a)]$ An instance of Leibniz's Law in bivalent logic

6b. $\triangledown(a = b) \supset [\neg\triangledown(a = a) \supset \neg(a = b)]$ From 6a, contraposing by propositional logic

6c. $\triangleright\{\triangledown(a = b) \supset [\neg\triangledown(a = a) \supset \neg(a = b)]\}$ From 6b by necessitation

6d. $\triangleright\triangledown(a = b) \supset \triangleright[\neg\triangledown(a = a) \supset \neg(a = b)]$ From 6c by the S5 principle for conditionals

6e. $\triangleright[\neg\triangledown(a = a) \supset \neg\ (a = b)]$ From 2 and 6d by *modus ponens*

6f. $\triangleright\neg\triangledown(a = a) \supset \triangleright\ \neg(a = b)$ From 6e by the S5 principle for conditionals

7. $\triangleright\neg(a = b)$ From 6 and 6f by *modus ponens*

The view discussed in this book is untouched by the argument. This is because the argument is not relevant to it. The view discussed in this book holds that indeterminacy in a state of affairs results in lack of truth-value of any sentence articulating that state of affairs; the view under attack in the argument holds that indeterminacy in a state of affairs results in a truth-value for a sentence that articulates it, though not determinately. These are too different for a refutation of one to carry over to the other.

Evans's argument is sometimes discussed as a refutation of the view that there can be *vagueness* in the world, at least, vagueness of identity. It is a viable option (though certainly not inevitable) to think that vague sentences *have* truth-values, and that of such statements, some are vague and some are not. (For example, Williamson (1994) holds that *all* meaningful statements have truth-values, and some are vague and some not.) Suppose we take the antonym of 'vague' to be 'precise', and we take 'precisely' to mean 'precise and true'. If we then interpret the 'definitely' of the argument above to mean 'precisely', it appears to be a view according to which no identity statement with singular terms that are used *de re* can be vague.

A natural response to the argument as a refutation of *vagueness* is to say that it runs afoul of higher-order vagueness. A statement may be vague without being precisely vague (it may be vague even if it is vague whether it is vague). If so, the reduction rules of S5 would not apply to a logic of vagueness, since you should not be able to infer '$\triangleright \triangledown S$' from '$\triangledown S$'. However, if this were the *only* objection to Evans's argument, the argument would still be of great interest to the vagueness theorist, for two reasons. First, the case against the S5 reduction principles is not that firm; for example, Fine (1975: §5) develops systems for vagueness both with and without these principles. Second, although the above argument does not refute vague identities, it constrains them in a severe fashion. Here is why. The reduction postulate of S5 is used only once, in step 2 above. Suppose we reclassify line 2 as a premiss. Then every step in the proof is valid, and it results in a contradiction. What this now shows is not that line 1 is inconsistent, but that lines 1 and 2 together are inconsistent. That is, the negation of line 2 follows from line 1. The proof shows, in other words, that this is valid:

$$\frac{\triangledown(a = b)}{\neg\triangleright\triangledown(a = b)}.$$

But the following is trivially valid (recall that '$\triangleright S$' entails 'S'):

$$\frac{\triangledown(a = b)}{\neg\triangleright\neg\triangledown(a = b)}.$$

Conjoining these gives:

$$\frac{\triangledown(a=b)}{\neg\triangleright\triangledown(a=b)\ \&\ \neg\triangleright\neg\triangledown(a=b)}$$

which, by definition of '$\triangledown$' is:

$$\frac{\triangledown(a=b)}{\triangledown\triangledown(a=b)}.$$

The argument shows, in other words, that if it is vague whether a is b, it is vague whether it is vague whether a is b. So higher-order vagueness is not only possible, it is forced. Further, this argument iterates. Take the argument just given and replace '$\triangledown(a=b)$' everywhere by '$\triangledown\triangledown(a=b)$', and that argument, slightly expanded, is also valid. So here are all the things that can be inferred from the assumption that it is vague whether a is b:[9]

---

[9] Here is a sketch of how these results may be proved. It is easiest to do this by employing some lemmas. The logic in question is S5 except that none of the reduction axioms is used. So in addition to the logic of the ordinary propositional calculus we assume the following principles:

Necessitation of theorems of logic: infer '$\triangleright$S' if 'S' is proved by logical
                                      principles alone.
Necessary truths are true: from '$\triangleright$S' infer 'S'.
Definition of '$\triangledown$' in terms of '$\triangleright$'.
Necessitated contrapositive of Leibniz's Law (see earlier footnote):
                                      From $\triangleright\Phi a$ and $\triangleright\neg\Phi b$ infer $\triangleright\neg a=b$.

Lemma A: The following are all theorems of the logic:

$\triangleright\neg\triangledown a=a$
$\triangleright\neg\triangledown\triangledown a=a$
$\triangleright\neg\triangledown\triangledown\triangledown a=a$
etc.

The following proves the first two of these by a pattern of proof that is easily generalizable:

1. $a=a$	Truth of logic
2. $\triangleright a=a$	1, Necessitation
3. $\neg\neg\triangleright a=a$	2, propositional logic (Double negation)
4. $\neg\neg\triangleright a=a\ \vee\ \neg\neg\triangleright\neg a=a$	3, propositional logic (Addition)
5. $\neg(\neg\triangleright a=a\ \&\ \neg\triangleright\neg a=a)$	4, propositional logic (DeMorgans)
6. $\neg\triangledown a=a$	5, Definition of '$\triangledown$'
7. $\triangleright\neg\triangledown a=a$	6, Necessitation $\leftarrow$
8. $\neg\neg\triangleright\neg\triangledown a=a$	7, propositional logic (Double negation)
9. $\neg\neg\triangleright\triangledown a=a\ \vee\ \neg\neg\triangleright\neg\triangledown a=a$	8, propositional logic (Addition)
10. $\neg(\neg\triangleright\triangledown a=a\ \&\ \neg\triangleright\neg\triangledown a=a)$	9, propositional logic (DeMorgans)
11. $\neg\triangledown\triangledown a=a$	10, Definition of '$\triangledown$'
12. $\triangleright\neg\triangledown\triangledown a=a$	11, Necessitation $\leftarrow$
13.	

$$\frac{\triangledown(a = b)}{}$$

$\triangledown\triangledown(a = b)$
$\triangledown\triangledown\triangledown(a = b)$
$\triangledown\triangledown\triangledown\triangledown(a = b)$
$\triangledown\triangledown\triangledown\triangledown\triangledown(a = b)$
. . .

If vagueness is associated in any way with difficulty in knowing (as most vagueness theorists hold), then vagueness of identity entails maximal ignorance of every sort about itself: if it is vague whether a is b, it is vague (you can't know?) *whether* it is vague, and it is vague (you can't know?) *whether* it is vague whether it is vague, . . . I don't know quite what to conclude

Lemma B: The following is always a correct inference:

Φ /∴ $\neg\triangleright\neg\Phi$

Proof:

1. Φ	Given
2. Suppose $\triangleright\neg\Phi$	Hypothesis for refutation
3. $\neg\Phi$	By the "truth of necessities": $\triangleright$S /∴ S
4. $\Phi\& \neg\Phi$	1,3 propositional logic
5. $\neg\triangleright\neg\Phi$	RAA 2–4

With these lemmas in hand we can show from $\triangledown a = b$ these all follow:

$\triangledown\triangledown a = b$
$\triangledown\triangledown\triangledown a = b$
. . . . .

We give a proof for the first two conclusions, establishing a pattern for the rest:

0. $\triangledown a = b$	Premiss
1. $\triangleright\neg\triangledown a = a$	Lemma A
2. Suppose $\triangleright\triangledown a = b$	Hypothesis to be refuted
3. $\triangleright\neg a = b$	Necessitated contrapositive of Leibniz's Law
4. $\neg\triangleright\neg a = b$	0, definition of '$\triangledown$'
5. $\neg\triangleright\triangledown a = b$	RAA 2–4
6. $\neg\triangleright\neg\triangledown a = b$	0, Lemma B
7. $\neg\triangleright\triangledown a = b \ \& \ \neg\triangleright\neg\triangledown a = b$	5,6 propositional logic
8. $\triangledown\triangledown a = b$	7, definition of '$\triangledown$' ←
9. $\triangleright\neg\triangledown\triangledown a = a$	Lemma A
10. Suppose $\triangleright\triangledown\triangledown a = b$	Hypothesis to be refuted
11. $\triangleright\neg a = b$	Necessitated contrapositive of Leibniz's Law
12. $\neg\triangleright\neg a = b$	0, definition of '$\triangledown$'
13. $\neg\triangleright\triangledown\triangledown a = b$	RAA 10–12
14. $\neg\triangleright\neg\triangledown\triangledown a = b$	Lemma B
15. $\neg\triangleright\triangledown\triangledown a = b \ \& \ \neg\triangleright\neg\triangledown\triangledown a = b$	13,14 Propositional logic
16. $\triangledown\triangledown\triangledown a = b$	15, definition of '$\triangledown$' ←
17.	

from this, but it certainly gives vagueness of identities a status that other vaguenesses do not have. (Recall, however, that the above proofs are given within classical logic, and they will be irrelevant to at least some non-classical accounts.)

REFERENCES

Broome, John (1984) "Indefiniteness in Identity", *Analysis* 44: 6–12.

Burgess, J. A. (1989) "Vague Identity: Evans Misrepresented", *Analysis* 49: 112–19.

——(1990) "Vague Objects and Indefinite Identity", *Philosophical Studies* 59: 263–87.

Cook, Monte (1986) "Indeterminacy of Identity", *Analysis* 46: 179–86.

Copeland, B. Jack (1995) "On Vague Identity, Fuzzy Objects, and Fractal Boundaries", *Southern Journal of Philosophy* 33: 83–96.

Cowles, David (1994) "On Van Inwagen's Defense of Vague Identity", *Philosophical Perspectives* 8: 137–58.

Dummett, Michael (1978) *Truth and Other Enigmas* (Cambridge, Mass: Harvard University Press).

Evans, Gareth (1978) "Can There be Vague Objects?", *Analysis* 38: 208.

——and McDowell, J. H.(eds.) (1976) *Truth and Meaning* (Oxford: Oxford University Press).

Fine, Kit (1975) "Vagueness, Truth, and Logic", *Synthese* 30: 265–300.

French, Steven, and Krause, Décio (1995) "Vague Identity and Quantum Non-Individuality", *Analysis* 55: 20–6.

Garrett, B. J. (1988) "Vagueness and Identity", *Analysis* 48: 130–4.

——(1991) "Vague Identity and Vague Objects", *Nous* 25: 341–51.

Geach, Peter (1967) "Identity", *Review of Metaphysics* 21: 3–13.

Gibbons, P. F. (1982) "The Strange Modal Logic of Indeterminacy", *Logique et Analyse* 25: 443–6.

Johnson, Bruce (1989) "Is Vague Identity Incoherent?", *Analysis* 49: 103–12.

Keefe, Rosanna (1995) "Contingent Identity and Vague Identity", *Analysis* 55: 183–90.

——and Smith, Peter (1996) *Vagueness: A Reader* (Cambridge, Mass,: MIT Press).

Kripke, Saul (1975) "Outline of a Theory of Truth", *Journal of Philosophy* 72: 690–716.

Lewis, David (1988) "Vague Identity: Evans Misunderstood", *Analysis* 48: 128–30.

——(1993) "Many, but Almost One", in John Bacon, Keith Campbell, and Lloyd Reinhardt (eds.), *Ontology, Causality and Mind: Essays in Honour of D. M. Armstrong* (Cambridge: Cambridge University Press): 23–42.

216 *References*

Lowe, E. J. (1994) "Vague Identity and Quantum Indeterminacy", *Analysis* 54: 110–14.

Machina, K. F. (1976) "Truth, Belief and Vagueness", *Journal of Philosophical Logic* 5: 47–78.

Martin, R. L., and Woodruff, P. (1975) "On Representing 'True-in-L' in L". *Philosophia* 5: 213–17.

Mellor, D. H., and Oliver, Alex (eds.) (1997) *Properties* (Oxford, New York: Oxford University Press).

Noonan, Harold (1982) "Vague Objects", *Analysis* 42: 3–6.

——(1984) "Indefinite Identity: A Reply to Broome", *Analysis* 44: 117–21.

——(1990) "Vague Identity Yet Again", *Analysis* 50: 157–62.

——(1991) "Indeterminate Identity, Contingent Identity, and Abelardian Predicates", *Philosophical Quarterly* 41: 183–93.

——(1995) "E. J. Lowe on Vague Identity and Quantum Indeterminacy", *Analysis* 55: 14–19.

Over, D. E. (1984) "Vague Objects and Identity", *Analysis* 49: 97–9.

Parsons, Terence (1984) "Assertion, Denial and the Liar Paradox", *Journal of Philosophical Logic* 13: 137–52.

——(1987) "Entities without Identity", *Philosophical Perspectives* 1: 1–19.

——(1996) "Fregean Theories of Truth and Meaning", in Matthias Schirn (ed.), *Frege: Importance and Legacy* (Berlin, New York: Walter de Gruyter).

——(1997) "Meaning Sensitivity and Grammatical Structure", in M. L. Dalla Chiara *et al.* (eds.), *Structures and Norms in Science* (Kluwer, Dordrecht): 369–83.

——(2000) "Indeterminacy of Identity of Objects": An Exercise in Metaphysical Aesthetics", in Alex Orenstein and Petr Kotatko (eds.), *Knowledge, Language, and Logic: Questions for Quine* (Kluwer, Dordrecht): 213–24.

——and Woodruff, Peter (1995) "Worldly Indeterminacy of Identity", *Proceedings of the Aristotelian Society* 1995 (Winter): 171–91.

Peacocke, Christopher (1981) "Are Vague Predicates Incoherent?", *Synthese* 46: 121–41.

Pelletier, Francis Jeffrey (1984) "The Not-so-Strange Modal Logic of Indeterminacy", *Logique et Analyse* 27: 415–22.

——(1989) "Another Argument against Vague Objects", *Journal of Philosophy* 86: 481–92.

Quine, W. V. (1981) "What Price Bivalence?", *Journal of Philosophy* 78: 90–5.

Rasmusssen, Stig (1986) "Vague Identity", *Mind* 95: 81–91.

Sainsbury, R. M. (1988–9) "Tolerating Vagueness", *Proceedings of the Aristotelian Society* 89: 33–48.

——(1989) "What is a Vague Object?" *Analysis* 49: 99–103.

——(1991) "Is There Higher-Order Vagueness?", *Philosophical Quarterly* 41: 167–82.

——(1994) "Why the World Cannot be Vague", *Southern Journal of Philosophy* 33 (Suppl.): 63–81.

Salmon, Nathan (1981) *Reference and Essence* (Princeton: Princeton University Press).

Stalnaker, Robert (1986) "Counterparts and Identity", *Midwest Studies in Philosophy* 11: 121–40.

——(1988) "Vague Identity", in D. F. Austin, *Philosophical Analysis* (Dordrecht: Kluwer): 349–60.

Thomasson, Richmond (1982) "Identity and Vagueness", *Philosophical Studies* 42: 329–32.

Tye, Michael (1990) "Vague Objects", *Mind* 99: 535–7.

Van Fraassen, Bas (1966) "Singular Terms, Truth-Value Gaps, and Free Logic", *Journal of Philosophy* 63: 481–95.

Van Inwagen, Peter (1988) "How to Reason about Vague Objects", *Philosophical Topics* 16: 255–84.

Wiggins, David (1986) "On Singling out an Object Determinately", in P. Pettit and J. McDowell (eds.), *Subject, Thought, and Context* (New York: Oxford University Press): 169–80.

Williamson, Timothy (1994) *Vagueness* (London and New York: Routledge).

Woodruff, Peter W. (1969) *Foundations of Three-valued Logic* (Ann Arbor: University Microfilms).

——(1970) "Logic and Truth Value Gaps", in Karel Lambert (ed.), *Philosophical Problems in Logic*: 121–42.

——(forthcoming) ". . . And of Sets".

——and Parsons, Terence (1997) "Indeterminacy of Identity of Objects and Sets", *Philosophical Perspectives*: 11.

————(forthcoming) "Set Theory with Indeterminacy of Identity", *Notre Dame Journal of Formal Logic*.

Zemach, Eddy (1991) "Vague Objects", *Nous* 25: 323–40.

INDEX